MW00657189

Strive for
TRUTH!

Strive for
TRUTH!

PART SIX

PATRIARCHS OF A NATION (2)

Vayikra – Divrei Ha-yamim

מכתב מאליהו

RABBI
ELIYAHU E. DESSLER

Strive for
TRUTH!

MICHTAV ME'ELIYAHU

Selected writings of Rabbi E.E.Dessler
rendered into English and annotated by

ARYEH CARMELL

FELDHEIM PUBLISHERS
Jerusalem ☐ New York

Transliteration Key
$\underline{h}$ = ח
a = הָ
'a, a' = ע

Strive for Truth!
PART SIX

PARTS 5,6:
regular-sized hardcover, gift-boxed set
ISBN 1-58330-354-5
First Published 1999

PARTS 4,5,6:
pocket hardcover, gift-boxed set
ISBN 1-58330-555-6
First Published 2002

Published by permission
of the Committee for Publication
of the Writings of Rabbi E.E. Dessler

FELDHEIM PUBLISHERS
POB 35002 / Jerusalem, Israel

202 Airport Executive Park
Nanuet, NY 10954

www.feldheim.com

10 9 8 7 6 5 4 3 2 1

Printed in Israel

ספר זה מוקדש לזכרו של

ר׳ יעקב ברויאר ז״ל

מנהל ישיבת ״הרב שמשון רפאל הירש״
בניו יורק
בן הגאון מוהר״ר לוי יוסף ברייער זצ״ל
רב ואב״ד קהל עדת ישורון, ניו יורק

מורה ומחנך שקירב תלמידיו הרבים
לתורה למצוות ולדרך ארץ

אוהב את המקום

אוהב את הבריות

אוהב את הצדקות

ת נ צ ב ״ ה

contents

Preface

It is with feelings of endless gratitude to Hashem that I present here these two additional volumes in the *Strive for Truth!* series. The previous volume, PART FOUR (*Sanctuaries in Time*), was based on the first half of Volume II of *Michtav Me-Eliyahu*, containing Rabbi Dessler's insights on the special occasions in the Jewish year.

These present two volumes originally began as an adaptation of the latter half of Volume II, comprising essays on most of the weekly Torah readings and many of the other books in *Tanach*. At the suggestion of my son, Reb Avrohom Chaim ז״ל, I incorporated articles from the other three volumes of *Michtav Me-Eliyahu* to create *Strive for Truth!* FOUR and FIVE which now include Rabbi Dessler's thoughts on every one of the weekly portions and each of the remaining books of *Tanach*.

PARTS FOUR and FIVE, entitled *Patriarchs of a Nation*, deal with the giants of spirit whose lives serve as the template for the Jewish concept of greatness. As our Sages teach us, "Every Jew should ask himself, 'When will my deeds resemble the deeds of my forefathers Avraham, Yitzchak and Ya'akov?' " (*Tanna de-Bei Eliyahu Rabba* 1:25).

As in *Strive for Truth!* PART FOUR, some articles have been abbreviated and occasionally simplified for the present work. Since these lectures were given to a variety of audiences, they vary greatly in the depth of the ideas discussed. Many of them presume the reader is familiar with the principles developed by Rabbi Dessler in previous volumes. Cross references are given to other volumes where these ideas are further clarified. (I would strongly suggest that the reader familiarize himself with the section in *Strive for Truth!* PART TWO, "Sins of Great Men" [pp. 190-215] which contains the basic principles of Rabbi Dessler's approach to understanding *Tanach* through the eyes of our Sages.)

I pray to Hashem that He grant me renewed strength and good health to continue making the teachings of my beloved *rebbe* זצ"ל, available to the English reader. Together with my dear wife Gitel, שתי', who is a constant fountain of encouragement and loving support, we should merit to see our children and their families continue to follow the path of sincere service of Hashem charted out in these pages.

Aryeh Carmell
Jerusalem
Kislev 5759

Vayikra

[This essay is taken from *Michtav Me-Eliyahu* IV, pp. 173–174.]

The Offerings

Rambam's views on the purpose of the offerings, as stated in *Moreh Nevuchim*,[1] are well known. One of the reasons why the Torah commanded us to bring offerings, he suggests, is because people were accustomed, in idolatry, to bring offerings as a form of worship. People would not have been able to accept the idea of worshipping the One God without offerings, just as nowadays we would not be able to accept the idea of praying to God in thought and not by actually speaking.

Ramban disagrees with this idea and points to the fact that Cain, Hevel and Noah all brought offerings, although there was no hint of idolatry in the world. Furthermore, the mitzvot in the Torah are eternal. Rambam writes in *Mishneh Torah* that the *Mashiah* will rebuild the Temple "and then all the laws of the Torah will be reinstated in their previous form: offerings will be brought, etc."[2] This, too, does not seem in accord with the above reason, since in the time of the *Mashiah*, idolatry will be uprooted from the whole world.

Now this matter, like so many other mitzvot in the Torah, can be understood on various levels. The great man understands them on his level and the lesser person un-

derstands them on his. We experience this in our performance of many of the mitzvot of the Torah; at first we
perform them without understanding, like a servant
obeying his master, but ultimately we might grow to
grasp the inner meaning in some or all of its aspects.

HINTS

It is clear that the deeds we are commanded to perform in
connection with the offerings are of a symbolic nature.
The slaughtering of the animal, the throwing or sprinkling of its blood on the altar and so on, hint in a rather extreme manner at certain very deep and subtle concepts.
We can see some similarities here with the mitzva of *egla
arufa*.[3] A person has been found murdered somewhere in
the land of Israel. The suspicion is entertained that the
elders of the city where the murdered man had been stay-
ing failed to perform their duty to give the traveler provisions and a proper escort. A young calf is killed and the
elders of the city, in the presence of a delegation from the
Great Sanhedrin in Jerusalem and an assembly of *Kohanim*, have to wash their hands (symbolizing innocence)
and declare, "Our hands did not shed this blood." No one
suspects them of actually committing the murder. The sin
they are suspected of is very subtle in nature: perhaps
they failed to care sufficiently for one of their citizens.
But the symbolism is harsh and shocking. This is the way
of the Torah.

In another chapter of *Moreh Nevuchim*,[4] Rambam writes
that the goats brought as sin offerings on the New Moon
and Festivals come to atone for the sin of Yosef's brothers,
who "slaughtered a young goat,"[5]—that is, for the sin of
selling Yosef. Here Rambam clearly discusses the symbolic nature of offerings. He views offerings as a kind of

treatment for spiritual defects lodged deeply in the nation's subconscious. In a subtle sense, the sin must still somehow exist in the nation's psyche. As we know, to be effective, psychological treatment must reach the root of the problem.

THE *YETZER HA-RA'* OF IDOLATRY

We must, however, add that the matter is much more profound than this. We know that "the greater a person, the great his *yetzer ha-ra'*."[6] In his "Laws of Idolatry," Rambam describes the origins of idolatry. He explains that idolatry originated in a very subtle error. Since it is evident that God gave great powers to the heavenly bodies and the heavenly hosts in general, it was thought that by showing reverence to these heavenly powers—who are God's servants—one would be showing respect to their master, God Himself. Only later did this degenerate into worship of the heavenly hosts themselves, God Himself being forgotten. A very great man fell into this error: Enosh, the grandson of Adam, who was one of the three born in the divine image.[7]

During the times of the first Temple, the *yetzer ha-ra'* for idolatry was extremely powerful, sweeping away even people who had elevated concepts of God and the Torah.[8] Elsewhere we have explained[9] that the great strength of the *yetzer* of idolatry was needed in Israel in those times to counterbalance the power of prophecy and the revealed presence of God which characterized that period.

During the times of the Second Temple, when prophecy had disappeared from Israel and God's presence in the world was no longer obvious, the men of the Great Assembly succeeded in having the *yetzer* of idolatry abolished. The Gemara graphically describes how, through prolonged prayer, they succeeded in dislodging the *yetzer* of idolatry from its hold over the Jewish heart. "The appearance of a young lion of fire emerged from the Holy of Holies. The prophet told Israel: 'This is the *yetzer* of idolatry.'"[10] This seems amazing to us. How can the *yetzer* of idolatry have emerged from the Holy of Holies, of all places? After all, the Holy of Holies is the focal point and heart of the Temple!

The meaning is that this particular *yetzer ha-ra'*, as we said before, is associated with high levels of spirituality. If "fire" stands for enthusiasm, the Gemara may be hinting that it was misplaced enthusiasm in the service of God which, by some subtle error, became transformed into idolatry.

Rambam suggests that offerings are in some sense an antidote to idolatry. Idolatry in Israel, as we have seen, was associated with high levels of spirituality and the obvious presence of God. When *Mashiah* comes and once more we merit to attain the level of spirituality associated with the rebuilding of the Holy Temple, this will certainly be accompanied by an influx of the holy spirit and the spirit of prophecy as in the days of old. "After that, I will pour My spirit upon all flesh and your sons and daughters will become prophets."[11] We all hope with all our heart that we will merit this wonderful gift in our times. But we must realize that the resurgence of the holy spirit and all that is associated with this may possibly result in a resurgence in some form or another—most probably in a very subtle form—of the *yetzer ha-ra'* for idolatry. Therefore, the coming of *Mashiah* will certainly result in a revival of the Temple offerings.

notes

1 3:32.
2 Laws of Kings 11:1.
3 *Devarim* 21:1–9.
4 3:46.
5 *Bereshit* 37:31.
6 *Sukka* 52a.
7 *Bereshit Rabba* 23:6.
8 *Sanhedrin* 102b.
9 *Michtav Me-Eliyahu* IV, pp. 134–135.
10 *Yoma* 69b.
11 *Yoel* 3:1.

Tzav

[This essay is taken from *Michtav Me-Eliyahu* IV, pp. 39–42.]

Torah and *Middot*

"The *Kohen* shall wear his garment [*middo*] of linen"[1]—*middo* means *ke-middato*: according to his measurement. The *middot* [individual character traits] of a person should be like a garment, cut to his measure" (the Gaon of Vilna).

Rabbi Ḥayim Vital, the great disciple of the Ari *z"l*, poses a question in *Sha'arei Kedusha*. He asks why the Torah does not explicitly prohibit bad *middot*. For example, why do we not have a negative command, "You shall not be angry," or "You shall not be proud" and so on? The reason, he says, is that the perfection of *middot* is a prelude to the Torah and therefore cannot be included in the Torah itself.

The Rabbis say, "Who is a learned person [whose words can be trusted completely]? One who is particular to wear his outer garment on the right side [so that the seams do not show]."[2] This obviously has a deeper meaning. The Gaon of Vilna[3] explains that the inner side of a robe—that closest to the human body—represents inwardness, and is holy. The outer side represents the opposite, for "*resha'im* walk about on the outside."[4]

We would be at a loss to understand this comment were

it not for the brilliant interpretation of Rabbi Y. Haver, who writes (in part) as follows:

> The robe of the Rabbis is close to the person's skin. Skin, as we know from Adam's tunic, has a dual meaning: On the outside it is *'or* [skin] and on the inside it is *or* [light].[5] This corresponds to the Tree of Knowledge of good and evil. Elsewhere the Gaon explains that "being particular about one's robe" refers to the *middot* of a person, as it says, "The *Kohen* shall wear his garment [*middo*] of linen—to his precise measurement." This means that he must mold his *middot* and turn them into holiness. The Gaon has revealed a great depth of meaning here. The *middot* of a person are comprised of good and bad. For example, jealousy towards other people is bad, but on the other hand, to be jealous for the glory of God, as in the case of Pinhas, is very good. Similarly, anger can be very bad, but used against evil people anger can be good; and so with all the *middot*. The 365 negative commands of the Torah all refer to acts which are essentially evil, and therefore the Torah commands us to refrain from them completely, at all times. *Middot*, however, have two sides, as we have explained. Therefore the Torah does not forbid them explicitly, because our task is to change our use of them from evil to good.[6]

INWARD HOLINESS

From this fundamental insight we learn that every person has in him a source of holiness, and if he uses it, he has the power to change *middot* from bad to good. But if he distances himself from the inward truth and approaches "outwardness"—the desires of the world and other selfish motives—all his *middot* are bad. This is symbolized by the skin, which on the inward side is attached to the human being and on the outward side turns to the world outside us. Thus, "a learned person who is particular to turn his robe to the right side," refers to a *talmid hacham* who is in control of his *middot* and always succeeds in turning them to the good. But "*resha'im* walk about on the outside"; the essence of a *rasha'* is that he is in constant contact with the outwardness of life and never reaches his own internal source of holiness.

Incidentally, we see how Rabbi Haver answers the question of Rabbi Hayim Vital. It is not possible for the *middot* to be included in the negative commands of the Torah because *middot* are not essentially bad. Each *midda* can be, and should be, used for good.

Some people ask: Since the *middot* are based on psychological factors, it should be possible to treat them medically, either with drugs or brain surgery and the like. In this way, we could do away with bad *middot* or mitigate them considerably. (A religious physician told me that we already have the means to achieve this.) Would this not be desirable from a Torah point of view?

The answer is no. According to the insight gained above, this would not be acceptable from the Torah point of view. *Middot* are not diseases which need to be eradicated. On the contrary, they are all implanted in us for a good purpose. It is our task to use them only for the good, and this is possible if we make ourselves inward people.

But this is a very difficult and dangerous undertaking. How often do we see people making grave errors about their *middot*! Everyone who gets angry convinces himself that his motives are solely for the sake of a mitzva, and similarly with all the other *middot*. How can the Torah have imposed upon every one of us what seems to be an almost impossible task?

EVERYTHING IN THE TORAH

The solution is spelled out by Rabbi Avraham, the brother of the Vilna Gaon, in his book *Ma'alot Ha-Torah*, as follows:

> The Gemara says, "I, blood, stand at the beginning of all disasters; and I, wine, stand at the beginning of all cures. Where there is no wine, that is where medications are required."[7] "Blood" stands for desire, which is the commencement of all sins—the diseases of the soul. "Wine" stands for Torah learning, which is often compared to wine. "Where there is no wine" that is, in the absence of Torah learning, "medications are required," that is, a person has to work very hard on curing his bad *middot*. But a master of Torah does not need to deal with his *middot* individually, e.g., by fasting and other drastic methods. All he needs to do is occupy himself with Torah and the fear of God. "Turn it and turn it again, grow old in it and leave it not, for there is no better *midda* than this."[8] Torah learning supersedes all *middot* and includes all *middot*.

The meaning is as follows. A person who occupies himself with Torah and whose interest lies solely in Torah finds that the *middot* in their negative aspect simply do not interest him. Nothing else attracts him, nothing else is worth desiring, there is nothing that is worth getting angry about. In the course of time, from lack of use, the *middot* will lose their potency and be forgotten, like a limb that atrophies when it is not used. When this occurs, a person reaches a stage where it is relatively easy to control his *middot* and to use each *midda* only as the Torah requires it to be used — for the sake of Torah and the service of God. In this way, the Torah becomes the all-round cure for our *middot* problems. We see the wisdom of <u>H</u>azal who said, "Everything is in it."[9]

Happy are those who learn Torah and are devoted to it with all their hearts. What was the response of Rabbi Elazar ben Shamua[10] when he saw a disciple very eager to add to his knowledge? "His eyes filled with tears and he said, 'Happy are you, disciples of the wise, who show such great affection for the words of the Torah!' He applied to him the verse: 'How much I love Your Torah, all day I talk of nothing else.'"[11] These are the people who willingly and joyfully give up all the vanities of the world in order to enjoy a life of Torah learning. With this they have insured their success in this world and the ultimate reward awaits them in the World to Come.

notes

1 *Vayikra* 8:3.
2 *Shabbat* 114a.
3 *Lekkutei Ha-Gra* p. 228.
4 *Tehillim* 12:9.
5 In *Be'er Yitz<u>h</u>ak* ad loc.
6 See *Bereshit Rabba* 20:12.
7 *Bava Batra* 58b.
8 *Avot* 5:22.
9 Ibid.
10 *Mena<u>h</u>ot* 18a.
11 *Tehillim* 119:97.

Shemini

Nadav and Avihu

The greatness of Nadav and Avihu, Aharon's two older sons, can hardly be questioned. The order of those who "went up" towards God at Har Sinai was: (1) Mosheh and Aharon; (2) Nadav and Avihu; and (3) the seventy elders of Israel.[1] And when, at the dedication of the Sanctuary, God struck them down with fire, Mosheh comforted Aharon by saying, "I knew the House would be sanctified by those close to Hashem. I thought it would be either you or me. Now I see that *they* were greater than both of us."[2] The Torah contains no exaggerations. Since Mosheh said this, there must have been aspects in which Nadav and Avihu were indeed greater.

THEIR DEATH AND ATONEMENT

The Torah commences the *parasha*, which discusses the atonement of Yom Kippur, with an allusion to the death of Nadav and Avihu.[3] This hints to us, says the Zohar,[4] that their death was an atonement for the sins of Israel in all generations.

And yet they sinned. The verse that records their death tells us that they sinned by "bringing before God strange fire which He had not commanded them."[5] Our Rabbis reveal many additional sins of which they were guilty. And yet they were still so great! And their death still atones for us after so many thousands of years! This puzzle calls for a solution.

THE SINS

Many and various sins are indeed attributed to them in the Midrash.[6] We have summarized most of them below. Our Rabbis deduced from various indications in the Torah that they:

(1) Decided a law in the presence of their teacher.

(2) Entered the Holy of Holies without permission.

(3) Brought an offering which they had not been commanded to bring.

(4) Brought "strange fire"—from their own hearths.

(5) Acted independently, without even consulting each other.

(6) Entered after drinking wine.

(7) Entered without proper garments, in particular the blue robe of the *Kohen Gadol* (the *me'il*).

(8) Had not married.

(9) Looked forward to the time when Mosheh and Aharon would die and *they* would lead the generation.

(10) Feasted their eyes on the glory of the *Shechina*, which they beheld at Har Sinai.

THE COMMON FACTOR

What is common to all these apparently disparate acts and attitudes? It is the sin to which even the greatest are prone: being aware of one's greatness. This can lead to a drop in the proper level of humility, and this—in a subtle and refined sense, as befitting their elevated status—was the underlying sin of Nadav and Avihu.

When we consider the "offenses" listed above, we can quickly perceive that this is the common thread running through most of them. We shall now discuss those in which the connection is not so obvious.

THEY HAD NOT MARRIED. Why did they not marry? They simply could not find suitable mates. They said: "Our father's brother is the king of Israel; our mother's brother is the prince of a tribe;[7] our father is the high priest and we are second in command. Where are the women who are fit for us to marry?"

THEY ENTERED WITHOUT PROPER GARMENTS. Why the reference to the missing garments? If they wanted to take on the functions of the *kohen gadol* and bring incense into the Holy of Holies, then they should have worn the garments of the *kohen gadol*.[8] One of these was the *me'il*, which is distinguished by the golden bells surrounding its lower hem. They were attached there "so that his sound shall be heard when he goes into the holy place and when he comes out, and he shall not die."[9] The *kohen gadol* is in mortal danger if he enters the holy place without a proper feeling of awe and trembling, prompted by the tinkling of the bells. This is what Nadav and Avihu apparently lacked.

"THEY FEASTED THEIR EYES ON THE *SHECHINA*."[10] This should be contrasted with what is said of Mosheh Rabbenu: "He hid his face for he was afraid to look..."[11] It is known that Mosheh was the humblest of men.[12] It seems that Nadav and Avihu were in some sense lacking in this respect.

DEEPER LEVEL

When they were walking in the procession with Mosheh and Aharon in front and the seventy elders behind,[13] the Midrash attributes to them the thought (or the words): "When will these two old men die so we can take over the leadership of the generation?"[14] However, the *Hafetz Hayim*, in his commentary on *Torat Kohanim*, points out that the reading in *Torat Kohanim* is: "These elders will one day die and we will have to lead the community." The *Hafetz Hayim* explains that we should not entertain even for one moment the idea that Nadav and Avihu actually said or even thought the words attributed to them by the Midrash. What they meant was: "Mosheh and Aharon are already old and after a time they will certainly die, and then the burden of leading the congregation will fall on us. Are we really worthy of this task?" This was a very commendable thought, but the way they expressed it was less creditable. They should at least have said: "...and, *God forbid*, Mosheh and Aharon may die..." The way one expresses things often reflects what is going on in a person's subconscious mind. The reading in the *Torat Kohanim* refers to their conscious thoughts, while the Midrash refers to the thoughts and feelings hidden deep in their subconscious.

But can a person be held responsible for what occurs on his subconscious level?

SYMBOLISM OF FIRE

Both the sin and death of Nadav and Avihu are associated with fire. "Fire," according to some interpretations, may symbolize the attribute of strict justice.[15] It seems that Nadav and Avihu, conscious of their truly great spiritual achievements, wished—like Ya'akov Avinu before them[16]—to be judged by the standard of *middat ha-din*, strict justice, leaving mercy and the various forms of heavenly aid to lesser mortals. To be able to stand up to the judgment of *middat ha-din*, a person must be completely pure and free of all selfish thoughts, both on the conscious and subconscious levels. It seems that here, in some subtle sense, Nadav and Avihu were found wanting.

ENTHUSIASM—TWO FORMS

One of the sins they are said to have committed was that they drank wine before entering the Sanctuary. The law against *Kohanim* drinking wine before their service had not yet been given.[17] Nevertheless, they were being held to a higher standard and they should have known that the heightened emotions resulting from drinking wine might be dangerous. Enthusiasm also is often symbolized by fire.[18]

Enthusiasm in the service of Hashem is praiseworthy. But there are two kinds of enthusiasm. There is the enthusiasm of outward excitement. This can easily be recognized because it is invariably only temporary and fades out after a short time. Inner enthusiasm results from recognizing God in one's innermost heart—"having the *Shechina* in one's heart." This is a pure and strong inner enthusiasm for the word of God, and its characteristic is that it does not fade with time. Bearing in mind their high level, and the strict standards to which they were being held, it seems that their excitement was judged to be of the lower quality. The "fire of God"—the *middat ha-din*—rejected their "strange fire," and they died.

In a sense they sacrificed themselves for an ideal. And this is why their death remains an atonement for all generations.

notes

1 *Shemot* 24:9.
2 Rashi on *Vayikra* 10:3.
3 *Vayikra* 16:1.
4 III, 56.
5 *Vayikra* 10:1–2.
6 See *Midrash Rabba* and *Tanḥuma parashat Aḥarei Mot*.
7 *Shemot* 6:23.
8 *Teshuvot Ha-rosh, klal* 13 (end).
9 *Shemot* 28:33–34.
10 See *Shemot* 24:11.
11 Ibid. 3:6.
12 *Bemidbar* 12:3.
13 See note 1, above.
14 *Sanhedrin* 52a.
15 Rabbi M. Recanati on *Vayikra* 10:2.
16 See above "Inwardness and Outwardness," near end.
17 See *Vayikra* 10:8–9. It was given immediately after the death of Nadav and Avihu, which led our Rabbis to conclude that this had been their sin.
18 *Michtav Me-Eliyahu* IV, p. 174.

Tazria'—Metzora'

[This essay is taken from *Michtav Me-Eliyahu* III, pp. 173–175.]

Material and Spiritual Sickness

When the people of Israel were on the level of miracles—that is, a very clear and complete perception of the ways of Hashem in the world—diseases were dealt with on the spiritual level. When King Asa was afflicted by a disease in his feet (apparently gout), he was criticized for "not seeking God, but the doctors."[1] Ramban cites this to prove that in the time of the First Temple, when prophecy and miracles were frequent, the normal thing to do when stricken with sickness was to "seek God," that is, to inquire of a prophet.[2]

When a person was stricken with a plague of *tzara'at* which, as we see from the episode of Miriam,[3] was a punishment sent by Hashem for wrongful speech [*lashon hara'*], one turned not to a physician but to a *kohen*. The whole procedure, as described in *parashat Tazria'*, was designed to guide the patient towards *teshuva*. If he had to be shut up in the house for a period of time to see if the plague would spread, this was to give him an opportunity to be on his own and consider his actions and turn to *teshuva*. If he succeeded in this, the plague would recede and he would be declared pure. If he did not succeed and he was established as a *metzora'*, he had to live in isolation outside the camp (or later, outside the city) and call out "*tamei, tamei!*" ["impure, impure!"] if he saw anyone approaching. This was to impress on him the necessity of doing *teshuva* and also to warn others to keep far from sin.

In our time, we rarely associate the onset of sickness with sin. We tend, rather, to attribute the sickness to bacteria or the like, and the conquest of the physical cause is our main or sole concern. But in truth, things have not changed. The true cause of our disease, and all disease, is the spiritual factor. The physical factor—such as the spread of germs or a virus—is merely a consequence of the spiritual defect. There is a "cause-effect reversal" here. What we consider the cause is, from a spiritual perspective, the effect.[4] <u>Hazal</u>, with their exceptional insight into the human situation, often reveal to us the sin associated with any particular disease.

But before a person can recognize which spiritual defect is the cause of his illness, he has to be on a very high level of holiness approaching *rua<u>h</u> ha-kodesh* [the holy spirit]. In the First Temple Period, people were close to this *madrega* and were able to identify the spiritual defect which had led to their sickness. Or if not, they went to the prophet, who would assist them in this and also give them a blessing for a quick spiritual and physical recovery. Ramban[5] tells us that in our time, too, the true "servant of God" can act in this way.

TO LEARN OF HIGHER LEVELS

This is how things should be. But we must not deceive ourselves. We are on a much lower level than this. Our very mind is diseased and corrupted with false ideas of the supremacy of physical factors. To think in terms of the true spiritual factors is very far from our grasp.

But even a person on the lower *madrega* needs to learn of the existence of higher levels of living than his own. He needs to clarify for himself that on the higher level the world looks very different from the way he is used to. Armed with this knowledge, he can guard himself from much confusion and misunderstanding about the ways of Hashem. He learns about the high attainments of previous generations, who turned to the prophets rather than to the physicians and who followed the prophet when he told them which spiritual defect they should rectify. Knowing this, even though in his present state he naturally turns to the physician to solve his problem, he may still remain aware that the function of the sickness is to arouse him to remedy his spiritual failings. He may even come to gain an inkling of the cause-effect reversal which we have referred to above, and accept that spiritual failings are the cause of evil in the world.

In practice, every person has to behave in accordance with his true spiritual level. Only after he has perfected himself on one level can he dream of rising to a higher level. No one should try to jump levels or attempt to adopt behavior which is not in accord with his personality. But we still have to learn and understand conceptually the behavior of those who are on the higher levels. This will help us to regard our present *madrega* as only provisional and preparatory. We must grasp that the truth lies on levels far above ours.

notes

1 *Divrei Ha-yamim* 16:12.
2 See on *Vayikra* 26:11.
3 *Bemidbar* 12:10.
4 See *Strive for Truth!* II, pp. 177–178, 202–203.
5 See note 2, above.

Aharei Mot

[This essay is taken from *Michtav Me-Eliyahu* II, p. 52.]

Torah Obligations

"You shall keep my statutes and my judgments which a human being shall do, and by which he shall live."[1] God gave the Torah to us at Har Sinai. This means that the spiritual Torah was brought down to us in the form of mitzvot. This is why the children of Israel were praised so highly for saying, "We will do and we will hear."[2] They realized that they could come to "hear" the inner spiritual voice of Torah only if they first accepted upon themselves the yoke of the practical mitzvot. As the Gemara says, "Greater is the person who does a mitzva because he is commanded than the one who does a mitzva without being commanded."[3] The constant awareness that he is responsible to Hashem for what he is doing and the way he is doing it gives him a closer attachment to Hashem than the one who is pursuing his own ends.

If the person sincerely pursues the path of mitzvot, he will eventually be able to hear the inner voice which points to the highest spiritual goals of the Torah. But he will only achieve this so long as he observes the mitzvot as divine commands, conscious that he is fulfilling the divine will. If he performs them out of habit without thinking, he will never get to hear that inner voice. Even if a person has committed the same sin many times, and therefore no longer perceives it as a sin,[4] he may still go on keeping mitzvot and avoiding *averot* out of habit. But since he has shown that he is prepared to abandon one or more aspects of the Torah, he no longer will consider his mitzvot as divine commands. The person who perceives mitzvot as divine commands realizes that they call for complete obedience. The fact that he has abandoned the yoke of Torah in one respect casts a grave doubt on the seriousness of the rest of his mitzva observance.

In the verse we cited in the beginning of this essay, our Rabbis emphasize the words "which a *human being* shall do." We learn in a *beraita*:

> Rabbi Meir said: How do we know that even a non-Jew who occupies himself with Torah is equivalent to a High Priest? Because the Torah says "which a human being shall do and by which he shall live [in the World to Come]." The verse refers neither to Priests, Levites, nor Israelites, but to human beings. We learn from this that even a non-Jew who occupies himself with Torah is equivalent to a High Priest.[5]

The "non-Jew who occupies himself with Torah" must be one who learns Torah with a view to observing its mitzvot and who, in fact, observes them in practice. The Torah which he learns must refer to the seven mitzvot which obligate all the descendants of Noaḥ.[6] He learns them, with all their ramifications, from the Torah itself. And what is more, he learns them as divine commands—as the way of serving the Almighty.

Rambam writes that a non-Jew who observes the seven mitzvot of *bnei Noaḥ* receives a portion in the World to Come, but he restricts this to the non-Jew who keeps the mitzvot because he realizes that they have been commanded by God.[7] There seems to be no obvious source for the Rambam's restriction. Rabbi Yosef Karo in *Kesef Mishneh* suggests that Rambam derived this through his own reasoning. It seems possible however that Rambam derived it from this very passage in the above *beraita*. Rabbi Meir does not refer merely to "the non-Jew who observes the commandments" but to "the non-Jew who occupies himself with the Torah." This means, as we mentioned above, that the non-Jew derives his knowledge of the seven mitzvot and the obligation to perform them from the Torah itself. This implies that he performs them as divine commands. He is the one of whom the Torah says, "He shall live by them—in the World to Come." This seems to be the source for Rambam's statement.

We see that the fact that the Torah was given at Har Sinai eases the path of the non-Jew, too, to reach levels of truth and sincerity. First he realizes the truth of the Torah, feels the obligating command of Hashem, and accepts the "we will do." If he perseveres in this course, he may eventually reach the level of "we shall hear." This is what Rabbi Meir calls "occupying himself with Torah." The greatness of our Fathers was that they attained all the levels of the Torah by dint of their own efforts before the Torah was given. The level of their constant service was so great that God Himself refers to them as "Avraham, Yitzhak and Ya'akov, who ran before Me like horses."[8]

Now that the Torah has been given to us here below, it is impossible to reach any true spiritual level except by means of the Torah. The levels of the holy spirit and prophecy, too, are revealed to those worthy of them only through the power of the Torah. This is the meaning of the words: "The Torah is not in heaven."[9] It is the power of the Torah which enabled Rabbi Yehoshua‘ to overrule a heavenly voice [*bat kol*] which spoke in favor of Rabbi Eliezer in a famous episode.[10] Similarly, the Gemara cites Rabbi Ḥananya ben Gamliel who said: "If a person has committed a sin for which the punishment is being cut off from Israel [*karet*] and has now received the punishment of lashes at the hand of *beit din*, this absolves him from the punishment of *karet*." On this the Gemara asks: "Who went up to heaven and returned with this information? [*Karet* is a punishment given by God]... By expounding the verses of the Torah can we obtain this information too."[11]

notes

1 *Vayikra* 18:5.
2 *Shemot* 24:7; and see *Shabbat* 88b.
3 *Kiddushin* 31a.
4 *Yoma* 86b.
5 *Avoda Zara* 3a.
6 *Tosfot* ad loc. s.v. *she'afilu*.
7 Laws of Kings 8:11.
8 *Sanhedrin* 96a.
9 *Devarim* 30:30.
10 *Bava Metzia* 59b.
11 *Makkot* 23b.

Kedoshim

[This essay is taken from *Michtav Me-Eliyahu* III, pp. 88–90.]

You Shall Love Your Neighbor as Yourself

The mitzva "You shall love your neighbor as yourself"[1] can be understood on three different levels, each one more profound than the other.

DOING AWAY WITH JEALOUSY

Ramban explains that loving your neighbor as yourself cannot be taken literally. A person naturally loves himself more than anyone else. We have a law that "saving one's own life takes precedence over saving someone else's life."[2] Ramban therefore explains that the mitzva is to remove all jealousy from one's heart. A person should want his friend to have all the good things he wants for himself. These are Ramban's words:

> A person may love his neighbor to the extent that he wants him to be blessed in some respects and not in others. He may want him to be rich but not clever, or vice versa. Even if he wants him to have all kinds of good things...riches, property, honor, knowledge, and wisdom, but not to the same degree that he himself has them [he is not observing this mitzva]. In his heart he

still wants himself to have more than his neighbor. The mitzva of the Torah is that the person should remove from his heart this defect of jealousy. He should be as happy when his friend is blessed with good things as he is when he himself is blessed in this way... We find an example of this unselfish love in the case of Yonatan's love for David, of which the verse says: "He loved him as he loved himself."[3] And how do we know this? Because he was well aware that David would reign over Israel in his place, but no jealousy entered his heart.[4]

The meaning is as follows. We know that an ordinary person wants everything for himself and nothing for his neighbor. One might think that the mitzva is to want everything for one's neighbor and nothing for oneself. But this is too much to ask of a person. Every person naturally feels that he is special, and he is always searching for something, some virtue, however small it may be, by which he can feel himself superior to others. This is extremely important to him and he will fight with all his strength to get other people to recognize his special qualities.[5] It hurts him if anyone else comes near or surpasses him in any way. The holy Torah reveals that this attitude is the character defect called jealousy. What does a person really lack if his friend is his equal in any quality? It is only in his imagination. He wants to honor himself at the expense of others.

The holy Torah therefore commands that a person should be prepared to give up his imagined advantage over his neighbor. If he is rich, his mitzva is not to give up his riches, but to want his neighbor to be as rich as he is and to recognize the truth—that his uniqueness would not be diminished by this; and similarly with wisdom and all the other qualities.

LIKE YOURSELF—WITHOUT DISTINCTION

There is a higher aspect of this mitzva. We have already explained[6] that love is a consequence of giving. When a person gives, it is as if he is giving part of himself. He therefore loves the recipient because he finds in him something of himself. If his giving assumes great proportions and he lavishes *ḥessed* on his neighbor with abundance, he will then find himself included entirely in the other. Then he can love his neighbor "as himself—completely, as himself—without any distinction" as Rabbi M. Ḥ. Luzzato wrote in *Mesillat Yesharim*.[7] Loving one's neighbor as oneself "without any distinction" can come only from self-identification with one's neighbor, both in heart and soul.

We find this idea in the *Talmud Yerushalmi*:

> The Torah asks us not to take vengeance or bear a grudge against the members of our nation. How is this possible? [*How can a person come to such an elevated level that he does not even bear a grudge against a person who has wronged him?*] If a person was chopping meat and the knife slipped and cut his hand, would that hand turn around and avenge itself on the other hand? [*A person should consider all Israel as one body. Just as one part of the body does not take vengeance against another, so it should be unthinkable for one Jew to take vengeance against another: It would be like taking vengeance against oneself!*][8]

How can a person come to look upon himself and other Jews as one body? Only if he acts with *ḥessed* toward everyone with all his being. He will then feel himself completely united with them, so that no feeling of resentment enters his heart against the person who wronged him; he and the other person are, after all, parts of one whole. Is a person resentful against himself? *Love of Israel leads to loving one's neighbor as oneself.*

LOVING ONE'S NEIGHBOR IS A RESULT OF LOVING GOD

We can understand this commandment on still a higher level. We learn in *Bereshit Rabba*:

> Rabbi Akiva said: "You shall love your neighbor as yourself"—this is an all-embracing rule in the Torah. One should not say: Since I have been insulted, my friend should be insulted too; since I have been cursed, my friend should be cursed too. Rabbi Tanhuma said: If you have done this [if you have allowed your friend to be insulted with you], you should know whom you are insulting: He who made [man] in the image of God.[9]

It follows that if a person loves his neighbor, who is made in the image of God, he is in fact loving God and honoring Him.[10]

Love of one's neighbor is a byproduct of close attachment to Hashem. A person who sees how small he is, compared to Hashem, should feel the same towards his neighbor, who is made in the image of God.

notes

1 *Vayikra* 19:17.

2 *Bava Metzia* 62a.

3 *Shemuel I* 20:17.

4 Ibid. 24:21.

5 See *Strive for Truth!* IV (*Sanctuaries in Time*), p. 178.

6 See *Strive for Truth!* I, "Discourse on Lovingkindess," Chapters 4 and 5.

7 Ibid., Chapter 11, see also note 6.

8 *Nedarim* 9:4.

9 Sec. 24, end.

10 Rabbi M. Recanati, *parashat Kedoshim*.

Emor

[This essay is taken from *Michtav Me-Eliyahu* IV, pp. 143–145.]

Shabbat and Redemption

"Six days work shall be done and on the seventh day, a Shabbat of rest."[1] Our Rabbis tell us: "If Israel were to keep only two Sabbaths according to their laws, they would immediately be redeemed."[2] "Two Sabbaths" means two levels of Shabbat: the higher Shabbat and the lower Shabbat, or in other words, the inner Shabbat and the outer Shabbat. "They would immediately be redeemed," since if one has attained Shabbat both outwardly and inwardly—that is perfection, and that too is redemption.

What do we mean by the "outward Shabbat"? If a person is not yet cleansed of his material desires and Shabbat comes to him as a holy gift from on high—this is called the outward Shabbat. Shabbat is called "inward" when the person has Shabbat in his heart even before it arrives. Then he can contribute something of his own holiness to Shabbat. When Shabbat complained that seven was an odd number and it had no companion among the days, God told it that the congregation of Israel would be its companion: "Israel sanctifies the Shabbat."[3]

REDEMPTION

In redemption, too, we find the same two aspects. We read in the Talmud: "The pupils of Rabbi Yannai say that the name of the *Mashiaḥ* will be 'Yinnon,' while the pupils of Rabbi Ḥanina say his name will be 'Ḥanina.'"[4] "Ḥanina," from a root meaning "grace," means redemption as a gift completely undeserved. As we know, *Mashiaḥ* may come in a generation which is "completely guilty,"[5] where all comes from "above" and very little from "below." This is also the aspect of *Mashiaḥ*, who comes as "a poor man riding on a donkey," when our actions do not merit redemption.[6] But "Yinnon" expresses kingship and mastery.[7] This refers to the scenario in which the people of Israel provide the impetus from below; they deserve *Mashiaḥ* by their own actions.

SHABBAT THE BRIDE

It is remarkable that the same two *Amora'im* who describe these two aspects of *Mashiaḥ* express themselves in a similar manner regarding the two aspects of Shabbat. "On Friday afternoon, Rabbi Ḥanina would envelop himself in his *tallit* and say: 'Come, let us go out to meet Shabbat the Queen!' Rabbi Yannai put on his Shabbat clothes and said: 'Come, o' bride, Come, o' bride!' "[8]

"Shabbat the Queen" implies Shabbat bestowing upon us an influx of holiness from above, just as a queen stands above her people. This is on the level of what we referred to above as the outer Shabbat. It is indeed remarkable that this is the same Rabbi Ḥanina who thought of *Mashiaḥ* as a gift from above.

Rabbi Yannai, who thought *Mashiaḥ* would come as a result of an impetus from below, also thought of Shabbat as the "inner Shabbat." According to him, Israel, as a bridegroom, contributes to the holiness of Shabbat, his "bride": "Shabbat shall be your companion." He has Shabbat in his heart and is therefore in a position to bestow some holiness back on Shabbat itself.

TO SANCTIFY THE SHABBAT

Even on the lower level, where the influx of holiness comes completely from above, there is still much that we have to do. We have to experience the holiness of Shabbat and "return it into our hearts." Thus we have it in our power to make the outer Shabbat an inward experience. This is the task which has been allotted to us. The combination of these two aspects is the "double Shabbat" which we referred to at the beginning of this essay, and which, if Israel were to observe, would result in their immediate redemption.

notes

1 *Vayikra* 23:3.

2 *Shabbat* 118b.

3 *Bereshit Rabba* 11:9.

4 *Sanhedrin* 98b.

5 Ibid.

6 Ibid.

7 Rashi on *Tehillim* 72:17.

8 *Shabbat* 119a.

Behar—Behukotai

[This essay is taken from *Michtav Me-Eliyahu* IV, p. 179.]

Shemitta and *Yovel*

The Torah prescribes a seven-times-seven-year *shemitta* cycle, followed by the *yovel* in the fiftieth year.[1] The institution of *shemitta* is referred to briefly in *parashat Mishpatim*: "Six years you shall sow your land and gather in its harvest. In the seventh year, you shall let it go and abandon it..."[2] These are the two main mitzvot of the *shemitta* year: to "let it go," that is, not to work the land; and "abandon it," that is, to treat whatever grows as *hefker*—ownerless—and let anyone take it. (The "owner" may take no more than his immediate needs.) The aim of this mitzva, which involves great sacrifice and great trust in God, is clearly to teach us to moderate our sense of "attachment" to our material possessions.

The two main mitzvot of the *yovel* year are: (1) to return to its original owners all land purchased during the past fifty years, and (2) to grant freedom to all Jewish slaves, allowing them to return to their homes and families. "Proclaim freedom throughout the land to all its inhabitants."[3] Here, too, a great sacrifice is demanded. One has to have the strength of character to divest oneself of land and individuals considered for decades to be part of one's personal wealth. One senses here a sublime purpose: to rectify all that has gone wrong in the preceding fifty years—to restore things, so to speak, to their pristine state.

WORLD CYCLES

The masters of *kabbala* have indicated that this cycle, which is to dominate the life of Israel in its land, also reflects a vaster, universal cycle.[4] Each year of the *shemitta* cycle represents a thousand years of world time. As the Gemara states: "This world lasts for six thousand years, then for one thousand it will cease to exist," corresponding to "Six years you shall sow...and in the seventh let it go..."[5]

But this is only the beginning. After seven thousand years, God renews His world.[6] Six seven-thousand-year cycles, or worlds, follow, each on a higher level than the preceding,[7] until the fiftieth thousand, which is the *'Olam Ha-tikkun* — the World of Rectification.

SHEMITTA

As we saw above, the main purpose of the mitzva of *shemitta* is to loosen one's attachment to material things. The less one is attached to material things, the higher one can strive to achieve attachment to the Almighty. For the same reason, each six-thousand-year cycle is succeeded by a thousand years during which the material world ceases to exist. Nothing can teach the transience of material things more effectively than to see the whole physical world suddenly come to an end![8]

The need for such a vast forty-nine-thousand year cycle bears witness to the stubbornness of human attachment to the material. The task is renewed each cycle at ever higher levels of refinement. As we have often seen in these essays, there is no end to the refinement of a *midda*.

YOVEL

The *'Olam Ha-tikkun* is the climax of the whole drama of creation. It implies the unification of all created beings. All the vast numbers of individual acts of *gillui*—revelations of God's glory—combine to form one stupendous, all-embracing *gillui*, as we explained in detail in the essay "Unity of Creation and Unity of the Human Heart."[9]

At this stage, mankind reaches such an elevated level of self-sacrifice and outpouring of *ḥessed* that each is willing and eager to give up all individualism. Each conceives his own ego no longer as something separating himself from others, but as part of the universal ego of all created beings. This universal ego then merges itself in the glory of a song of praise to the Creator.

notes

1 *Vayikra* 25:1–13.
2 *Shemot* 23:10–11.
3 *Vayikra* 25:10.
4 Ramban and R. Be<u>h</u>ai, *parashat Behar.*
5 *Sanhedrin* 97a.
6 Ibid. 97b.
7 See R. Yisral Lifschutz, author of the famous *Mishna* commentary *Tiferet Yisrael*, who explains in his *Derush Or Ha-<u>h</u>ayyim*, that the emergence of new human beings in each new world to fulfill the tasks of humanity on a higher level is what is commonly referred to as the resurrection of the dead.
8 See *Michtav Me-Eliyahu* IV, p. 152.
9 See *Strive for Truth!* III, pp. 231–233.

Bemidbar

"The Apple of His Eye"

"And God spoke to Mosheh in the desert of Sinai..."[1]

The Midrash comments: "Before the *Ohel Mo'ed* was erected, God spoke with Mosheh at the burning bush...in Egypt...in Midian...in the desert of Sinai... Once the *Ohel Mo'ed* was erected, He said: 'Modesty is a good thing, as it says, "Walk modestly with your God...the King's daughter is all glorious within."' From then on, He spoke with him only in the *Ohel Mo'ed*."[2]

Mosheh Rabbenu worried for many years about the fate of his people in Egypt, until—in response—God appeared to him at the burning bush and showed him that the bush was not consumed, meaning that Israel would survive its troubles.[3] After he told Yitro that he wished to visit his brothers in Egypt, God responded again by giving him further instructions.[4] Again, in Egypt, when he saw how the people suffered because Pharaoh refused to give them straw, he cried out to God and received the prophecy of the four expressions of redemption.[5] Subsequently, God spoke to him at the giving of the Torah and the division of the camp in the desert of Sinai.

All these prophecies came about through external circumstances and the pressures of the moment. The perfection of prophecy is when it is independent of external factors and arises out of inward, spiritual considerations alone. This is the meaning of "modesty"—inwardness.

In another *midrash*, which we quoted in connection with the ordering of the desert camp of Israel,[6] emphasis is laid on the *Mishkan* as a "protection."

> "He guards them as the apple of His eye!"[7] Happy are the ears which hear this! How much did He guard them! How much did He protect them! As if it were possible to say this: Like the apple of His eye! Come and see how He lavished affection on them, how He guarded them, how He protected them...telling them to make a Tabernacle for Him to dwell among them![8]

Outwardness is greatly in need of protection. It is always vulnerable. Since the spiritual achievement it brings about is dependent upon outside factors, it is liable to disappear when the outside factor no longer operates. But an inward achievement suffers no dangers of this sort. When "God is in one's midst" no further protection is necessary. This is the meaning of *Ohel Moed*, the Tent of Meeting, synonymous with *Mishkan*, dwelling place.[9] "I will dwell among them," that is, "within them." From then on, God communicated with Israel only in privacy. This is a sign of inwardness.

notes

---

1 *Bemidbar* 1:1.

2 *Bemidbar* 1:3.

3 *Shemot* 3:3. See *Shemot Rabba* 2:5.

4 Ibid. 4:18–19.

5 Ibid. 6:6–7.

6 See *Strive for Truth!* I, p. 265.

7 *Devarim* 32:10.

8 *Yalkut Shimoni, Bemidbar* #687.

9 See *Strive for Truth!* V, *Teruma—Tetzaveh*, the essay "*Mishkan* and *Mikdash*."

Naso

[This essay is taken from *Michtav Me-Eliyahu* IV, pp. 268–269.]

A Very Expensive Hotel

A person who takes upon himself not to drink wine, not to cut his hair, and not to become defiled by contact with a corpse for a minimum period of thirty days is called a *nazir*. This means literally "one who is crowned." The Torah states explicitly: "The crown of his God is upon his head...he is holy to God."[1] Our Rabbis comment: "Everyone who sanctifies himself here below is sanctified from above. This person who denied himself wine and endured the discomfort of refraining from cutting his hair in order to guard himself against sin is considered by God to resemble the High Priest..."[2] On the other hand, we find that the *nazir* is called a sinner because he denied himself wine.[3]

This apparent inconsistency occurs in several other contexts. On the one hand: "Rather than praying that Torah should enter his mind, one should pray that tasty delicacies should not enter his body."[4] And on the other hand: "One will have to face judgment for everything his eyes saw and he did not eat."[5] Similarly: Rabbi swore on his deathbed that he had not enjoyed this world even by as much as his little finger.[6] And yet: "Whoever undertakes a voluntary fast is called a sinner."[7] We are told: "Withdraw your hand from the meal you enjoy most,"[8] while on the other hand, "The world is given to human beings to enjoy—after making the appropriate blessing."[9]

[These contrasts do not represent different trends in Judaism, the ascetic and the non-ascetic. There is no conflict here. Each statement is true and valid—in its particular context.]

TWO LEVELS

The solution is that there are two levels in this matter. A person may feel that he is in danger of being swept away by physical desires. In this case, he should minimize his physical pleasures as much as possible. This follows the rule of our Rabbis regarding physical desire: "Gratify it and it is hungry; starve it and it is satisfied."[10] All the statements praising abstention apply to this level.

The ideal, however, is that when a person has put physical desire behind him, he should still make a point of tasting the pleasures of this world to some extent. This is so that he can bless God with deep gratitude for the pleasure he has enjoyed. Rabbi Yehuda Halevi writes in *The Kuzari*[11] that the higher a person's spiritual *madrega*, the more pleasure he gets from eating. The reason for this is that the higher his *madrega*, the more he appreciates the food as a gift from God, which he expresses in his blessings.

THE EXPENSIVE HOTEL

However, it is not advisable to have too much of a "good time" in this world. Rabbi Simḥa Zissel wrote in the name of his father that this world is a very expensive hotel. Sometimes one may have to pay for what one enjoys here using very precious currency—the currency of the spiritual world, which is eternal. So long as Rabbi Eliezer the Great enjoyed unblemished success in this world, his greatest *talmid*, Rabbi Akiva, was concerned that he was paying for this with his eternal reward.[12]

Even pleasant feelings can cost someone dearly. "A bad man is shown good dreams," says the Gemara.[13] This is so he will enjoy himself and use up his eternal reward.[14] Conversely, "a good man is shown bad dreams" for the opposite reason.[15]

EXPENSE ACCOUNT

Rabbi Simḥa Zissel added in the name of Rabbi Yisrael Salanter that the only way out of this dilemma is to become essential to the community. If many people need someone, he may not have to pay his expenses out of his own pocket. If he works day and night for the community, it is normal for the community to pay his expenses. The meaning of Rabbi Yisrael's parable is this. A person may not be worthy of receiving heavenly aid on his own; his personal merits may not be sufficient. But if some very important project is needed for the good of the community and he is the only person prepared to undertake it and devote his energies wholeheartedly to it, he may find tremendous heavenly aid being showered upon him. In such a case, he may "enjoy the fruits in this world," that is, he may be allowed a reasonable amount of material benefit to enable him to carry out his job, while "the capital remains intact for him in the World to Come." These benefits are not drawn against his eternal reward, because, so to speak, they "go with the job."

A person who acts only for himself may find that whatever material benefits he obtains in this world make him a "taker" and severely reduce his spiritual stature. That is why this world is such an "expensive hotel." However, a person who devotes his life to the public good, especially if this involves disseminating Torah on a large scale, will find that his giving will always be in excess of his taking. Any benefits he receives along the way are absorbed by his efforts to make the great project a success. He is the one who is "happy in this world and in the next."

notes

1 *Bemidbar* 6:7–8.

2 *Bemidbar Rabba* 10:11.

3 *Nazir* 19a.

4 *Tanna de-Bei Eliyahu Rabba*, #26; *Tosefot Ketubot* 104a.

5 *Yerushalmi*, end *Kiddushin*.

6 *Ketubot* 104a.

7 *Ta'anit* 11a.

8 *Gittin* 70a.

9 *Berachot* 35a.

10 *Sukka* 52b.

11 III, 15–17.

12 *Sanhedrin* 101a.

13 *Berachot* 55b.

14 Rashi ad loc.

15 See note 13, above.

Beha'alotecha

[This essay is taken from *Michtav Me-Eliyahu* IV, pp. 177–178.]

Levites and Firstborn

"Take the Levites out of the children of Israel and purify them."[1] The verse goes on to list several kinds of purification: sprinkling with sanctified water, shaving hair, washing clothes, etc. All these acts are intended to add purity upon purity, refinement upon refinement.[2] The Torah concludes with the words "and they shall purify themselves," indicating the main point: that they should purify themselves in their own hearts.

THE *MADREGA* OF THE LEVITES

The purpose of the whole procedure, as the Torah indicates, is: "The Levites shall be Mine."[3] Ibn Ezra comments: "This is a great dignity." "Mine" means "devoted to Me,'" which implies service that is completely and absolutely for the sake of Heaven—*lishma*. This is indeed a great *madrega*.

Seforno remarks: "They and their descendants shall be ready for My service." Their readiness must be so deeply felt that it is capable of influencing even future generations. The Levites must be *permanently* available for the service of Hashem.

"For they are given—*given*—to Me from among the

children of Israel..."[4] The repetition of "given" is explained by Seforno as follows:

> Given of themselves—for they gave themselves up for My service—as the verse testifies when [Mosheh] proclaimed: "Who is for Hashem—to me!", all the Levites gathered to him.[5]
>
> Given—also from among the children of Israel, who would provide the livelihood of the Levites in the form of *ma'aser rishon*, the first tithe—"in exchange for their service,"[6] so that My service shall be jointly performed by all.

On the same lines, we find in the Midrash: "Take the Levites—for leadership, for My name's sake." [*To merit serving the Kohanim is leadership!*] God raises no one to leadership without first examining and testing him... So it was with Avraham...Yitzhak...Ya'akov...Yosef...and similarly, the tribe of Levi, who gave their lives to sanctify God's name and to save the Torah."[7]

THE *MADREGA* OF THE FIRSTBORN

Had it not been for the sin of the Golden Calf, service would have stayed the responsibility of the firstborn of every family.[8] Seforno supplies the reason: "It was an ancient tradition that service be performed by the firstborn. They are the most honored in their home and service belongs to them."[9] As we know, greater advantages—more *kelim*—mean more obligations.

But the Torah gives an additional reason for the sanctity of the firstborn. "On the day I struck down every firstborn in the land of Egypt, I sanctified for Myself every firstborn in Israel."[10]

On this verse (3:13), Seforno says something remarkable. He tells us that the firstborn of Israel might well have been stricken on that night together with the firstborn of Egypt. Being the most honored among the people, they might have had to suffer for the sins of the generation. Also, one has to have very special merits to escape a general catastrophe, as we see from Lot and Sodom.[11] God explains that He saved the firstborn of Israel from this fate by investing them with a special sanctity. He devoted them to Himself, so that they were not allowed to engage in any common task, just as a holy object may not be used for any nonholy purpose. When the danger was past, God ordered them to be redeemed from this special status, but the obligation of service remained. Only when Israel sinned with the Golden Calf did the firstborn forfeit this obligation, which was taken over by the tribe of Levi.[12]

Seforno is addressing the puzzling fact that already in Egypt we were given the commandment to redeem the firstborn,[13] although the firstborn were not rejected until the sin of the *Egel*. And why another redemption here in *parashat Beha'alotecha*? His answer is that there are two forms of sanctity. Originally the firstborn, because of their elevated status, were given the obligation and privilege of performing the service of *korbanot*. This did not involve a personal status of holiness. Then, in Egypt, on the night of the plague of the firstborn, they were given a status of personal sanctity in order to save them from the plague. Thus two redemptions became necessary.

In Torah life, also, we see that there are two forms of sanctity. Everything we have, though not holy in itself, should be used as a *keli* to serve the purpose of holiness in the world. This corresponds to the original status of the firstborn. But in the time of the Temple, things could also become *hekdesh*, completely devoted to the Sanctuary, and could not be used for any nonholy purpose whatsoever. This corresponds to the special status of the firstborn in Egypt and also to the status of the *kohanim* and *levi'im*, whose whole lives were to be dedicated to the service of God, as we saw above.

This latter status has been taken over by those stalwart souls in our time who devote themselves entirely to learning and teaching Torah. As Rambam writes:[14]

> ...And not the tribe of Levi alone, but any person, of all who come into the world, whose spirit moves him...to stand before God and to serve Him...dismissing all worldly calculations...he is sanctified, holy of holies, and God is his portion forever... and he will be given what he needs in this world, as the *kohanim* and *levi'im* were.

REDEMPTION AND FIRSTBORN TODAY

The mitzva of redeeming the firstborn throughout the generations seems to teach us that there is some residual sanctity in the firstborn even today. A human being sees the hand of God most clearly in the first appearance of anything—be it the first fruit to ripen on the tree, the first grain of the new harvest, or the first portion of the dough the housewife prepares for her family's bread. To celebrate these special moments, the Torah has given us three mitzvot: *bikkurim*,[15] *teruma*,[16] and *halla*.[17] Similary, the Jewish father sees in his firstborn son the first continuation of his line. Here again he sees clearly the gracious hand of God, and the mitzva of *pidyon ha-ben* "captures" these holy thoughts. It may also give expression to the yearning of the Jewish father that his firstborn should be able to devote his life to the service of God.

By the money he gives for "redemption" on behalf of his son, he associates his son with the upkeep of the *kohen*, the man of *ḥessed*, the servant of Hashem. In this way, his infant child is contributing to the welfare of *Klal Yisrael*. Maybe the Torah is teaching us that the best way to advance in the spiritual life is to attach ourselves to *ḥessed*.

notes

1   *Bemidbar* 8:6.
2   See Rashi on 8:7 in the name of R. Mosheh Ha-darshan.
3   Ibid. 8:14.
4   Ibid. 8:16.
5   *Shemot* 32:26.
6   *Bemidbar* 18:21.
7   *Yalkut* ad loc.
8   Rashi on 8:17.
9   On 8:17.
10 *Bemidbar* 3:13; echoed in 8:17.
11 See *Bereshit* 19:15.
12 From commentary on *Bemidbar* 3:13.
13 *Shemot* 13:13.
14 "Laws of the Seventh and Fiftieth Years," 13:13. See also *Mishna Berura, Oraḥ Ḥayim* #156, *Biur Halacha*, end.
15 *Shemot* 23:14.
16 *Bemidbar* 18:12.
17 Ibid. 15:21.

Shela<u>h</u>

[This essay is taken from *Michtav Me-Eliyahu* V, p. 322.]

Repentance and Its Limitations

After the sin of the ten spies and the nation's refusal to enter Eretz Yisrael, it was decreed that they would wander in the desert for forty years until a new generation arose. When they heard this, they were very remorseful. The next morning they armed themselves and told Mosheh they realized they had sinned. They were now ready to enter the land and conquer it, as God had commanded. But Mosheh told them that this was wrong: "You are disobeying God; you will not succeed... You refused to follow God; now He will not be with you." Their attack failed and they were beaten back with great losses.[1]

This is difficult to understand. All the ingredients of *teshuva* seem to have been present. There was confession, remorse, and resolution for the future. Why was their repentance not accepted?

ADAM'S REPENTANCE

One could ask the same question about *Adam Ha-rishon*. We know that Adam repented for one hundred and thirty years, but this did not free him from the decree of death nor return him to *Gan 'Eden*.[2] Why not?

R. Yesha'ya Horowitz writes in the name of his father

that Adam was first created to be like an angel and live forever. However, after he sinned, his body took on a more physical nature and this prevented him from achieving eternal life. This explains why his repentance could not restore him to his original state. Even though his repentance was complete, the decree of death could not be lifted, because his new physical state made it impossible for him to achieve eternal life.[3]

However, we might still ask, why did his perfect repentance not succeed in changing his state back into the angelic form in which he was created?

THE TEST HAS TO REMAIN IN PLACE

To resolve these difficulties, we must understand a basic principle. There is a law in creation: "A person is led along the way in which he wants to go."[4] It follows that a person has to create his *tikkun* on that very level which he chose for himself when he first transgressed. The *gillui*—the revelation of God's glory—must emerge from the depths of darkness which the sinner created. This was the purpose of creation: that light should come out of darkness.[5] Therefore, the temptation which caused his test in the first place—his *beḥira*-point—must remain in place. He has to overcome his temptation and all its consequences, fighting a long-term battle against the darkness which he created. This is the only way in which the purpose of creation can be fulfilled. Decrees cannot be cancelled; there can be no easy return to a person's state before the sin.

This explains why Adam could not return to *Gan 'Eden*, at least not until all the consequences of his choice were thoroughly worked through by his descendants. Only thereafter, in the fullness of time, will mankind be able to return to *Gan 'Eden*.

A similar consideration accounts for the refusal to accept the repentance of the generation which had turned its back on the "Land of Desire."[6] They had made their choice, and they and their children had to accept the consequences and fight their battles on the chosen level. They had to live in the desert for a generation until their desire for Eretz Yisrael was fully restored. Only then could they be allowed to resume the conquest of the land.

THE GOLDEN CALF AND ITS CONSEQUENCES

In the case of the Golden Calf, we find that the people's repentance and Mosheh Rabbenu's self-sacrificing prayers succeeded in restoring the people almost to the level which existed before the sin. The *Shechina* was once again in their midst.[7] Nevertheless, accounts were not quite settled. God told Mosheh: "On the day I remember, I will remember their sin against them."[8] As Rashi explains: "I have agreed not to destroy them, but from now on, whenever I tally up their sins, I will remember a little of this sin along with the others. No punishment comes upon Israel which does not contain some punishment also for the sin of the *'Egel*."

This too can be explained as above. When a person fails his test, his *behira*-point is lowered accordingly. "Punishment" means "correction." Correction must always suit the level which the sinner chose for himself. A disease is only cured when the root cause of the disease has been addressed. Similarly, spiritual correction must address the root of the problem.

notes

1 *Bemidbar* 14:39–45; *Devarim* 1:41–45.

2 *Bereshit Rabba* #22, end.

3 *Shnei Luḥot Ha-brit, Masechet Rosh Hashana, Torah Or, Kuntres* 2.

4 *Makkot* 10b.

5 See *Strive for Truth!* V, "Adam's Test and Its Lessons for Us," subhead "Adam's Temptation."

6 *Tehillim* 106:24.

7 *Shemot* 33:17.

8 Ibid. 32:34.

Korah

[This letter is taken from *Michtav Me-Eliyahu* IV, pp. 305–306.]

The Fox and the Lion

On an ocean liner
En route to America
Third of parashat Koraḥ, 5690 [1930]

My dear pupils,

I started writing to you several times, but had to stop. I was unwell the first few days, but even now that I feel better, thank God, it is still difficult to write—the movement of the ship makes my hand unsteady.

I want to write to you on an extremely important matter—something that will be useful to you all your lives. You would do well to fix it firmly in your memory. Please notice who wrote this: Rav Hai Gaon, the greatest of the *geonim*, wrote it in his Responsa 13. I will copy it out for you word for word.

> There is a parable about a lion who wanted to eat a fox for his dinner. The fox said to the lion: "What good can I be to you? I will show you a very fat human being whom you can kill and you'll have plenty to eat."
>
> There was a pit covered with branches and grass and behind it sat a man. When the lion saw the man, he said to the fox: "I'm afraid this man may pray and

cause me trouble."

The fox said: "Nothing will happen to you or to your son. Maybe your grandson will have to suffer for it. Meanwhile you can eat and be satisfied; until your grandson comes along, there is still plenty of time."

The lion was persuaded and ran towards the man. He fell into the pit and thus was trapped. The fox came to the edge of the pit and looked down.

The lion said: "Didn't you tell me that the punishment would only come upon my grandson?"

"Your grandfather may have done something wrong and you are suffering for it," replied the fox.

"Is that fair?" asked the lion. "The father eats sour grapes and the children's teeth ache?"

"So why didn't you think of that before?" replied the fox.

How much *mussar* there is in this fable!

It seems amazing to us that the great Rav Hai Gaon should have taken the trouble to write out—in his Responsa—what seems to be no more than a children's fable. There must be some great message in this which escapes us.

There is another puzzle in this week's *parasha, parashat Korah*. We know that Korah was a very intelligent man and a great man, one of those chosen to carry the holy Ark. With him were two hundred and fifty heads of the Sanhedrin in the great generation which had received the Torah at *Har Sinai*. How could they all have made such an obvious mistake? How could they accuse Mosheh and Aharon of "taking them out of a land flowing with milk and honey"—Egypt? Had they enjoyed the "milk and honey" of Egypt? Had they not seen with their own eyes how Israel was enslaved in Egypt, how they were beaten and persecuted, their children slaughtered or buried alive in the walls of buildings? And all Israel joined in this cry, not only the mixed multitude of Egyptians and others who accompanied them. After all, in the desert they had all they needed. How could they present such a foolish argument, implying that they had been better off in Egypt? They presented it with such force, as though its truth was obvious to all!

This kind of question can be asked in every generation, including our own. When we study the sciences, we see how very intelligent people bring into their studies arguments which contradict the basic tenets of our holy Torah. It is not difficult to see their errors, but they proclaim their arguments with great vigor and obstinacy as though their words were true beyond a shadow of a doubt. We must understand that even the views of the most intelligent people cannot be trusted when their personal desires block the truth. Not only does their intelligence not keep them from erring, but they use their intelligence to mislead others into accepting their foolish conclusions as if they were based on the most rigorous logic. Every sinner wants to lead others to sin.

Maybe this is one of the lessons which Rav Hai Gaon wanted to teach us with his parable. The lion, king of the beasts, fell into the fox's trap simply because he was attracted by the sight of some fat meat. His desire prevented him from seeing what he afterwards realized was the truth.

If we take a clear look at our own times, we shall see that those who run blindly after material things lose touch with the truth. Both scholars and scientists can drown in a sea of materialism and use their knowledge and cleverness to draw others after them by mixing anti-

Torah ideas with their science. But a critical person can soon distinguish between wisdom and foolishness. In the mind of one who is guided by faith in the Torah, "the fear of sin comes before wisdom." If Hashem is near to him in his heart and God's Torah is his delight, he will not easily fall into the traps laid for him by his *yetzer*.

In every generation, those who were seduced by their *yetzer* wanted everyone else to follow them—even great people like the spies and Kora<u>h</u> and the heads of the Sanhedrin. We have to pray with intensity for Hashem to save us from the *yetzer ha-ra'* and draw our hearts to Him always. If we really want this, then He "fulfills the wish of those who fear Him. He hears their cry and saves them..."

Hukkat

"Get Yourself a Teacher"

A person is surrounded by many teachers. Everything that happens to him, everything that his senses perceive, is sent so that he can learn from it. A person can learn about the greatness of God, His power, and His love from all that surrounds him. So everything—everything without exception—is like a *rebbe* for a person.

This is what is meant by the words "God owns everything—*koneh ha-kol*."[1] The meaning is that we have to hand over everything to Him—to realize that His kingdom extends over everything—in other words, to learn from everything the immensity of His kingship.

Sometimes what a person may not be able to learn for himself from his environment requires a living rabbi to do this for him. His rabbi should be a great man whose eyes see the world in its true perspective. But what the rabbi cannot see is certainly lost to the pupil.

WHAT THE RABBI SEES

In *parashat Ḥukkat*, we find the song Israel sang about the well that accompanied them on their desert wanderings. The song begins: "Then Israel sang this song..."[2] This is in contrast with the song at the Red Sea which begins:

"Then Mosheh and the children of Israel sang this song to God..."³ The Midrash comments:

> "Then Israel sang." Why is Mosheh not mentioned? Because he was punished in connection with water.⁴ A person cannot praise his own executioner. And why is God's name not mentioned? This can be likened to the high official who made a banquet for the king. The king asked him: "Is my friend going to be there?" "No," the official replied. "If my friend is not there," said the king, "then I also will not be there."⁵

At the Red Sea, Mosheh saw God's wonderful lovingkindness from his own elevated perspective. Through him, Israel was also elevated and thus able to sing their "song to God." The clarity of their vision was such that they saw God's loving acts throughout creation, as the Rabbis say: "Even a maidservant saw at the sea more than Yehezkel and all the prophets."⁶ But at the well, they failed to reach this elevated degree of clarity because Mosheh their teacher could not achieve it. With all his greatness, he was unable to see God's lovingkindness with absolute clarity on that occasion because he had suffered from the severity of *middat ha-din* in that very connection. "If my friend is not there, I will not be there." Since Mosheh could not achieve this, Israel also lacked the ability to see God in the miracle with absolute clarity.

SEEING THE RABBI

A person can also learn from observing his rabbi. If he has a comprehensive appreciation of his rabbi, seeing his purity of heart, his devotion and attachment to spiritual values, this can have a great effect on the pupil's own way of looking at the world.

But what if the pupil is not serious about his own service of God? What if his fear of God is nothing but lip service, as Yesha'ya says: "These people honor Me...with their lips, but their heart is far from Me. Their fear of Me is like a command of human beings learned by habit."[7] What is God's response? "The wisdom of their wise men shall be lost." The pupil will lose his rabbi.

But we know that punishment is for rectifying the wrong. How is losing his rabbi going to help him? One would think that the opposite is the case. But maybe the pupil has been relying on his rabbi too much. Maybe the loss of his rabbi will challenge him to draw upon his own inward spiritual resources. The loss of his rabbi may act as the necessary shock, the overwhelming stimulus that he needed to begin his own spiritual ascent.

LOSS OF THE RABBI

In *parashat Hukkat*, Israel is attacked by the Canaanites of Arad in the Negev—the Amalekites in disguise. Israel fights back, defeats them and destroys their cities. They name the place *Horma*—"destruction."[8]

The point of naming a place after a major event that occurs there is to preserve the spiritual effect of that event so that its positive influence will not be lost.[9]

So it is with one's rabbi. One must fix the lessons one has learned from his rabbi in his mind and heart so that their influence never fades.

It is extremely important for the pupil to recognize the greatness of his rabbi. Unless he does, he will never learn from him the spiritual truths on which to base his life. "Get yourself a teacher" is the title of this essay; literally: "Make yourself a teacher."[10] If he harbors the slightest doubt about his rabbi, he will never learn from him.

In the episode where Mosheh struck the rock (which we referred to briefly above),[11] at one point Mosheh says to the people: "Listen you rebellious ones, shall we bring water for you out of this rock?"[12] This seems to imply that there was some doubt about which was the correct rock. And indeed Rashi explains that when Mosheh and Aharon came to speak to the rock, it went away and they spoke to another rock. That rock gave no water, so Mosheh decided to hit it instead. At that point the original rock returned and they hit it and it eventually gave its water.[13] We may wonder what this is supposed to teach us.

The Vilna Gaon explains that Mosheh was in some doubt about whether he was only meant to speak to the rock. The rock symbolized the stony heart of Israel, and Mosheh believed that when dealing with the *yetzer ha-ra'*, words are insufficient. "A slave cannot be disciplined by words."[14] Or perhaps Israel was on the level of "children," for whom words are sufficient. Since Moshe was in doubt which lesson was to be derived, the rock disappeared. However, once he was clear about the lesson that could be derived from striking the rock, it returned.[15]

This teaches us that one can only learn from someone or something one is sure about. As we said above, if one entertains any doubt about his rabbi, then this person ceases to be his rabbi and he can no longer learn from him.

And since all Israel lost the lesson they should have learned from Mosheh's speaking to the rock, they lost other great lessons as well. One of the consequences of Mosheh's doubt was that "no one knew his burial place."[16] Hence, all Israel forfeited the great lessons which could have been learned had we been able to stand at the grave of Mosheh, the man of God.

To sum up: There are many factors that can disrupt our learning. Therefore we have to be very careful to preserve our relationship with our rabbi, and similarly to nurture all the opportunities for learning that we are offered.

---

notes

1 See *Bereshit* 14:19,22. Prayer book, *Amidah* (first blessing).

2 *Bemidbar* 21:17.

3 *Shemot* 15:1.

4 *Bemidbar* 20:10–13.

5 *Yalkut Shimoni* ad loc.

6 *Mechilta* on 15:2.

7 *Yesha'ya* 29:13.

8 *Bemidbar* 21:1–3.

9 Rabbi Mosheh H̲. Luzatto, *Megillat Setarim* ad loc.

10 *Avot* 1:6.

11 *Bemidbar* 20:7–13.

12 Verse 12.

13 Rashi on verses 10–11.

14 *Mishlei* 29:19.

15 *Aderet Eliyahu* (Sinai, Tel Aviv), p. 202.

16 Ibid.

Balak

[This essay is taken from *Michtav Me-Eliyahu* IV, pp. 14–15.]

Bil'am's Offerings

"Bil'am said [to God]: I built the seven altars and I offered a bull and a ram on each."[1] Why "*the* seven altars?" Bil'am was hinting that he had built for God as many altars as had all the *Avot* put together: Avraham built four, Yitzhak one, and Ya'akov two. These are "the seven altars" to which Bil'am was referring. And Avraham offered only one ram, while he, Bil'am, offered a bull and a ram on each altar.[2]

An offering to God is a symbol. It shows a recognition of God's oneness. Maharal writes: "When we offer a *korban* to God, this acknowledges that everything belongs to Him...there is no one but Him; He is uniquely One." And furthermore: "This service...symbolizes that the person is offering himself to God. Even though he is not in fact offering himself to God, but only something he owns...by this service he is declaring himself a slave who belongs to his owner; he and his property all belong to his master."[3]

Quality counts a great deal in a *korban*. One who says, "It is only a symbol, so what does it matter what I bring?"—like Cain who brought his offering from low quality fruit[4]—is only betraying his own stinginess. He is keeping the best for himself, and his *korban* merely serves to cover up his inner defect.

On the other hand, recognition of oneness resides in the purity of heart of the one who brings the *korban*. This is true "quality." Excessive quantity, or even excessive emphasis on external quality, distorts the meaning of the *korban*.

According to a *midrash* cited by Maharal, Bil'am argued before God that it was surely better for Him to be worshipped by seventy nations than by one nation.[5] The seventy nations would offer to Him thousands of rams and a myriad rivers of oil rather than the one small measure of oil offered by Israel. God replied, in the words of *Shelomo Ha-melech*: "Better dry bread and peace with it than a house full of offerings with strife."[6]

There are two reasons why God preferred Israel. First, because the nations used the excessive quantities to cover up the evil within, as we mentioned above. And further, what God desires is motivation which is completely *lishma*. A person who acts *lishma* attributes no value or importance to his deeds. For him, the service of God in truth is self-understood and the most obvious thing in the world; truth is reality and falsehood is nothing. This is true oneness and unity in the service of God. As soon as he feels that his actions have value, he becomes conscious of himself and his importance. Since it is no longer God alone Who is involved, it no longer is a service of "oneness." True *lishma* exists only where there is a complete absence of any hint of self.

notes

1 *Bemidbar* 23:4.
2 Rashi ad loc.
3 *Netivot Olam, Netiv Ha-avodah*, ch. 1.
4 Rashi on *Bereshit* 4:3.
5 *Tanḥuma Balak* #11.
6 *Mishlei* 17:1.

Pineḥas

[This essay is taken from *Michtav Me-Eliyahu* V, pp. 104–105.]

The True Zealot

God said to Pineḥas: "I give him My covenant of peace...a covenant of everlasting priesthood."[1] Seforno writes that death occurs because of incompatibility between the different parts of an organism. Where complete peace reigns, death is delayed. In fact, we find that Pineḥas lived much longer than all his contemporaries; and if he is to be identified with Eliyahu, he is indeed still alive.[2]

In the Zohar we also find that a person who is zealous for God is immune to the Angel of Death. Since Pineḥas is Eliyahu, this explains why he did not die.[3]

We need to understand, however, what there is about zeal which endows the person possessing it with such high levels of being. Normally we find that zeal is connected with anger, and this is surely not an attractive trait.

PRAYING FOR KIDDUSH HASHEM

Rabbi Menaḥem Mendel of Vitebsk writes that the madrega of the true zealot is that he never feels any lack of material things. He realizes that everything is from Hashem, and in this context the whole concept of "lack" is simply inappropriate. What breaks his heart is the ḥillul hashem that exists in the world as a result of human action and the fact that the glorious *Shechina* of God is in exile. He cannot bear to see how limited God's influence seems to be in the world.[4]

The *tsaddik* who sees this constantly prays and begs that God's name will be sanctified once more and that all obscurity will be removed. He does not even consider praying for his own material needs because these count as nothing in his eyes compared with the immensity of his pain over the exile of the *Shechina*.

This is the person who, if he sees the opportunity to right some terrible wrong, will stride forward and act with zeal for the honor of Hashem. It is not anger that moves him, but an influx of power from Hashem. As Rashi puts it: "He takes upon himself the anger which God Himself should have vented."[5] His anger is "God's anger," that is, it is completely for God's sake, with no thought or hint of personal motives. This is the true zealot.

notes

1 *Bemidbar* 25:12.
2 Ad loc.
3 I, 209a.
4 *Pri Ha-aretz, parashat Pinehas.*
5 On 25:11.

Mattot—Mass'ei

The Tribes of Gad and Reuven, I

We know that every person's task is to increase the amount of *kiddush Hashem* in this world. As we have explained previously in this volume,[1] everything in the world can serve as a *keli* for this sublime purpose.

In our holy books we find that there are holy sparks in exile, in the darkness of the world, and it is the task of Israel to release these sparks and restore them to their place of origin.[2] We learn, too, that there are some sparks which are meant for each particular individual to redeem; they are sparks of his own *neshama* which have been taken captive by the *Sitra Aḥara*[3] — the focus of evil in creation.

We are aware that these ideas allude to very lofty concepts whose full import is far beyond our comprehension. However, we shall try and make them, as much as possible, a little more comprehensible.

THE POWER OF FREE WILL

All the obscurity in creation is capable of being transformed into a revelation of God's glory through human free will. Everything in creation holds within it the potential for *kiddush Hashem*. Every human being can change an item from impure to pure by making it a vehicle for serving Hashem. Say we are faced with this-worldly matters which hold a fatal attraction for human beings. If a person makes use of them only to the extent that they are needed for His service and no more, then he has created a revelation of God's glory and a sanctification of His name. He has shown that there is someone in the world who has seen the true purpose of creation.

The *yetzer ha-ra'* itself is nothing but a vehicle for *kiddush Hashem*. Its purpose is to challenge the person to exercise his free will to defeat it.

It is written that the power of defilement feeds on the sparks of holiness that it contains. *Tum'a* continues to exist only by virtue of its potential for *kiddush Hashem*. This is its raison d'etre—its purpose in life. Without *kiddush Hashem* there is no point in anything existing, and therefore no existence. If you could imagine anything that had no longer any potential for *kedusha*, it would cease to exist—and that itself would be its *kiddush Hashem*. It is in this sense that *tum'a* "feeds" on the holy sparks it contains; it continues to exist only by virtue of its potential for *kedusha*.

The idea that an individual has holy sparks which are his particular duty to redeem means that each person has his own allotted portion in *kiddush Hashem*. All his abilities, his *middot*, and the tests he has to undergo are suited to this basic task. This task is assigned to him from Above; it constitutes his full spiritual potential, which in some context is referred to as his *neshama*. In this sense, a person's *neshama* is not his ego, but—the particular ideal to which he should devote his life and the totality of spiritual powers granted him to complete his task. He becomes aware of his potential through the circumstances in which he is placed and the tests he is given. Each test challenges him to realize part of his spiritual potential, or in other words, releases one of the holy sparks contained in his *neshama*.

THE SPIRITUAL TASK OF GAD AND REUVEN

The tribes of Gad and Reuven belonged to the "generation of knowledge," who had received the Torah at Sinai and were constantly aware of the presence of God in their midst. When they asked Mosheh to be allowed to settle in Transjordan because of the vast quantity of livestock that they possessed,[4] one may be sure that it was not merely economic considerations which moved them.

Mosheh objected very strongly to their request because he understood they wanted to opt out of fighting for the Land of Canaan. This, he felt, would be bad for the morale of the nation.[5] When they assured him that they would fight alongside the other tribes in conquest of Canaan, he was prepared to grant their request.[6]

If their motives for wishing to settle in Transjordan were not merely economic, what were they? The tribes of Reuven and Gad certainly realized that the great number of sheep and cattle they had been given were meant to be vehicles for *kiddush Hashem*. Their first concern was to insure that their property would not cause a *hillul hashem*. It is not advisable to pasture sheep near arable land because of the damage they are likely to do to the crops. In fact, it later became prohibited to raise sheep in the arable parts of Eretz Yisrael.[7] Transjordan, however, had large areas of pastureland[8] and therefore was very suitable for raising sheep and cattle. There they would cause no damage to their neighbors.

A HASTY INHERITANCE

Nevertheless our Rabbis criticize their decision. They apply to them the verse: "An inheritance which is overly hasty at the beginning will not be blessed in the end."[9] Rashi comments on this verse: "An over-hasty inheritance: One who rushes in confusion to be the first to take, like the tribes of Gad and Reuven who hastened to take their portion in Transjordan and spoke in confusion, putting their sheep before their children (see next paragraph),[10] will not be blessed in the end, as we find that they were exiled several years before the rest of Israel." They are also accused of "separating themselves from their brethren because of their money."[11]

Their motives were certainly of the highest level. But because of their high spiritual level, our Rabbis find cause for criticism. It may well have been the right inheritance for them, but why did they have to rush to take it so soon? Why not wait until the division of the land was on the agenda? To the keen eyes of *Hazal*, this shows that subconsciously there were other motives in operation. In however subtle a form, economic considerations also played a part. To confirm this, our Rabbis note that the tribes of Gad and Reuven said to Mosheh: "We shall build sheepfolds here for our livestock and cities for our children,"[12] putting their livestock before their children. Of course this may well have been just a slip of the tongue. But our Rabbis were well aware that slips of the tongue are significant and betray the speaker's subconscious thoughts. It shows that they had their priorities confused.

Anyone who has to busy himself with the affairs of this world because this is where his portion lies, even if his motives are basically for the sake of Heaven, has to be very much on guard that his business does not develop into love of this world for its own sake, at the cost of his serving Hashem. We see that even the children of Reuven and Gad, in spite of their very high level, were misled by their slight, subconscious attachment to their property into making hasty decisions and getting their priorities wrong.

As a result, they "lost their blessing." Blessing means the expansion of *kelim* used for spiritual purposes. It is heavenly aid which the *Mishna* calls "the fruits of a mitzva in this world."[13] If a person becomes attached to material things for their own sake, then the blessing is withdrawn, for it no longer is good for that person.

THE RIGHT PRIORITIES

Rabbi Yitzhak 'Arama[14] illustrates this with a parable. When workmen build a house, they construct gangways with rough timber, even hammering together broken planks for this purpose. But for the interior decorations and furniture, only the best polished wood is used. No one is particular about things which are temporary and serve a secondary purpose, but only about things which are permanent and primary. Our stay in this world is only temporary, while our spiritual life is permanent and primary. It is surprising, therefore, how many of us make our material occupations primary and our Torah secondary.

"When the tribes of Reuven and Gad entered the land [of Canaan] and saw the wheat fields and the orchards, they said: 'Surely a spoonful of this land is worth more than a double handful in Transjordan!' Then they said, 'But still, we chose it for ourselves. It was our decision.'"[15] A person feels bound by any choice he makes, even when he begins to realize it could have been a mistake.

All this was said about the people of that great generation, whose very sins could be considered to be of a spiritual nature. How much greater is the danger in our times. A person should ponder well before deciding what the main thrust of his life will be—material affairs or Torah.

Everyone knows in his own heart what for him is primary and what secondary. One has to educate himself in such a way that he will be able to direct his life toward the primary and not, God forbid, toward the secondary.

notes

1 See the essays, "Noaḥ" and "Avraham and the King of Sodom" in *Strive for Truth!* V.
2 For a previous reference to "raising the holy sparks," see *Strive for Truth!* III, p. 100.
3 Literally, "the other side."
4 *Bemidbar* 32:1–5.
5 Ibid. 32:6–15.
6 Ibid. 20–24.
7 *Bava Kamma* 79b.
8 *Bemidbar* 32:4.
9 *Mishlei* 20:21.
10 *Bemidbar* 32:16.
11 *Bemidbar Rabba* 22:9.
12 See note 9, above.
13 *Pe'ah* 1:1.
14 *'Akedat Yitzḥak, parashat Mattot*.
15 *Vayikra Rabba* 3:1.

The Tribes of Gad and Reuven, II

From the exemplary way they kept their promise to Mosheh, one can see the greatness of these two tribes.

"The tribes of Reuven and Gad formed part of Yehoshua's retinue and [when they returned to Transjordan], he accompanied them as far as the Jordan. When they saw that his retinue was depleted, they accompanied him back to his home."[1] We see that they formed the main part of his retinue and paid him the highest honor.

According to the arrangement, they were to fight with their brethren and return home after the conquest.[2] But they undertook more than this. "We shall not return to our homes until each member of Israel has received his inheritance."[3] And they kept their word. They stayed with Yehoshua' after the conquest for another seven years, until they finished dividing up the land.

HOW TO FULFILL ONE'S TASK

The greatness of their *madrega* is evident. Why did they stay on those extra seven years? They did not feel able to return to their homes before the other tribes of Israel had received their inheritance.

All their actions were for the sake of Heaven. They viewed their inheritance in Transjordan as fulfilling their portion in *kiddush Hashem*, as we described in the previous essay. They also saw their military service as a *kiddush Hashem*. They took their task so seriously that they became the main retinue of Yehoshua' and volunteered their services in the difficult task of apportioning the land.

REMORSE HAS ITS DANGERS

When they finally returned home, before they crossed the Jordan, they built a large altar as a monument.[4] When they discovered this altar, the people of Israel were very disturbed. The temple of Shiloh was already standing and no offerings could be brought anywhere else. For what purpose had they built such an altar?

The people of Israel suspected them of building a rival altar, which they thought implied a rebellion against the God of Israel. Before launching a military attack, the tribes of Israel sent a high-level delegation to Gilead to investigate the matter. They told them of their suspicions, and added: "If you find the land of your inheritance unsuitable, come over here and settle here with us...but do not rebel against God."[5]

The tribes of Reuven and Gad explained that the altar was not meant for sacrifice, but only as a memorial to remind future generations that they had fought with them in the conquest of Canaan and were definitely part of the nation. This was to prevent later generations from saying that, since they lived on the other side of the Jordan, they were not part of *Klal Yisrael*. Far from being a rebellion against God, the altar was intended to reinforce their identity as an integral part of the nation.[6] The delegation accepted this explanation and the matter ended amicably.

The question remains: Since all Israel had witnessed their greatness and their praiseworthy devotion to duty, how could they suspect them of idolatry? There is something very profound here which we need to understand.

When someone becomes overly attached to the things of this world, regrets it, and wishes to do *teshuva*, he faces a new danger. We remember that when Elisha ben Abuya—Aher—had thoughts of doing *teshuva*, he heard a heavenly voice proclaiming, "All Israel can do *teshuva*, but not Aher." (We have explained elsewhere[7] that the voice came from Aher's own subconscious resistance to *teshuva*.) His reaction was: "If I'm not going to be accepted in the next world, I might as well enjoy myself in *this* world," and he abandoned the Torah completely.[8]

The tribes of Reuven and Gad were experiencing some regrets about their decision. The people of Israel were concerned that if they were suffering pangs of remorse but were finding it too hard to do *teshuva*, they might abandon Torah altogether.

This goes to show how difficult it is to free oneself from attachment to material things. We can succeed only if we remain determined not to be deflected from our path of Torah and *yir'at Shamayim* and to turn to God in prayer for heavenly aid—a prayer which is never refused.

notes

1 *Yalkut Shimoni, Yehoshua‘* #31.
2 *Bemidbar* 32:20.
3 Ibid., v. 18.
4 *Yehoshua‘* 22:10.
5 Ibid., v. 15–20.
6 Ibid., v. 21–29.
7 *Michtav Me-Eliyahu* IV, p. 289.
8 *Hagiga* 15a.

Devarim

[This essay is taken from *Michtav Me-Eliyahu* IV, pp. 105–106.]

Perspectives of Mercy

In the very first verse of *Sefer Devarim*, one of the place-names mentioned is Di-Zahav (meaning: "enough gold"). Our Rabbis take this as an allusion to the Golden Calf. "Thus did Mosheh say before God: Lord of the Universe! The silver and gold [*zahav*] that you showered on Israel until they said, 'Enough [*dai*]!'—this caused them to make the Golden Calf."[1]

They illustrate this with a parable. "There was a man who had a son. He bathed him, anointed him, fed him well, hung a purse full of money around his neck and set him down at the entrance to a house of harlots. What could that son do but sin?"[2]

Eliyahu, in his prayer on Mount Carmel, also said: "It is You who have turned their hearts backwards" to worship idols,[3] thus expressing a similar idea. And the Gemara concludes:[4] "God eventually agreed with Mosheh, as it says: I gave them much silver and gold—they made it into a Baal."[5]

What does all this mean?

There are two ways of looking at things: the way a master views the work of his servant and the way a father looks at the deeds of his son. The master looks at his servant with a critical eye; he is interested only in whether or not the servant fulfilled his task. But the father looks with merciful eyes. If the son fails, the father will blame himself for giving the son too hard a task or think of other far-fetched excuses. If the son does something good, however small, the father's love will magnify it.

TWO MODES OF *KIDDUSH HASHEM*

Every individual, every generation, and all generations together have a portion in the purpose of creation—the *kiddush Hashem* which God has allotted to them. It is their task to reveal this by choosing the good against all the temptations and obstacles He has placed in their path. If they fail—and God has left it entirely in their hands to fail or succeed—God can view the situation with merciful eyes. He can say that the tests they were given were indeed very difficult and they can hardly be blamed for failing under those circumstances.

But the purpose of creation will not be fulfilled without some positive contribution from human free will; there must be some "arousal from below." God will therefore look upon the little good that they did as sufficient to provide the "arousal from below," through which He can shower upon the world the influx of holiness required to bring the world to its perfected state. In this way, all the *kiddush Hashem* which mankind was supposed to produce will have been accomplished. What has not been produced by the direct action of human beings will be made up through the revelation of God's great mercies—our Father's mercy on His children. By magnifying their good deeds and minimizing their failures, He will reveal His lovingkindness to such a tremendous degree that all the *kiddush Hashem* required from creation will have been achieved.

Eliyahu adopted the first approach: magnifying their achievements. He drew out of the people, by means of a miracle, the acclamation "Hashem is God!"[5] and asked God to accept this as their full repentance. Mosheh Rabbenu followed the other approach: minimizing their failures.[6] He argued that, taking into account the masses of silver and gold they had been given and the fact that they had lived among the idol-worshipping Egyptians for so long, they had been given a greater temptation than anybody could be expected to overcome.

THE ESSENTIAL CONTRIBUTION OF THE *TSADDIK*

One more thing is needed to bring about such a drastic change in God's perspective. There must be a *tsaddik* in the generation who is prepared, so to speak, to challenge God to look at the world from a different viewpoint. This *tsaddik* is convinced that we could not withstand the darkness that would befall the world if the standard of strict justice were enforced. He is prepared, as Mosheh was, to sacrifice himself for the sake of God's people, Israel.

And God, whose love so vastly exceeds any human love, may agree.[7]

notes

1 *Berachot* 32a.

2 Ibid.

3 *Melachim* I, 18:37.

4 *Berachot* ibid.

5 *Hoshea'* 2:10.

6 *Melachim* I, 18:39.

7 Compare "Avraham's Prayer for Sodom," subtitle "How *Tsaddikim* 'Do Battle' in Prayer" in *Strive for Truth!* V.

106 |

Va-ethanan

[This essay is taken from *Michtav Me-Eliyahu* III, pp. 235–237.]

The Purpose of Suffering

"God will scatter you among the nations...and there you will worship gods made by human hands, of wood and stone... And from there you will seek God, your God, and you will find Him if you search for Him with all your heart and soul."[1]

Suffering and exile are sent by Hashem for various purposes. They may be punishment for sins; and punishment, as we know, is meant to teach us and correct our faults. "God chastises the one He loves."[2] "God chastises you as a man chastises his son."[3]

On the other hand, wrongdoing may have reached such a stage that hope for repentance is virtually lost. Divine judgment may then decide to remove all support and let matters take their course, even if this leads to utter destruction, moral—and ultimately—also physical. This is the process of "one sin brings on another sin."[4] Mercy also decrees this course, as the Mishna tells us: "Death for the wicked is good for them and good for the world."[5] Good for them—because they can do no more evil; and good for the world—because it no longer has to suffer from their wrongdoing. [This may have been the fate of the Ten Tribes of Israel,[6] but such a solution can never be applied to *Klal Yisrael* as a whole, concerning whom there is a divine promise: "I shall never reject them nor utterly destroy them..."[7]]

The Torah describes the consequences of abandoning the mitzvot in material terms: poverty, being conquered, and ultimately being exiled. Rambam explains this as follows:

> We are told in the Torah that if we deliberately abandon the Torah... the true Judge will remove from those who have done this all the good things of this world which encouraged them to rebel against God [this is the first alternative: corrective punishment]; and He will bring upon them all the misfortunes that prevent them from acquiring 'Olam ha-ba so that they shall perish in their wickedness [this is the second alternative: a sin draws in its wake another sin].[8]

EVIL DESTROYS ITSELF

At first sight, it may seem as if these two alternatives contradict each other. But this is not necessarily so. The way of corrective punishment is effective for the person who is likely to learn from suffering to change his life. For the one who is not prepared to do this, suffering may become destructive. Sin multiplies until the limit is reached. This is what the Rabbis mean by "the measure [of sin] is full."[9] When evil has destroyed all the good, the evil itself must disappear. Something that is completely evil cannot exist. This is a safety-valve built into the universe: evil must eventually destroy itself.

But there may be a happier outcome. Suffering may have the effect of destroying the evil in the person while leaving the person intact. This may be what Rambam meant when he wrote: "The true Judge will remove from them...all the good things of this world...which encouraged them to rebel." Some people, when they see that the bottom has dropped out of their world and they despair of ever experiencing the "good life" for which they yearned, may come to see the vanity of the aims of the *yetzer ha-ra'*. They may even come to inward repentance.

This may also happen on the moral plane. There may be another meaning behind the verses which head this essay. "There you will worship gods made by human hands... And from there you will seek God, your God."[10] When you realize the depths of degradation which you have reached—this may be the strongest impetus for you to return in all sincerity to God. As the Talmud puts it: "'When the plague covers all the body, the person is pure.'[11] When the generation is wholly guilty—then redemption comes."[12]

LEARNING BEFORE SUFFERING COMES

Our Rabbis teach us to be sensitive to everything that befalls us in everyday life. God is continually giving us hints and it is up to us to take the hints.

> If a person goes out to the market [where there are squabbles and shouting], he should consider it as if he had been summoned to court for judgment. If he has a headache, he should consider it as if he was being hauled off in chains. If he is unwell and has to take to his bed, he should consider it as if he was being judged on a life and death charge. If he really was in such a predicament, only great lawyers could get him acquitted. What are the "great lawyers"? Repentance and good deeds.
>
> Even if there are 999 accusers and only one in his defense, he will be saved... Even if in that one angel in his defense there are 999 points of guilt and only one point

in his favor, he will be saved.[13]

This seems strange. The Talmud begins by saying that he needs "great lawyers" to acquit him. How, then, can it go on to say that even a thousandth thousandth part of merit will suffice to save him?

The meaning is this. When they say that if a person has a headache or is confined to bed he should consider it as if he were facing the scaffold, they mean that a person should be very sensitive to everything that happens to him. If something occurs that may seem to hold only a remote chance of danger, he should take it as a hint from Hashem that his spiritual life is in danger.

If he takes the hint now and sets about finding what is wrong and rectifying it, even a small merit will serve to save him from a great danger. However, if he waits until the danger is already a reality, he may need to take much more drastic measures to save himself.

ADVANTAGES OF EARLY LEARNING

We have learned that suffering is sent to serve an end—that a person should mend himself and mend his ways. It is clear that this cause is best served by "early learning." If a person waits until the troubles are already upon him, he is less likely to learn from them. The *yetzer ha-ra'* may persuade him to harbor resentment against Hashem for sending him these troubles and he will be in no mood to draw the right conclusions. In a state of suffering, too, it is extremely difficult to concentrate.

The time to learn and to rectify one's faults is when the danger is only a possibility.

There is another advantage. If a person does *teshuva* when the troubles are already upon him, his *teshuva*, though it may be real, is of a lesser quality. The impetus for his *teshuva*, in a sense, came from outside himself—from the sufferings sent him by Hashem. If a person repents at the stage when the suffering is only a possibility, the impetus for his repentance comes from himself—from his own being. His repentance is of a higher quality because he rectifies his evil choice at its source. The impetus to sin came from himself and his repentance likewise comes from the depths of his being.

If a person does not arouse himself to *teshuva* and repents only when sufferings have broken him mentally and physically and virtually crushed his *yetzer ha-ra'*, only a small part of his *teshuva* can be attributed to his own *behira*. Hashem's providence has provided the lion's share.

MASHIAḤ WITHOUT *TESHUVA*?

Earlier in this volume,[14] we discussed the argument of Rabbi Eliezer and Rabbi Yehoshua' about the redemption of Israel. Rabbi Eliezer maintained that there could be no final redemption without *teshuva*, while Rabbi Yehoshua' insisted that *teshuva* was not necessary.[15] Yet eventually Rabbi Yehoshua' conceded that Israel will do *teshuva* because of "the decrees of a king as bad as Haman."[16] It is clear that they were arguing about the value of suffering-induced *teshuva*.

When the time for the final redemption arrives, the Gemara seems to imply that Israel will be within a hairsbreadth of moral degradation. But this will not be allowed to occur, as explained in the first part of this essay. Before this can happen, God forbid, God will begin to show the light of *Mashiaḥ* before his actual coming. The hand of God will be revealed in the stirring events of that time.

Those of the people of Israel who are still attached to their heritage, even by a hairsbreadth, will acknowledge the clear evidence of God's intervention in history. Masses of people will do *teshuva* and go forward to meet *Mashiah*.

It is true that a *teshuva* of this sort contains a large contribution from Above and a minimal contribution from below, but at this critical juncture in world history, Hashem will accept our repentance and usher in the Messianic era.

notes

1 *Devarim* 4:27–28.
2 *Mishlei* 3:12.
3 *Devarim* 8:5.
4 *Avot* 4:2.
5 *Sanhedrin* 8:5.
6 See *Divrei Ha-yamim* II 17:7–23.
7 *Vayikra* 26:44.
8 Laws of Repentance 9:5.
9 See *Bereshit* 15:16 and Rashi ad loc.
10 *Devarim* 4:28.
11 *Vayikra* 13:13.
12 *Sanhedrin* 97a.
13 *Shabbat* 32a.
14 See *Strive for Truth!* V, *parashat Shemot*, in the essay "Hardening Pharaoh's Heart," subtitle "Two Forms of *Teshuva*."
15 *Sanhedrin* 97b.
16 Ibid.

Ekev

[This essay is taken from *Michtav Me-Eliyahu* IV, p. 44.]

Eretz Yisrael: Greatness and Responsibility

The greatness of Eretz Yisrael lies in the fact that it "corresponds to the Eretz Yisrael of above."[1] This means that in Eretz Yisrael, one has direct access to the highest Torah ideals meant to be realized in the land.

The Torah tells us that "God's eyes are upon this land from the beginning to the end of each year,"[2] meaning that in Eretz Yisrael one can perceive more clearly than anywhere else the direct providence of Hashem—*hashgaha pratit*. Through this, one can approach more closely the ideal of complete and selfless purity of service—*lishma gamur*.

The influx of holiness into people's minds is different here, in Eretz Yisrael. If a person is willing to think deeply about Torah in Eretz Yisrael, he will find his efforts rewarded with a flow of ideas much deeper and more abundant than he would achieve with the same effort elsewhere.[3] This is the meaning of the "change of angels" Ya'akov Avinu experienced when he left *hutz la-aretz* and arrived in Eretz Yisrael.[4] God is closer here than anywhere else. This is why the Rabbis say: "Whoever lives outside Eretz Yisrael resembles one who has no God, while whoever lives in Eretz Yisrael resembles one who has a God."[5]

THE LOSS OF THE HIGHER ERETZ YISRAEL

We have described something of the greatness and holiness of Eretz Yisrael. Yet—for our sins—many have grasped the "Eretz Yisrael of below" and completely ignored the "Eretz Yisrael of above." They are satisfied—so far—with a "secular" Eretz Yisrael. This means that the forces of evil have succeeded in capturing the love of Eretz Yisrael which resides in every Jewish heart.[6] Not only have they secularized this holy feeling, they have misused the whole concept of Eretz Yisrael for their own anti-Torah purposes. Terrible!

RESPONSIBILITY

A tremendous responsibility rests upon us, the *bnei Torah*. Our Rabbis tell us that exile, too, is a desecration of God's name:[7]

> This, too, is *hillul hashem*... When people say of them: "These are God's people and they have left His land."[8] They desecrate My name...when the nations among whom they are exiled say: "See, these are the people of God and He could not save them from exile." The name of God is desecrated and His honor diminished.[9]

Punishment is a lesson for the sinner and a correction for the sin. Its source is holy. But since it was caused by sin, the forces of evil can use it to bring about a great defilement. And who is responsible? The sinner whose sin brought the punishment, which can then be used by dark forces for *hillul hashem*.

We see holy sparks held prisoner by the forces of darkness.[10] Who is responsible? Those who learn Torah but fail to practice what they learn in everyday life. As Rabbi M. H. Luzatto wrote, heavenly lights which are left unused and are not engaged in the world of action are prey to the forces of evil.[11] The result is utter confusion and instability.

The remedy is in our own hands. Our learning must be for the furtherance of God's purposes in the world. "May God rejoice in His works."[12] "His works" refers to the lower worlds, that is, the world of the subconscious. If Torah penetrates our subconscious, then it can engage with the world of everyday life, of human relations, of friendliness, of honesty, of giving—the world which thirsts so much for Torah values. If we apply our Torah to this world, then we are helping to fulfill the purpose for which it was given. "The main thing is not the learning, but the doing."[13]

> A person should study Scripture, Mishna, and Talmud and serve the disciples of the wise, and insure that at the same time his business dealings are honest and his speech is friendly to all. What do people say about him? Happy is his father who taught him Torah, happy is his *rebbe* who taught him Torah... About him God says: You are My servant, Israel, by whom I am glorified.[14]

Such a person creates a great *kiddush Hashem* in the world and restores holiness to its rightful place in Jewish life. At the same time, he weakens and drives away the powers of evil. He shows his love of God by making God's name beloved to all.[15] Such a person helps to realize the purpose of creation. If only more of us—all of us—would adopt this program, our world would be very different.

notes

1 Zohar III 72a.
2 *Devarim* 11:12.
3 Rabbi Dessler *zt"l* reported this as his own experience when he first came to Eretz Yisrael.
4 Rashi, and *parashat Vayetzei*.
5 *Devarim Rabba* 7:10.
6 See *Strive for Truth!* I, p. 55.
7 *Yoma* 86a.
8 *Yehezkel* 36:20.
9 Rashi, Yoma 86a.
10 See above *parashat Mattot-Mass'ei*.
11 *Adir Ba-marom*, Warsaw ed. p. 22.
12 *Tehillim* 104:31.
13 *Avot* 1:17.
14 See note 7, above.
15 Ibid.

Re'ei

[This essay is taken from *Michtav Me-Eliyahu* V, pp. 11–12.]

Two Kinds of Joy

King Shelomo prayed: "Give me neither poverty nor riches; give me my allotted bread. If I am satisfied, I might deny and say 'Who is God?' If I am poor, I might steal and take the name of my God [in vain]."[1]

Troubles arouse a person and turn him towards God. If all his needs are satisfied, he may imagine that he can do without God, and from that to denial is not very far. It is clear that human beings have a strong tendency to deny God. If a person whose needs have been satisfied for the moment has this tendency, how much more so a rich man who thinks his prosperity is guaranteed far into the future.

Because this danger was so clear to him, Shelomo Ha-melech prayed that he would not have riches nor even the complete satisfaction of his physical needs, but only the essential minimum: "my allotted bread." The implication is that he would have much preferred to be poor and lack even essentials, were it not that poverty has its own dangers. He might be tempted to steal and lie, and so eventually also come to deny God by taking a false oath.

SUKKA OF PEACE

"You shall make a festival of Sukkot...when you gather your harvest..."[2] Everyone is happy when the harvest is in and they feel that their livelihood for the year is assured. The danger of denying God is self-evident. To obviate this danger, the Torah commands us to "dwell in *sukkot* for seven days."[3] This is to teach us that safety is not in material things, but in our closeness to God. Our shelter is not the roof, but God's *sukka* of peace. We realize that true satisfaction comes only from banishing material ambitions from our hearts and filling our lives with *avodat Hashem*.[4]

REJOICING IN THE FESTIVAL

Instead of rejoicing in the harvest, the Torah tells us to "rejoice in your festival."[5] This means spiritual joy, as another verse says, "You shall rejoice *before God, your God*."[6] The Talmud learns from this verse—"and you shall rejoice in your festival"—that one is not allowed to celebrate a marriage during a festival: "Rejoice in your festival and not in your wife."[7] It is all the more obvious that our joy should not be in our harvest or in our sense of physical security. The joy of the festival is spiritual joy. It is joy in the heartfelt fulfillment that comes from transcending material desires and putting in their place the service of Hashem.

But how is it possible to change one's joy from joy in the material to joy in the spiritual? There is only one way in which to do this, which we shall now explain.

THE FIELD OF THE HEART

My *rebbe* told me this in the name of the Vilna Gaon, of blessed memory. It is impossible to sow a field unless it has first been plowed. Similarly, the blockage in our heart—*timtum ha-lev*—prevents spiritual feelings from penetrating it. The hard peel surrounding the heart must first be pierced. Only then can spiritual insights be sown, and only then can fruit be expected to grow, in the form of changed attitudes.

How can the hard soil of the heart be plowed? *With strong emotional upheaval*. This can come from sudden disaster or from great joy. When a person is in a state of great excitement, for whatever reason, his heart opens. A person can now impress on it whatever he likes. He can say to himself: Now is my chance! The hard casing of my heart has been broken open. Quick! I must sow in it what I want.

The origin of the great joy may have been nothing more than a good harvest. But now that the heart is excited and aroused, its habitual blockage is removed. This provides the opportunity to show one's heart that the joy of spiritual success far exceeds the joy of material success. Here is the chance to transform one's joy into another, higher level of joy.

The water-drawing ceremony which took place during the nights of the Sukkot festival was one of the highlights of the service in the Holy Temple in Jerusalem. "One who has never seen the water-drawing ceremony in the Holy Temple has never seen joy in his life."[8] This ceremony and the water libation—*nissuch ha-mayim*—that followed it were in essence a prayer for rain for the coming year. But our Rabbis transformed it into a celebration of the spirit. "Why is it called 'the joy of the water-drawing'? Because from it they used to draw the holy spirit."[9] Prophets used to draw their inspiration from this dramatic and joy-inspiring ceremony.[10]

So we see what the Torah meant by "Make a festival...when you gather..."[11] Use the physical joy of gathering the harvest as a springboard to reach spiritual joy. Then your joy will be complete. You will experience the supreme happiness of transforming the lower into the higher—the darkness of denial into the great light of faith in God.

HASSIDIC CUSTOMS

With this in mind, we can now understand the custom prevalent among Hassidim to arouse joy and good humor through external means, such as the judicious use of liquor. They use joyous occasions to speak words of Torah and serving Hashem. Whoever instituted this obviously understood the secret of opening the heart and sowing seeds of Torah and *hessed*—as we discussed above.

It is wonderful to see how all Jewish customs, in every section of Jewry, have the same goal—to further Torah and deepen our *avodat Hashem*.

notes

1 *Mishlei* 30:8–9.
2 *Devarim* 16:13.
3 *Vayikra* 23:42.
4 See *parashat Shoftim*, end.
5 *Devarim* 16:14.
6 *Vayikra* 23:40.
7 *Mo'ed Katan* 8b.
8 *Sukka* 51a.
9 *Bereshit Rabba* 70:8.
10 *Yerushalmi Sukka* 5:1.
11 See note 2, above.

Shoftim

[This essay is taken from *Michtav Me-Eliyahu* IV, pp. 5–7.]

Jealousy and Its Consequences

Maharal equates the "evil eye" with the "mean eye."[1] The person with the mean eye—*tsar 'ayin*—eyes his neighbor with distaste. He does not want his neighbor to have anything good. In fact, he would prefer that his neighbor not be there at all. (This is the opposite of *tov 'ayin*, the person with a good eye, who wants his neighbor to have only good, and is happy when he sees his neighbor blessed with all of Hashem's bounties.) There are many sources throughout the Talmud and Midrash which describe the unfortunate effects of the evil eye. First of all, there is the disastrous effect on the person who possesses an evil eye. "The evil eye, the evil inclination, and the hatred of other people take a person out of this world."[2]

The effect of the evil eye on other people is often described by *Hazal*. For example: "The first tablets of stone, which were given with great publicity, were subject to the influence of the evil eye and were broken."[3] The evil eye belonged to the nations of the world who were jealous of Israel's glory at *Mattan Torah*. The evil eye can also work subconsciously. "A person should not walk by the field of his neighbor when the wheat is fully grown and ready for harvesting, since he may look upon it with an evil eye."[4]

HOW *'AYIN HA-RA'* WORKS

The effectiveness of *'ayin ha-ra'* is based on the fact that on a spiritual plane people are closely joined to each other. Without their knowing it, people are—to a considerable extent—interdependent.

If A is jealous of B and looks upon him with a "mean eye," as we described earlier, it shows that A does not want B to have the good thing which he happens to have at the moment. But it means much more than that. It means that A wants B to have only bad things from now on, and indeed A would prefer that B didn't even exist. We explained before that, in a sense, everyone is dependent on everyone else. Therefore, to the extent that B's good fortune is dependent upon how A feels about it, it may well be that when A looks upon B with such loathing, this may adversely affect the flow of life which maintains B in existence and may even make him more prone to injury and accident.

Earlier in this volume, we refer to the mitzva of *egla arufa*.[5] When a corpse is found near a city, the elders of that city must come out and declare that they are innocent of the death of this unknown traveler. "Our hands have not shed this blood, etc."[6] Our Rabbis comment on this: "The *egla arufa* comes only because of those who are mean of eye." The elders have to say: "Our hands have not shed this blood, etc." Did anyone really think that the elders of the *beit din* were murderers? No. This comes to tell us that they must declare their innocence of treating the stranger who came to their city negligently. They must announce that: "When he came to us, we did not let him go without provisions and we did not see him and allow him to leave without company." Rashi explains that the murder may have occurred because the traveler was allowed to leave without sufficient provisions and on his journey he saw somebody who had food. Perhaps because of his hunger, he attempted to take the food away from the man, and in the ensuing fight he got killed. If the elders of the city had seen to it that he was not left to travel alone without provisions, the murder might not have happened.[7]

Why is this negligence on the part of the city elders called "meanness of eye"? Maharal explains that the city elder who does not care about the stranger in his city and fails to provide for his minimal needs, resulting in his death, is in a sense guilty of murder.[8] The evil eye with which he looked at his neighbor caused bloodshed.

Why is this called "meanness of eye"? Maharal teaches us that a person who is completely indifferent to the needs of his fellow can be said to look upon him with an evil eye. Someone who recognizes that his neighbor has rightful needs and has the power to help him, yet remains indifferent, declares by his very indifference that he is not interested in his neighbor whatsoever. The other person's existence is a nuisance to him; he does not want to be bothered to provide him with the little that he needs. This is meanness of eye which borders on bloodshed.

HOW CAN ONE AVOID 'AYIN HA-RA'?

We have explained how a person who is jealous of his neighbor and looks upon him with an evil eye can cause him damage and injury. But the world is run along just lines. A person is never able to injure someone else unless that someone else deserves it in some way. What fault does that person affected by the evil eye have? Why should the attribute of justice find him deserving of the hurt caused by the person with the evil eye?

There may, of course, be many reasons. He may be liable, by the standards of strict justice, because he in some way made another person jealous. If a person became jealous of his property, maybe he was not modest enough in its use and people thought he was ostentatious. It is a well-known fact that a person who does not act only for himself, but whose whole behavior is based on giving rather than taking—such a person never arouses jealousy. If others suspected that in one way or another he was taking things for himself, they would automatically feel that he was taking something away from them. However irrational, this is how people think, and if one causes these thoughts, one has to accept the consequences.

We are told that the descendants of Yosef are not subject to the evil eye. The evil eye has no power over Yosef because he never wanted to take anything that was not his. Some learn this from Ya'akov's blessing: "They shall multiply like fish." "Just as fish in the sea are completely covered by water and consequently are not subject to the evil eye, so the seed of Yosef, etc."[9] There are two points about fish: they are out of sight, and also they live, so to speak, in another world. They do not compete with land dwellers even for the air they breathe.

The lesson here is that the person who lives a modest life devoted to mitzvot and good deeds, taking nothing from anyone, but only interested in bestowing good upon everyone else, is never an object of jealousy. The evil eye can have no power over him.

THE *BEN TORAH*

It works both ways. The person who has rejected worldly ambitions and seeks and finds fulfillment in a life of learning and spreading Torah will have no jealousy in his heart for other life styles. His eye will not look with evil on others, but will seek only the good in everyone else. And in response, others, too, will look upon him only with a good eye.

This describes the *ben Torah* of our times, whose sole desire is to be left in peace to pursue the goals of Torah and to grow in spiritual stature. He has to say *Enough!* to the search for worldly success, *Enough!* to all that would deflect him from his goal, *Enough!* to materialism, *Enough!* to vain dreams. In this way, he will distance himself from jealousy and the evil eye. He may even reach the *madrega* of the good eye, that most splendid of all human characteristics. By freeing himself from the desire for material goals, he also frees himself from the jealousy of those who pursue those goals. Though those who follow material ambitions may often appear to be successful, *he* knows that this does not bring with it genuine fulfillment. True, deep satisfaction is granted only to he who turns his back on material strivings and the world of taking, and in their place seeks spiritual progress and a life of giving. It is only those who "love God...and serve Him with all their heart and soul" who will "eat and *be satisfied*."[10]

This is an open miracle. Seeking the spiritual life is what gives happiness in this world, while seeking material success produces the opposite! This miracle is available to anyone who sincerely wants to experience it in his own life.

notes

1 *Netivot 'Olam, Netiv 'Ayin Tov.*
2 *Avot* 2:11.
3 *Midrash Tanḥuma, Ki Tissa* #31.
4 *Bava Metzia* 107a.
5 *Parashat Vayikra*, in the essay "The Offerings," p. 12.
6 *Devarim* 21:7.
7 *Sota* 38b.
8 See note 1, above.
9 *Berachot* 20a.
10 *Devarim* 11:13,15.

Ki-Tetze

[This essay is taken from *Michtav Me-Eliyahu* III, pp. 216–218.]

The Memory of Amalek

> Remember what Amalek did to you...they attacked
> you on the way and cut off all the stragglers...showing
> no fear of God.... [Therefore]...you shall blot out all
> memory of Amalek from under the heavens...[1]

We have noted elsewhere[2] that every nation has a dominant characteristic which can, in theory at least, be used
to further God's purposes in the world. Pride can be used
to foster good works. Aggressiveness can be turned
against the forces of evil. Pleasure seeking, too, can be
good if its aim can be turned to spiritual pleasure. And so
on. At present, all these possibilities for good are merely
in their potential stage, but when *Mashiah* comes, the potential will be realized—the "holy sparks" will be liber-
ated[3]—and these powers will be used to help Israel. In
this way, the nations can become *kelim* for holiness and
contribute to the purpose of creation. Their motivation
may not be pure, but their actions will at least give them
some connection to the divine purpose and justify their
existence.

Amalek, however, is different. Its memory must be
"blotted out." What is it about Amalek that gives them

apparently no justification for existing? Egypt, in spite of its moral degradation,[4] was capable of knowing God: "Egypt shall know that I am God."[5] Immorality can be overcome, as we see from the law that permits the grandson of an Egyptian to marry a Jewess.[6] The Canaanites had to be utterly destroyed,[7] but only in Eretz Yisrael. If they emigrated, they were left undisturbed.[8]

Only concerning Amalek was the decree given: "Blot out their memory..."[9] and "The war of God against Amalek lasts from generation to generation."[10] And our Rabbis say: "God's name is not complete nor is His throne complete until Amalek's name is blotted out."[11] What is the characteristic of Amalek which makes it different from all other nations?

DIFFERENT REACTIONS

[When Israel emerged on the world scene amid dazzling miracles, all the surrounding nations were dumbfounded.

> Nations heard and were frightened,
> The dwellers of Philistia were seized with dread.
> Then were the chieftains of Edom confounded,
> Trembling seized the mighty ones of Moab;
> All the dwellers of Canaan melted in fear.[12]

Amalek, however, refused to be impressed. On the contrary, it decided to "cool off" the other nations' excitement about Israel and convince them that Israel was just a nation like any other. The Rabbis point out that the word *karecha*—"attacked you"[13] contains the root *kar*—"cold."

> Amalek gathered all the nations of the world and asked them to come and help him against Israel. They replied: "We cannot stand against them. Pharaoh

tried...and he and all his army were drowned..."
Amalek said: "I will give you some advice. [I will engage them in battle first.] If they defeat me, you can escape... If I defeat them, come and join me against
them."[14]

As it turned out, the Amalekites were defeated, but not
before they succeeded in killing some of the Israelites.
They had succeeded in their design by showing that Israel, too, was vulnerable to attack.]

IDEOLOGICAL STRUGGLES

It was not political or military ends which motivated
Amalek to be the first nation to attack Israel. It was something much deeper than that. Amalek was the archenemy
of spirituality and holiness. It could not tolerate the rise of
the power of holiness in the world. Therefore, it felt impelled to attack the bearers of that power—the people of
Israel.

The Amalekites were engaged in an ideological struggle. Impudence, blasphemy, and mockery were their
weapons. On the words "they cut off the stragglers"[15], our
Rabbis comment: "They cut off the circumcised members and threw them towards heaven, saying 'This is
what You wanted; here, take it.'"[16]

The Rabbis detect in the word *karecha*[17] (in addition to
the idea of *coldness*, which we referred to above) two other
nuances. *Karecha* contains the root *mikreh*—"chance."
According to Amalek's ideology, there is no supervision
or design in the universe; everything happens by chance.
Furthermore, the Rabbis detect in this expression the
word *keri*—"defilement," particularly the homosexual defilement to which they subjected their Israelite captives.

It is not difficult to see how these three concepts are linked. A person may be nominally an observant Jew, but if he is cold towards Torah and mitzvot, he will also tend to be cold towards the signs of God's supervision in the world and will see everywhere only the hand of chance. As a result, he will be susceptible to the lure of the worst type of defilement, which he will find more exciting.

To sum up, Amalek's main characteristic was arrogant mockery of all that is holy. One can see why it is so difficult for this trait to be transformed into a positive force, unlike the other *middot* we referred to at the beginning of this essay. Such a person perceives spiritual truth as a threat to his overweening egotism, and the more he knows about it, the more he will belittle it and mock it. Most people tend to follow what they are told, and with people of "Amalekite" allegiance in positions of influence, it is not difficult to envisage that God's "name" and "throne"—His prestige and authority—will be diminished[18] in the eyes of many people.

THE FINAL TEST

With their prophetic vision, the masters of *kabbala* foresaw that this attitude would be prevalent in the time of the "footsteps of the *Mashiah*," which is the era in which we now live. With amazing prescience, they foretold that in this era the political leaders of the Jewish people would adhere to the "Amalekite" ideology.[19]

In this era, darkness obscures the spiritual world. Materialistic ideas gain power. Science progresses at a dizzying pace, allowing the world's resources to be increasingly exploited, seemingly for human benefit. Anti-Torah ideas of human supremacy flood the world. Many openly attack religious beliefs and practices. Believers in God and

His Torah are despised. This is the nature of the last exile of the Jewish people.

God returns many Jews to Eretz Yisrael. They gain power and sovereignty. Many are afflicted with arrogance and plan to replace Torah with anti-Torah. This is the final test of the exile of the *Shechina*—the hardest test of all.

Our task in this time of challenge is to remain steadfast in our faith—to recognize constantly the truth of the spirit and the falsity of its challengers. Some say: "We have done our part, we have conquered Eretz Yisrael. Now Hashem will do His part and restore the people of Israel to faith in the Torah and the fear of God." The error of this attitude should be self-evident. "Everything is in the hands of God *except* the fear of God."[20] God does not effect spiritual change in the world without someone making a correct *behira* choice.[21] Wars are won by God,[22] but rekindling the spirit of faith is in *our* hands. If we remain steadfast and show in our own lives how Torah transforms a person into an elevated human being, then we have done all that lies within the power of *behira*. Only then can we expect God to do the rest.

notes

1 *Devarim* 25:17–19.

2 *Strive for Truth!* IV, *Sanctuaries in Time*, pp. 64–65.

3 See above "The Tribes of Gad and Reuven – 1" and *Strive for Truth!* III, p. 100.

4 See *Strive for Truth!* IV, *Sanctuaries in Time*, p. 12.

5 *Shemot* 14:18.

6 *Devarim* 23:8–9.

7 Ibid. 20:16–17.

8 *Talmud Yerushalmi*, *Shevi'it* 6:1.

9 See note 1, above.

10 *Shemot* 17:16.

11 Ibid., Rashi.

12 *Shemot* 15:14–15.

13 See note 1, above.

14 *Mechilta* on *Shemot* 17:8.

15 See note 1, above.

16 *Yalkut Shimoni*, on *Devarim* 23:8.

17 See note 1, above.

18 See note 11, above.

19 Zohar III, p. 279a (*Raya Mehemna*).

20 *Berachot* 33b.

21 See Chazon Ish notes, end of *Orach Hayyim*.

22 *Avoda Zara* 2b.

Ki-Tavo

[This essay is taken from *Michtav Me-Eliyahu* V, pp. 78–79.]

The Joy of a Mitzva

It is said that the basis of the creation is *hessed*. God is good, and it is the way of the good to *do* good. God therefore created His world in order to bestow good on His creatures.[1] "The world is built on *hessed*."[2] But some ask: If God created everything for the sake of *hessed*, does this not imply that before creation something was lacking? But surely God, the only thing that existed before creation, never lacks anything?

This question is based on an error. In the "Discourse on Lovingkindness,"[3] we asked a similar question. In that essay, we contrasted the giver and the taker. The life of the taker is a sequence of needs and gratifications. His sole interest is taking, that is, gratifying his perceived needs. The giver, on the other hand, is interested only in giving, that is, in *hessed*—in bestowing happiness on all.

THE ORIGINS OF *HESSED*

The question was raised: Is not the desire to do *hessed* also a need? By being kind to others surely the giver is gratifying his needs, just as the taker gratifies *his* needs?

We answered this question by pointing out a profound distinction between the giver and the taker. The taker is mostly unhappy, because he perceives his needs most of the time and only occasionally gratifies them.

> The quality of giving [however] is inherent only in the person who is *happy*...with his lot. He is happy because his life is filled with the joys of spiritual pursuits, before whose riches all other interests pale... In his happiness, he resembles a river in flood whose life-giving waters overflow all its banks... Firmly rooted in the spiritual life, his eyes ever turned towards the heights, he sees in everything, great and small, "the lovingkindnesses of Hashem which are unending..." Consequently, his joy in these gifts knows no bounds and his life is unendingly happy. Out of his fullness of joy and happiness flow giving and love. Thus the urge to do good to others...is not produced by a lack or deficiency... It is an outflow of the ecstatic devotion by which the happy man is attached to Hashem.[4]

THE SECRET OF CREATION

So we see that the <u>h</u>essed of the giver is an overflow of his happiness. It comes, not from lack or deficiency, but from fulfillment.

Now we can see clearly the mistake we made when we asked: "Did God lack <u>h</u>essed that he had to create a world to give Him the opportunity to do <u>h</u>essed?" If we can envisage a human being whose <u>h</u>essed flows from fulfillment rather than from need, surely, with infinitely more justification we can envisage this in the Creator Himself. It is difficult for us to speak of God, for we can have no conception of Him as He truly is. We can speak of Him only by way of analogies and parables. But, by analogy to the human giver, we can certainly understand that the divine Giver also is not moved by need, for He has no needs.

His ḥessed and the worlds to receive that ḥessed are an outflow of — if we can say such a thing — His own inner
happiness in the fullness and perfection of His being. We
can conceive that this happiness overflows, and from it
universes of ḥessed stream forth. This is the secret of the
creation of the universe.

JOY OF BEING

In His goodness, God created us in His image.[5] He implanted in us the potential for just such a joy as this—the
joy of being, the joy of fulfillment. It follows that the elevated human being—the true giver—resembles his Creator. In this very fundamental aspect, the human being's
giving may flow from an inner joy akin in some sense to
the joy of the Almighty.

A person who does a mitzva may feel happy about this
for various reasons. He may feel happy because he has
"chalked up" another mitzva to his credit. Another may
feel happy as a result of the mitzva itself. In learning Torah, it often happens that one enjoys the learning itself,
and not just the fact that he has learned something. There,
inner joy resembles the intrinsic joy we spoke about
above.

This gives us a way of judging the intrinsic qualities of
the mitzvot we do. Maybe this will help us to understand
the difficult verse in *parashat Ki Tavo* which seems to imply that the gravest sin of all is not serving God with joy.
"Because you did not serve God, your God, with joy and
with a good heart, when you had everything in abundance, you will serve your enemies in hunger and
thirst...lacking everything."[6] Service without joy—without heart—is no service at all. It shows that the person is
still primarily self-serving. He has not even started on the

road to true service of God. And this is the root of all sin.

A person should examine the quantity and quality of his joy in doing mitzvot and compare them—or contrast them—with the joy he experiences after gratifying his physical desires. Then he will be able to assess his true *madrega*.

Similarly, learning *mussar* can be a real joy, because this is how a person comes to recognize himself—his true existence.

notes

1 Rav Saadya Gaon, *Emunot Ve'deot*, III, beg. Rabbi M. H̱. Luzatto, *Da'at Tevunot*, beg.

2 *Tehillim* 89:3.

3 *Strive for Truth!* I, pp. 141–142.

4 Ibid. p. 142.

5 *Bereshit* 1:27.

6 *Devarim* 28:41–42.

Nitzavim—Vayelech

[This essay is taken from *Michtav Me-Eliyahu* IV, p. 257, and III, p. 45.]

The Power of Words

> This commandment...is neither hidden from you nor distant. It is neither in the heavens...nor is it over the ocean... It is very close to you; [it is] in your mouth and your heart to do it.[1]

We can readily understand the statement "It is in your heart to do it." We know that in Torah everything depends on the heart,[2] that is, on the feelings and emotions which motivate a person to come closer to God. But "It is in your mouth to do it"? How can one draw closer to God and His Torah by using one's mouth?

TOILING WITH ONE'S MOUTH

Iyov teaches us that "Man is born for toil."[3] The Rabbis comment on this in the Talmud:

> Man is born for toil, indeed; but for what kind of toil? Is he created for toiling with his mouth or maybe for physical labor? Since another verse states: "[The soul of the toiler toils for him,] for he has directed his mouth towards this,"[4] we see that what is meant is toiling with the mouth. But I still don't know whether this means the toil of Torah or maybe the toil of conversation. Since another verse states: "This book of the Torah

shall not depart from your mouth,"[5] we see that what is meant is the toil of Torah.[6]

"Man became a living spirit"[7] is translated by Onkelos as "...a speaking spirit." Speech is the distinguishing characteristic of man. But man does justice to his status as a "speaking spirit" only when he uses his gift as a means of spiritual elevation—that is, to toil in Torah.

Great power resides in the faculty of speech. If a person gets used to speaking about Torah and holiness, this will have a tremendous influence on his thought patterns and also on his emotions.

Let us imagine: A heavy truck starts to roll backwards down a hill. Its brakes have failed and its engine, too, has stalled. There is only one way of stopping it. If someone could jump into the driver's seat and start the engine, he might be able to save the situation. Speech is the engine of the soul. Speech has the power to bring our knowledge to bear upon our heart. If only we would fill our speech with Torah, with wisdom, and *mussar*! This is the "toil of the mouth" which our Rabbis refer to above.

Now we know what Mosheh Rabbenu meant by: "It is in the power of our mouth and our heart to do it!"

---

notes

---

1 *Devarim* 31:7–11.

2 *Sanhedrin* 106b.

3 *Iyov* 5:7.

4 *Mishlei* 16:26.

5 *Yehoshua* 1:8.

6 *Sanhedrin* 99b.

7 *Bereshit* 2:7.

Ha'azinu

[This essay is taken from *Michtav Me-Eliyahu* III, pp. 56–57.]

Torah and Mitzvot

There is a *mishna* in *Massechet Pe'ah* which we recite every morning:

> These are the things for which one enjoys the fruits in this world while the capital remains secure in the World to Come: Honoring one's father and mother, bestowing good on others...and learning Torah." And the passage continues: "Learning Torah is equal to them all."[1]

On this the *Yerushalmi* comments: "Even all the mitzvot of the Torah are not equal to one word of Torah."

This would appear to be an amazing statement. Surely it is well established that "The main thing is not the learning, but the doing,"[2] and "They voted and decided: Learning is great because it leads to action"?[3] How can anyone possibly maintain that "All the mitzvot in the Torah are not worth one word of Torah"?

TWO VALUE SYSTEMS

There are two ways of evaluating mitzvot: one intrinsic and one according to their difficulty. The intrinsic value is the spiritual energy that Hashem has implanted in every mitzva. It is this intrinsic value to which the *mishna* refers when it says: "No one knows the true reward of mitzvot."[4] Mitzvot are also measured by the degree of difficulty experienced in performing them. It is well known that "One mitzva done with effort is worth a hundred done with ease."[5] My revered father, *z"l*, commented that there may be many degrees of difficulty involved in doing a mitzva, starting with physical effort, persevering in spite of tiredness, resisting pressure from friends and associates, risking financial loss and so on. For each additional degree of difficulty, the reward—which is the spiritual energy acquired—is multiplied a hundredfold. So if for the first degree of difficulty and effort the factor is one hundred, for the second degree the factor will be a hundred times that, or ten thousand, while for the third degree the factor will be a million, and so on.

It follows that the main reward for a mitzva—the most important element in the spiritual power it contains—lies in this exponential growth rate. This in turn depends entirely upon the degree of effort that is invested in the mitzva.

When the *Yerushalmi* told us that the reward for learning Torah was greater than the reward for all the mitzvot, it revealed an important insight. The resistance of the *yetzer* to learning Torah is stronger than its resistance to performing all the mitzvot put together. This is why the reward for learning is greater than the reward for all the mitzvot.

STUDYING THE ORAL TORAH

[The *Midrash Tanḥuma*[6] eloquently describes the personal difficulties likely to be encountered by one who resolves to dedicate himself to mastering the *Torah she-be'al peh*.

These are the words of the Midrash:

> Of the Oral Torah (*Torah she-be'al peh*), it is said: Longer than the earth is its measure and wider than the ocean.[7] And also: It is not found in the land of the living.[8] ...This means that it is not found among those who wish to live a life of ease, self-indulgence, and honor in this world... God made His covenant with Israel only concerning the Oral Torah...which is difficult and requires great effort and is compared to darkness, as it says, "The people who walk in darkness have seen a great light."[9] This refers to the masters of Talmud, who [first walk in darkness, but afterwards] see a great light, for Hashem enlightens their eyes... No one studies the Oral Torah unless he loves Hashem with all his heart and soul and might... Whoever loves riches and pleasure cannot learn the Oral Torah, for it demands immense effort and banishment of sleep. For its sake many are prepared to degrade themselves in this world. Their reward is in the spiritual world... The people who walk in darkness have seen a great light—this is the light of the spirit. It is in their merit that the world stands.]

The *yetzer* knows that the way to spiritual regeneration is found through learning Torah. This is why it makes learning Torah ("keeping Torah") harder than all the mitzvot. The prophet Yirmeyahu declared in the name of God: "They have abandoned Me...and have not kept My Torah"[10] on which our Rabbis comment: "Even if they abandoned Me, if they kept My Torah, there is still hope. The light in the Torah might return them to the right path."[11]

There is thus no happiness and no pleasure in the

world that can equal the happiness and reward and pleasure of the person who overcomes all difficulties and devotes himself to Torah. This is the meaning of the *Yerushalmi* which states that all the mitzvot in the world cannot equal one word of Torah.

THE LIGHT AT THE END OF THE TUNNEL

One who learns Torah, but without devoting all his strength to his learning, will not succeed. Eventually he will realize his weakness, become miserable and fall prey to despair, God forbid. But instead of seeking the cause of his downfall within himself and making a drastic change in his attitude, he will grow resentful and blame external factors rather than himself.

Towards the end of *parashat Ha'azinu* Mosheh Rabbenu exhorts the Jewish people: "This Torah...is not empty for you [literally, "from you"] for it is your life..."[12] We began this essay with a quotation from the *Yerushalmi* and we shall conclude it with another.

The *Yerushalmi* interprets this verse as follows: "The Torah is not empty. If you find it empty, it is 'from you'; it is your fault, because you do not toil in it sufficiently. 'It is your life.' And when is it your life? When you toil in it."[13]

Only when one labors and toils in Torah, in depth and in breadth, will one succeed in mastering it. Only then will the Torah become his source of unbounded life and happiness.

notes

1 *Pe'ah* 1:1.
2 *Avot* 1:17.
3 *Kiddushin* 40b.
4 *Avot* 2:1.
5 *Avot de-Rabbi Natan* 3:6.
6 *Parashat Noah* #3.
7 *Iyov* 11:9.
8 Ibid. 28:13.
9 *Yeshaya* 9:1.
10 *Yirmiyahu* 16:11.
11 *Yerushalmi, Hagiga* 1:7.
12 *Devarim* 32:47.
13 *Pe'ah* 1:1.

Ve'zot Ha-beracha

[This essay is taken from *Michtav Me-Eliyahu* III, pp. 19–20.]

Alacrity in This World and the Next

> God came from Sinai
> And shone to them from Se'ir;
> Appeared from the mountain of Paran...[1]

The beginning of *parashat Ve'zot Ha-beracha* describes the eagerness with which God approached Israel in order to give them the Torah. Since we know that God's actions reflect our own attitudes,[2] such eagerness can only reflect the eagerness on Israel's side to welcome God into their midst. Where do we find such eagerness here below?

> God said to Avraham: As a reward for the three occasions on which you ran [to do *ḥessed*], I will run three times towards your children at *Mattan Torah*. The three occasions when Avraham ran were: He saw and ran towards them; to the cattle Avraham ran...; and Avraham hurried to the tent...[3] And how did God repay it to his children? He came from Sinai, shone from Se'ir, appeared from Mount Paran.[4]

Avraham Avinu, shortly after his circumcision, was hardly able to move because of the pain. But in his eagerness to show *ḥessed* to strangers, who he thought were passing Arabs, he ran towards them, despite his pain, to make sure they did not pass by without entering his home. And when he had already sat them down under the shade of the tree, still in great haste because of his intense desire to show _ḥessed_, he ran to the cattle to select a fine, tender calf to serve to the guests. He then gave it to "the lad"—his son Yishmael[5]—to hurry along with its preparation. By this, he wished to teach him the importance of eagerness and alacrity in doing _ḥessed_.

This eagerness became an established trait that appeared in Avraham's descendants.[6] It was this trait in the people of Israel which called forth God's eagerness when He—so to speak—"ran" to meet His people at Sinai.

VALUE REVERSAL

It is this eagerness, this alacrity in learning Torah and doing mitzvot which increases one's spiritual reward in the World to Come. "According to the effort is the reward."[7] And the verse in _Mishlei_, which we have discussed before, states: "The toil of the toiler toils for him."[8] It is the toil of the toiler—not intellectual brilliance—which amasses his spiritual reward in ʿOlam ha-ba.

Let us imagine a student with a brilliant mind, a first-class memory, and broad knowledge, who finds Torah studies easy. In the eyes of the world, he would be considered to be a successful _talmid ḥacham_. However, if he does not toil to use his gifts to gain greater profundity in Torah, when he comes to the spiritual world, where greatness is measured by toil, he will be considered an ignoramus. On the other hand, a student with a mediocre intellect, weak memory, and little prior knowledge, who eagerly invests a lot of effort in his learning, will find in the next world that he possesses a superlative grasp of the spiritual Torah taught in that world. As someone who caught a glimpse of the spiritual world reported: "I saw a world in reverse: those who were high in this world were low in that world, and vice versa."[9]

notes

1 *Devarim* 33:2.
2 See *Michtav Me-Eliyahu* III, p.285.
3 *Bereshit* 18:2,6,7.
4 *Yalkut Shimoni, parashat Vayera.* (See *Tanḥuma* ibid. and correct accordingly.)
5 Rashi on 18:7.
6 Compare Vol. I, pp. 54–56.
7 *Avot* V, end.
8 *Mishlei* 16:26.
9 *Pesaḥim* 50a.

Yehoshua'

The Fall of Jericho's Walls

The essence of *bitaḥon*—the mitzva of trust and confidence in Hashem—is to know that everything comes from Hashem. True, we engage—and we are commanded to engage—in activities directed towards achieving certain results in the physical world. But we must realize that these actions are not the true causes of the results which seem to flow from them. The true cause is always the will of Hashem. We are instructed to pursue economic and medical activities and so on, only in order to disguise this basic fact. If it was obvious that everything came directly from Hashem, there would be too little scope for *beḥira*.[1]

NO MORE WORRY

A person who sees the world in these terms and has perfect faith that everything (except *beḥira*—"moral choices") comes from Hashem will never succumb to worry. He knows that Hashem has already decided the amount of worldly goods he needs for his spiritual service and there is, therefore, nothing to worry about. A person only worries about a situation which he thinks he can change. If the outcome is accepted as inevitable, a person may be apprehensive, but he does not worry. This is why people are not normally worried about the fact that they are going to die. A person who knows that all that happens to him comes from Hashem and nothing he does in the physical sphere can possibly change it has no cause to worry.

Shabbat is given to us to help us absorb this truth. On Shabbat, we desist from practical activity to remind ourselves that this kind of activity has no causative effect. We should see the reality of the spiritual within the physical and dedicate all our activity to Hashem: "It is a Shabbat for Hashem your God."[2]

When the Torah says "Six days you shall labor *and do all your work*,"[3] our Rabbis say this means that when Shabbat enters, "it shall be as if all our work were done."[4] Even if a person is faced with a great worry, when Shabbat comes his worry should evaporate. How can this happen? Because he has already worked on himself to recognize and understand that Hashem is the sole cause of all that happens. Secure in this knowledge, he will trust in Hashem's goodness and feel confident that Hashem has already prepared everything so that the outcome will be the best possible outcome for him. Shabbat will be the test. If his worries truly evaporate with the onset of Shabbat, it is clear that he has internalized this lesson. He no longer worries about what he did or might have done during the week, or what might happen next week, but places his trust in Hashem above.

THE CONQUEST OF JERICHO

With this understanding we can grasp what Hashem wanted to teach us through the detailed steps involved in the conquest of Jericho.[5]

I AM THE PRINCE OF THE ARMY OF GOD: NOW I

HAVE COME. The angel came to Yehoshua', encamped outside Jericho, to warn him and Israel not to relax their efforts in Torah learning. This battle was to be won by spiritual achievements only.[6]

TAKE YOUR SHOE OFF YOUR FOOT; THE PLACE WHERE YOU STAND IS HOLY. This was to prepare him for a communication from God (see 6:2). The same message was given to his master Mosheh at the burning bush.[7]

JERICHO WAS SHUT UP AND ENCLOSED. This is a parenthetical statement. It was clear that they could not conquer the city by natural means.

BEFORE THE CHILDREN OF ISRAEL. It seemed that even the merits of "Yisrael" were insufficient to merit a miracle of this magnitude.

AND HASHEM SAID. The special mercies associated with the name Hashem were required. [The angel had come to prepare Yehoshua' for this message from Hashem.[8]]

SEE! I HAVE GIVEN INTO YOUR HANDS... The first thing required of them was "to see." Their hearts had to see that Hashem, Who is the true cause of everything, had *already* given the city into their hands. God's will prevails against all difficulties, and since this is His will, it is as good as accomplished. We shall see it when its time comes.

JERICHO AND ITS KING, THE MIGHTY ONES. Once Israel realizes this, it will have no cause to worry about physical power. Israel will recognize the utter irrelevance of such power since the outcome is decided by God's will.

YOU SHALL GO AROUND THE CITY. They had to walk around the city to see the strength of its walls and to realize the impossibility of their conquering it through natural means.

ALL THE MEN OF WAR. The soldiers particularly had to learn this lesson.

SURROUND (*HAKEIF*)THE CITY. Make a complete circuit. *Hakeif* is spelled with an extra *yud* to indicate complete concentration on their spiritual task.

SIX DAYS. To realize that worldly power, symbolized by six days, would never suffice to conquer this city. And then:

SEVEN KOHANIM SHALL CARRY SEVEN RAMS' HORNS BEFORE THE ARK. The ark took part in the procession to impress upon Israel's hearts and minds the idea that they could succeed only if they observed and practiced the words of the Torah which the Ark contained (Ralbag).

ON THE SEVENTH DAY YOU SHALL GO AROUND THE CITY SEVEN TIMES. The seventh day was Shabbat. All this was to impress upon the people the primacy of the spiritual factor. "Seven" indicates the spiritual in the midst of the physical.

AS YOU HEAR (*BE'SHOM'ACHEM*) THE SOUND OF THE SHOFAR. The *kri* in the Torah is *ke'shom'achem*—"*when* you hear." But the *ktiv* (which always indicates the inner meaning, accessible only to those who can understand the deeper aspects of a word) is "*be'shom'achem*," which can mean "by," or "as a result of your hearing." *Because* you hear, because you recognize and remember the hidden power of God, hinted at by the shofar tone at Mount Sinai, therefore:

ALL THE PEOPLE SHALL UTTER A GREAT SHOUT. Only when you know that no power resides in human hands, and proclaim this fact with all your power, will you merit the miracle.

AND THE WALL OF THE CITY SHALL FALL IN ITS PLACE. Ralbag draws attention to the fact that loud noises can set off strong vibrations which might even cause walls to collapse. There is a lesson to be learned from this. If a person wishes to deny a miracle, he can always suggest far-fetched explanations which, to his twisted mind, can account for the miracle. In fact, in every miracle Hashem leaves an opening for the obstinate-minded to make such a mistake, so as not to eliminate free will completely. We find an example of this involving the miracle of the boy Elisha resurrected. It says: "He lay upon the child and put his face on his face etc.,"[9] which can be said to bear a resemblance to modern methods of resuscitation. The great shout of all the people was needed, but its purpose was to give vociferous expression to what they had learned: that human effort is of no avail; Hashem alone does everything.

YOU SHALL NOT SHOUT NOR SHALL YOUR VOICE BE HEARD NOR SHALL A WORD ESCAPE YOUR MOUTH. ONLY ON THE DAY I TELL YOU TO SHOUT SHALL YOU SHOUT. They were forbidden to utter a sound during the six days of circuits and during all the seven circuits of the seventh day. The enforced silence and heightened anticipation must have been almost unbearable. But if they had been allowed to give any premature expression to their feelings, this would have diminished the intense inwardness of their *madrega*. Only after the completion of the seventh circuit on the seventh day, when they realized in their utter purity of heart the vanity of believing in the certitude of physical power, were they permitted to give vent to their pent-up feelings. They acclaimed with the utmost conviction the supreme power of Hashem—and then the miracle happened.

notes

1 See *Strive for Truth!* II, p. 237 et seq.
2 *Shemot* 20:10.
3 Ibid., v. 9.
4 Rashi ad loc.
5 *Yehoshua'* 5:13–6:20.
6 *Eruvin* 63b.
7 *Shemot* 3:5.
8 Compare *Shemot* 3:2–4; *Shoftim* 6:12,14.
9 *Melachim* II 4:34.

Shoftim

The Power of Holiness

Holiness—*kedusha*—means separation from defilement of all kinds. "You shall be holy to Me...I separated you from the nations to be Mine."[1] "So long as you are separated from [the defilement of] the nations, you are Mine; if not, you belong to the rulers of the nations."[2] "To belong to God" means that all one's actions are directed towards God and His purposes: what we call complete *lishma*. On this level, one is free from the rule of the nations of the world.

CLOUDS OF GLORY

The desert generation came closer to this level of holiness than any other generation of Israel did or ever will until the coming of *Mashiaḥ*. Koraḥ said, with some justification: "All the congregation are holy and God is in their midst [that is, in their hearts]."[3]

Clouds of glory surrounded the camp of Israel in their desert wanderings. This was in the merit of Aharon.[4] They provided a special spiritual influx which protected Israel from any contamination from the environment. As a result, the people were, on the whole, impervious to the defilements of the nations. The lusts, urges, and desires which dominated the thinking of the nations of the world simply held no interest for them.

However, even in that great generation there were individuals who did not reach the same high level of holiness as the others. These individuals did not enjoy the protection of the clouds of glory. This is why we find that certain individuals were "rejected by the cloud." They were the "stragglers" that Amalek was able to attack.[5]

THE TRIBE OF DAN

Some of them belonged to the tribe of Dan. When Mosheh Rabbenu proclaimed: "Lest there is among you a man...a family, or *a tribe* whose heart turns away from Hashem," it is said that he was referring to the tribe of Dan.[6] It seems that there was even then an incipient tendency to idolatry among certain members of that tribe. Later on, an idolatrous temple was built in the territory of Dan in northern Israel, which remained a rival to the House of God in Shiloh for several centuries.[7] [This was later reestablished by Yarov'am (Jeroboam), after the death of Shelomo Ha-melech, to rival the Temple in Jerusalem.[8]]

Israel never served idols from a desire (God forbid) to deny Hashem. "Israel knew very well that idolatry was worthless. They indulged in it only because it gave them a license for immorality."[9] In this respect, too, we find a certain weakness—albeit in a very subtle form—in the tribe of Dan.[10]

But such individuals were rare. The tribe of Dan as a whole was given the title "rear guard to all the camps."[11] Their task was to restore to the clouds of glory's protection those Israelites who, because of some lack of *kedusha*, had lost this protection. Dan's function was to raise the stragglers' level until they equaled the rest of *Klal Yisrael*. In this respect, Dan's task resembled that of *Mashiaḥ*, which is to "bring back the outcasts of Israel."[12] This is why, when Yaakov Avinu saw Shimshon in the tribe of Dan, he thought he was the *Mashiaḥ*.[13]

Here we have a remarkable insight. We saw above that the *beḥira*-point of the tribe of Dan was at a slightly lower level that the rest of Israel. This was to aid them in their holy task of restoring the stragglers to the clouds' protection. It is known that if a *tsaddik* is to succeed in elevating holy souls who have become trapped in the depths of defilement, he has to lower himself somewhat so that he can communicate with them on their level. Thus, the very fact that the tribe of Dan was on a lower *madrega* than the others was for a holy purpose.

Nevertheless, this situation has its dangers. It can succeed only if the motives of the *tsaddik* are absolutely pure. We recognize Dan's greatness because we know Hashem entrusted the tribe with such a difficult and dangerous task.

SHIMSHON

Shimshon shared the task of his ancestors in the tribe of Dan. He had to lower himself in order to save the weaker souls of Israel. He also had to use his exceptional strength—derived from his very high spiritual *madrega*—to impress the non-Jews and raise Israel in their esteem. In these tasks, he resembled the *Mashiaḥ*, as we saw above.

This explains a unique feature of his spiritual life. The verse states: "The spirit of God began to chime in him [*le'fa'amo*]..."[14] This means that "the *Shechina* chimed in him like a bell [*pa'amon*]."[15] A bell rings and stops, rings and stops. So the *Shechina* took hold of him at intervals, alternately seizing him and leaving him alone. This was to train him for his future task in life. He would experience times of intense spiritual concentration, followed by periods when he would be alone, without heavenly aid.

Another characteristic of his was that he invariably acted alone; he looked for no help from others. (Ya'akov saw him as *ahad*—"unique";[16] "like the One Above, he needed no help."[17])

PREPARATIONS

Shimshon was destined for a very unusual and dangerous mission. Extraordinary preparations were needed to build up the power of *kedusha* within him, to enable him to meet all his challenges.

Shimshon was born to very exceptional parents. Manoah, his father, was also described as *ehad*—"ish ehad,"[18] hinting that he was unique in his righteousness in his generation.[19]

His mother, too, was an exceptional person. She merited to have an angel inform her of the impending conception and birth of Shimshon. She was told that the boy was to be a *nazir* from birth and that she was not to drink wine while she was carrying him.[20] This is the only time in all *Tanach* that a person had laws of *kedusha* apply to him *before* he was born!

Like Sara Imenu, Shimshon's mother was barren; she could not have children. Just as Yitzhak, the ancestor of Israel, could not come into the world by natural means, so it was with Shimshon. His *kedusha* was so powerful that it could enter the world only through a miracle.

SHIMSHON'S ACTIONS

The angel concluded his message to Shimshon's mother with the words: "He will begin to save Israel from the Philistines."[21] The Philistines at that time had occupied most of Eretz Yisrael and ruled over the Israelites with an iron hand.

The generation was not yet worthy of being redeemed from the yoke of the Philistines. Shimshon was only to "begin" the process of deliverance. His task was to cast terror upon the Philistines through extraordinary and fearsome acts, and so relieve the pressure on Israel. It was the will of God that he should wage a kind of "private war" on the Philistines, causing them considerable casualties while ostensibly avenging private wrongdoings.

MAINTAINING *KEDUSHA* INTACT

It was part of God's plan that Shimshon should marry a Philistine girl. By this means, he would become involved in disputes with the Philistines and so have opportunities to pursue his "private war."

This is stated explicitly in the narrative. When Shimshon asked his parents to arrange his marriage with a Philistine woman he saw in Timnata, they objected very strongly, but Shimshon persisted. "Get me this girl as my wife, for she is right in my eyes."[22] And the verse adds: "His parents did not know that *it was from God*. He was seeking an opportunity [to act] against the Philistines."[23]

[It is clear that the ability to carry on a one-man war against a whole nation can only be derived from a very high level of *kedusha*.] When circumstances demand this, certain laws may be temporarily suspended (on the authority of a *navi* or the *Sanhedrin*). This is called *hora'at sha'ah*.[24] That this was the situation here is indicated by the words "It was from God."[25] The power of Shimshon's *kedusha* was such that he could enter into a threatening situation and emerge from it with his *kedusha* intact.

The Torah warns us "not to follow after our hearts and our eyes, after which we go astray."[26] The heart and eye of every one of us goes astray after our desires and under no circumstances can we rely on them. But Shimshon's eyes were so pure that if he saw anything and it appeared right to him, he could be absolutely sure that it was holy and that it was the will of God that he should have it. "Get her...for she is right in my eyes... It was from God."[27] The verse confirms that this was true. Shimshon was not mistaken in the slightest.

SHIMSHON'S MISTAKE

Shimshon's mistake was of a different order. The Rabbis teach us in the Midrash: "Shimshon's punishment affected his eyes [the Philistines blinded him[28]] because he had been *proud* of his eyes."[29] That extraordinary and perhaps unique ability to be sure that whatever his eyes saw as right was indeed right and also the will of Hashem gave him a certain feeling of pride. Unfortunately, pride is fatal to all spiritual progress.

It was this failing alone which prevented Shimshon from completing his task. Pride affects the purity of a person's motivation. Once he is proud, his actions can no longer be completely *le'shem shamayim*. This defect weakened his defenses and ultimately led to his downfall, when he allowed himself to be ensnared by the wiles of Delila.[30] When he lost the power of his *kedusha*—symbolized by the crown of his *nezirut*, his hair—his physical strength also left him.

In his captivity, he realized his mistake and was determined to make amends by sacrificing his life for *kiddush Hashem*. He won his last great battle. The enemies of Hashem whom he killed in his death "were more numerous than he had killed during his life."[31]

THE IMPRESSION OF HOLINESS

Even though he failed, the impression of his tremendous *kedusha* was not lost. "He judged Israel for twenty years" comes twice in the narrative.[32] This teaches us, say the Rabbis, that the Philistines feared him twenty years after his death to the same extent that they had feared him during his life.[33] What were they afraid of after his death? Only his merits. Even the lowly, materialistic Philistines were so impressed by Shimshon's towering holiness that they feared the impact of that holiness even after he was gone.

This just goes to show how true inwardness can influence even the lowest of the low.

notes

1 *Vayikra* 20:20.
2 Rashi ad loc. from *Torat Kohanim*.
3 *Bemidbar* 16:3.
4 See *Strive for Truth!* IV (*Sanctuaries in Time*), p. 139.
5 See *Devarim* 25:18 and Rashi ad loc.
6 *Devarim* 29:17; *Midrash Tehillim* on psalm 101.
7 See *Shoftim* 17–18.
8 *Melachim* I, 12:29–30.
9 *Sanhedrin* 63b.
10 See *Vayikra* 24:1. "...The son of an Egyptian, the mother being from the tribe of Dan." This was the only case of this sort during the whole of their stay in Egypt. Although the

woman was innocent, having been deceived by the Egyptian into thinking that he was her husband (see Rashi on *Shemot* 2:11), in a subtle sense the innocence was not complete. Accidental sins happen only to those who have some sort of affinity with the sin.

11 *Bemidbar* 10:25.
12 *Yesha'ya* 27:13.
13 *Bereshit Rabba* 98:14.
14 *Shoftim* 13:25.
15 *Sota* 9b.
16 *Bereshit* 49:16.
17 *Bereshit Rabba* 99:11.
18 *Shoftim* 13:2.
19 *Bemidbar Rabba* 10:5. Although the Rabbis tell us that Manoaḥ was relatively ignorant of Torah (*Berachot* 61a), and the *mishna* in *Avot* (2:5) informs us that an *am ha-aretz* cannot be a *ḥassid* (who goes beyond what the law requires), Rabbenu Yona points out (commentary, ad loc) that he can nevertheless be a *tsaddik* (who scrupulously obeys all that the law demands).
20 *Shoftim* 13:3–5.
21 Ibid. 13:5.
22 Ibid. 14:3.
23 Ibid. 14:4.
24 *Sanhedrin* 68b.
25 See note 23, above.
26 *Bemidbar* 15:39.
27 See note 23, above.
28 *Shoftim* 16:21.
29 *Tanḥuma Beshalaḥ* #12.
30 Ibid. 16:4–20.
31 Ibid. 16:30.
32 Ibid. 15:20; 16:31.
33 *Bemidbar Rabba* 14:9.

Shemuel

[For the purposes of the present volume, the essay appearing under this heading in *Michtav Me-Eliyahu* II—"King David and the Building of the Temple"—has been replaced by the following, which is taken from *Michtav Me-Eliyahu* IV, pp. 102–104.]

Hanna's Prayer

We are by now familiar with the concepts *gillui*—"revelation of God's glory" and *hester*—"obscurity." We know that every moment, every day, every year, every generation has its potential *gilluim*.

All the possible *gilluim* throughout history are fixed in advance, and every soul that enters the world is given a share in the great combined *gillui* of all time.[1] Of course, each person has the choice whether or not to fulfill his allotted task.

TURNING POINTS

Sometimes a turning point may arise in the pattern of *gilluim* of one or several generations. At such a time it is possible for one person to experience a drastic change in the task allotted to him. This is what happened in the time of Avraham. His original name, Av-ram, meant that he was destined to be "father" (that is, the spiritual father) of Aram Naharayim—Mesopotamia. To fulfill this task, he was destined not to have children.[2]

However, he lived at a crisis point in history. Ten generations had turned against God. It was a turning point in the whole development of the scheme of *gilluim*. At this point, Avraham chose to be the first to reveal the meaning of pure faith in the one God and to teach His righteous ways to mankind. It was Avraham alone against the whole world. (This is why he was called "Avraham Ha-'Ivri," from *'ever*—"side." He was on one side and the whole world was on the other.[3])

THE CHALLENGE

Because of this, he received the reward of all the individuals in all the ten generations who had failed in their task.[4] "Reward" in this context means *gillui*. He had achieved the *gillui* which it had been *their* lot to achieve. *Gillui* is measured by quality and not by quantity. Mankind's consistent failure for so long a period had darkened the spiritual horizon to such an extent that a great barrier had been erected between God and the world. To break through this barrier required almost superhuman effort, and this raised the quality of Avraham's service immeasurably. Every sin committed by every individual in that whole period thus contributed to Avraham's greatness. In this sense "he took the reward of them all": the *gillui* they should have created was created instead by him. If all the people in all those generations had fulfilled all the tasks allotted to them, their combined *kiddush Hashem* would have been equal to the *kiddush Hashem*—the *gillui*—created by the superhuman efforts of this one man, Avraham, in the very challenging environment in which he had to operate.

So Avraham became *av hamon goyim*, "father of the multitude of nations."[5] The pattern of *gilluim* had changed and the purpose of creation was now channeled through him. His new role required him to have children. *Klal Yisrael* had to emerge from his progeny, leading eventually to the coming of *Mashiah* and the redemption of the whole world, in fulfillment of the blessing: "All the families of the earth shall be blessed through you."[6] Thus we understand the profundity of the statement: " 'Avram' cannot have children, but 'Avraham' can have children."[7]

HANNA AND *KLAL YISRAEL*

We find a similar situation in the case of Ḥanna, the mother of Shemuel. Ḥanna was unable to have children. Her portion in *gillui* was to bear the pain of this severe disability—including the mockery of her rival[8]—with love. She had to reveal the greatness of the Creator by showing how faith in Him enables one to overcome all difficulties.

She lived at the close of the period of the judges. It was at this time that the two terrible episodes described at the end of the *Book of Judges* occurred: those connected with the image of Micha and the concubine at Givʿa.[9] The second of these resulted in a bloody civil war between the tribe of Binyamin and the rest of Israel.[10] It was clear that the period of the judges had run its course. A turning point had been reached. The pattern of *gilluim* was about to change.

It was at this time that Ḥanna stood in the temple of Shiloh and prayed to God for a son.[11] Our Rabbis say that she "threw words up to God,"[12] meaning that in the bitterness of her heart she spoke harsh words. What were they? Some say she threatened, so to speak, to force God's hand. She said: "You wrote in the Torah that a *sota* who is found innocent will bear children.[13] I will make my husband Elkana jealous, he will make me drink the water, I will be found innocent, and then You will *have* to give me a child."[14] Or she said, "Everything...You created for a purpose: eyes to see, ears to hear, nose to smell, hands to work with, legs to walk with. These breasts you have given me over my heart—what are they for? To suckle a child. Give me a child and I will suckle it."[15] Or, according to another opinion: "O God of Hosts[16]...of all the hosts of creatures You created in Your world, is it so difficult for You to give me one son? This is like a king who made a banquet for his servants. A poor man came and stood at the door and asked for a piece of bread. They took no notice. He pushed his way into the presence of the king and said, My lord the king, from this whole banquet you have made, is it so difficult for you to give me one piece of bread?"[17]

THE PAIN OF THE *TSADDIK*

We have explained above[18] the meaning of "harsh words" spoken by a *tsaddik*. He expressed his inability to bear the *hester*—the dimming of God's glory—which would be caused by something that God seemed about to do. Of course, unless the *tsaddik* is completely free from personal motives and speaks only out of the pain he feels for the dimming of the glory of the *Shechina*, this would be very dangerous. We find that a great man—Levi, the disciple of Rabbi Yehuda Ha-nasi—once "threw words" up to God and was punished. In a time of drought, he stood up and prayed in these terms: "Lord of the universe! You seem to have ascended into the heights and no longer have mercy on Your children." His prayer was answered, but he was later punished and became a cripple.[19]

Hanna the *tsaddeket* did not pray merely for herself, but for the pain of the *Shechina* and for the good of the generation. She said: "O God of Hosts...if You will give Your maidservant male seed, I will give him to God all the days of his life."[20] By this she meant that the sole purpose of her son would be to care for and improve the spirit of the generation. We see this in the whole trend of her prophetic song of thanksgiving,[21] in which she speaks of the concerns of *Klal Yisrael*, the improvement of the generations, and the resurrection of the dead. She concludes: "He will give might to His king and exalt the power of His anointed." These words show that she foresaw the great changes that were soon destined to come over Israel and she prayed that her son would be instrumental in bringing about the redemption of the nation. As we said above, in a time of transition, when the pattern of *gilluim* are about to change, an individual who cares deeply about the situation and yearns to be able to help may receive heavenly aid quite disproportionate to his or her individual merits.

Ḥanna prayed at such a time. She was given a son who was in some respects equal to Mosheh and Aharon.[22] He unified the tribes of Israel and ushered in a new epoch in Israel's history—the period of the monarchy. He anointed two kings: Shaul, the first king of Israel, and David, the founder of the dynasty of the *Mashiaḥ*.

notes

1 See *Strive for Truth!* III, pp. 231–235.

2 *Berachot* 13a.

3 *Bereshit Rabba* 42:8.

4 *Avot* 5:3.

5 *Bereshit* 17:5.

6 Ibid. 12:3.

7 *Bereshit Rabba* 44:14.

8 *Shemuel* I, 1:6.

9 *Shoftim* 17–21.

10 Ibid.

11 *Shemuel* I, 1:10.

12 *Berachot* 31b.

13 *Bemidbar* 5:28.

14 *Berachot* 31b.

15 Ibid.

16 *Shemuel* I, 1:11.

17 See note 14, above.

18 See *Strive for Truth!* V, *parashat Vayera*, in the essay "Avraham's Prayer for Sodom."

19 *Ta'anit* 25a.

20 See note 16, above.

21 *Shemuel* I, 2:1–10.

22 *Tehillim* 99:6.

Melachim

[This essay is taken from *Michtav Me-Eliyabu* V, pp. 399–401.]

Courage and Miracles

Ahav was one of the worst, if not the worst of all the kings of the Ten Tribes of Israel. "There was none like Ahav, who sold himself to do evil in the eyes of God."[1] Ahav was worse than Yarov'am. Yarov'am acted out of fear ("the kingdom will return to the House of David"[2]), while Ahav served idols as a provocation. In Yarov'am's temples, the service was directed basically to the God of Israel, while in Ahav's temples, the service was exclusively to the Canaanite god Baal.[3] Ahav erased the name of God from the Torah scrolls, substituting the name Baal; thus: "In the beginning Baal created...," "And Baal said, Let there be light," and so on.[4]

THE QUALITY OF COURAGE

On the other hand, we find another side to Ahav. When Ben-Hadad, king of Syria, and the thirty-two kings who were his allies besieged Israel's capital city, Shomron, Ahav capitulated immediately. He realized that he did not have the slightest chance of defeating them in battle. When Ben-Hadad demanded that the king of Israel surrender his "silver and gold, his wives and sons," Ahav abjectly agreed.[5]

However, when Ben-Hadad insisted that he would not be satisfied with this, but would search Aḥav's palace and take away "all the desire of your eyes," Aḥav refused. He consulted the "elders of the land" and they, together with all the people, supported his refusal.[6] What was "all the desire of your eyes"?

Rashi explains that it was "the treasure of all treasures: the *sefer Torah*, which is more 'desirable than gold and much treasure.'[7] Aḥav said to himself, He is asking something too great. I cannot decide this myself. The decision must rest with the elders of Israel... *Although they worshipped idols, they honored the Torah.*"[8]

LEARNING FROM THE MIRACLE

Who merits a miracle? The one who is capable of learning from the miracle. The whole point of a miracle is that people should learn from it. This is what the *navi* meant when he said to Aḥav: "Thus said God: You see all this great multitude [the army of Ben-Hadad]? I am giving them into your hands today *so that you shall know* that I am God."[9]

[Our Rabbis see two divine messages here. One: "When Ben-Hadad falls into your hands, do not have mercy on him." (Remember: He who is merciful to the cruel will eventually be cruel to the merciful.[10]) Two: "I laid a trap to get him into your hands. If you let him get away, you will pay with your life for his life and your people for his people."[11] These messages are important for the later development of the narrative.]

To emphasize the lesson of the miraculous victory, the prophet announced that the battle should be fought by "the young men of the officers of the provinces,"[12] making it clear that it was not military might, but only the merit of Ahav's courage that was to win the day.

Ahav's question, "Who shall command the battle,"[13] is significant. As Redak points out, the question seems strange. Surely he is the king and who should command the battle but he? Ahav realized that since he was an idolater and the battle would be won by a miracle, maybe God had other ideas about who the commander should be. But the *navi* reassured him that he was the one, since the battle would be won by his merit.

We see that Ahav was certainly a person who could learn from a miracle [and even from the promise of a miracle]. What opened his eyes? His courage—and at what a risk!—in preserving the honor of the *sefer Torah*, the *sefer Torah* which he had previously desecrated! Although he remained an idolater, the point of truth which he perceived on his level was to his merit, as we have explained elsewhere.[14]

After the victory, the *navi* warned him: "Strengthen yourself and know and see what you have to do, because next year Syria will attack you again."[15] The meaning was: "Strengthen yourself with good deeds and uproot your idolatry; you have seen and recognized that the power belongs to God and horses are worthless for victory."[16] And although Ahav did not repent, since he had shown himself to be capable of learning from a miracle, God gave him another miraculous victory greater than the first.[17]

THE COURAGE OF THE *NAVI*

But Ahav failed to take this lesson to its logical conclusion by changing his idolatrous ways; eventually he was killed by the Syrians in the battle of Ramot Gil'ad.[18] It seems that it was decided in heaven that it was not worthwhile to grant him any more miracles, and the time had come for him to be punished for all his sins. What brought about this decision?

It was something that happened after the second victory. Ben-Hadad, the king of Syria, had fallen into Ahav's hands. [It was in his power—it was indeed his right and duty—to put him to death and so remove an extremely dangerous enemy of Israel]. Ahav however [— acting against the divine message previously given to him —] had mercy on Ben-Hadad and set him free to return to his kingdom.[19]

One of the disciples of the prophets disguised himself as a soldier, smearing dirt on his face. He commanded a friend in the name of God to strike him with his sword. The first person he asked refused, but the second obeyed, "striking and wounding." The *navi* wanted it to appear as if he had just come from battle. To make it more realistic, he wanted to be actually wounded and have blood running down his body.

He then approached King Ahav with a story. His officer, he said, had given him a prisoner to guard, warning him that if he escaped, his own life would be forfeit, and he had accepted this charge. Now the man had escaped; what was he to do? The king replied that he could not help him. "This is your judgment; you have decided your own fate."

Then he cleaned his face and Ahav recognized him to be a prophet. The story had been a parable for the Ahav. "Thus says God," said the *navi*. "Since you have sent away the man I wanted you to destroy, you shall pay with your life for his life and your people for his people."[20]

AHAV'S FAILURE

[In Hebrew, courage, steadfastness, and moral determination are all called by the one word *amitzut*.] Ahav's lack of
determination which led him to show mercy to Israel's
enemy indicated a failure in his *amitzut*—the virtue
through which he was granted the miracles. If he had the
courage once to stand up for the honor of the *sefer Torah*,
he might have learned from the resulting miracle to have
the courage to admit his sins and rectify them. But now
that he seemed to have lost that moral determination and
he was clearly even further away from *teshuva*, he met his
doom in Ramot Gil'ad.[21]

Although the prophet had said: "Your life shall be lost
for his life and your people for his people," in fact only
Ahav was killed. Why were the people spared?

It was the merit of the prophets' courage which saved
them. "The drop of blood which came from that *tsaddik*
Michayehu [the prophet], who was struck and wounded
by his friend, was an atonement for all Israel."[22]

There is a deeper meaning here. It takes courage to acknowledge the special Divine Providence of a miracle and
change one's life in response. Now that all Israel was able
to learn *amitzut* from the prophet, who persuaded someone to wound him in order to deliver God's message more
effectively, they were more likely to learn from a miracle.
Therefore God granted them a miracle and they were
saved.

The main point is: When learning [the narrative portions of] *Nach*, one must learn the inner meanings of the
events.

notes

1 *Melachim* I, 21:25.
2 Ibid. 12:26.
3 Redak, *Melachim* I, 21:25.
4 Redak, ibid. 21:20.
5 *Melachim* I, 20:3.
6 Ibid., v. 6–7.
7 *Tehillim* 19:11.
8 Rashi, *Melachim* I 20:6.
9 Ibid., v. 13.
10 *Yalkut Shimoni Shemuel* I #121.
11 *Tanhuma, parashat Emor* #3.
12 *Melachim* I, 20:14.
13 Ibid.
14 See *Strive for Truth!* II, pp. 54–58.
15 Ibid., v. 22.
16 Redak ad loc, second explanation.
17 Ibid., v. 28–30.
18 Ibid. 22:34–37.
19 Ibid. 20:30–34.
20 Ibid., v. 35–42.
21 Ibid. 22:34.
22 *Yalkut Shimoni Melachim* I #220. According to the Midrash quoted by Rashi and Redak on *Melachim* I 20:13, the prophet who was active throughout this narrative was Michayehu ben Yimla. See ibid. 22:8 et seq.

Yesha'ya

"Among a People with Unclean Lips"

"I said, Woe to me that I kept silent!"[1] The Yalkut Shimoni[2] explains that Yesha'ya saw the ministering angels praising God and did not add his praise to theirs.
[*He suspected that he was unworthy of joining his voice to the
voice of the angels.*] He was unhappy about this. "I am a
man of unclean lips," he said. If I had added my praise
to theirs, I would have lived forever as they do. [*Immor-
tality: all-round perfection.*] What came over me that I
was silent? While he was wondering about this [*a moment of deep repentance*], he uttered an unnecessary word
[*unnecessary but not forbidden!*]: "And I dwell among a
people with unclean lips." God said to him: You may
say "I am a man of unclean lips;" you may say what
you like about yourself. But can you say what you like
about My children? How could you say "And I dwell
among a people with unclean lips?" Immediately he received his punishment. The verse continues: "One of
the Seraphim flew to me with a glowing coal in his
hand." The verse does not say *gaḥelet* [*the usual word for
'glowing coal'*] but *ritzpa*...implying *retzotz peh*: crush the
mouth which spoke against My children.[3]

In the *Midrash Tanḥuma*[4] we read:

God said: Yesha'ya, how can you say such a thing about Israel, who said "we will do" before "we will hear" and who unify My name twice a day? And you call them "a people with unclean lips"!

It is apparent that God's criticism of Yesha'ya was of a very subtle nature. He had allowed himself to speak critically of Israel. We can learn from this that one is allowed to view another person only in his highest aspect—that he is the possessor of an immortal soul and that as a human being he is "beloved of God, being created in His image."[5] It is not for us to judge a fellow human being from the point of view of his weaknesses. Only God alone, Who knows everyone's innermost thoughts, is able to judge a person. We can and should judge ourselves, but we must refrain from judging others.

A HEAVENLY SIN

To get an idea of how far Yesha'ya's "sin" was from our everyday perceptions of right and wrong, we have to refer again to the above *midrash*. The *Tanhuma* continues as follows:

"One of the Seraphim flew to me." [*This was Michael, the high prince, known as Israel's "Prince"*[6]—*a particular aspect of love and mercy.*] "With a glowing coal in his hand; he had taken it with fire irons from the altar..." The angel went to take the coal and was burned. [*The fire on the heavenly altar is the fire of the souls of the tsaddikim*[7]—*the burning enthusiasm of their lishma. Michael is the Kohen there. His mission was to show that even an angel cannot compare to the fiery enthusiasm of the tsaddikim in their service.*] He took a fire iron and was burned. He took a second fire iron and put it into the first and took the coal and placed it on Yesha'ya's mouth... "With this your sin shall be removed..." A coal which the Seraph was unable to take without two fire irons touched Yesha'ya's mouth and he was not burned!

It is clear that by ordinary standards there was no sin. From the viewpoint of this world, his words were spoken in a sublime spirit of *teshuva*. The "sin" could be discerned only by the prophet approaching the heavenly fire of pure enthusiasm. Only there was it possible to discern the unnecessary words as an unwarranted criticism of others, [and even then it did not burn him.] The elevated vantage point gained by coming into contact with that heavenly fire was sufficient to remove the subtle defect as it taught him an even higher level of pure *lishma*.

A VESTIGE REMAINED

Menasheh, the idolatrous king of Yehuda, wanted to kill Yesha'ya. When the prophet heard this, he decided to escape. He pronounced the holy name of God and then was swallowed up in a cedar tree. Menasheh's men began sawing down the tree. Yesha'ya died when the saw reached his mouth, because he had said "I dwell among a people with unclean lips."[8]

A vestige of that sin still clung to him at the end of his life. Because of this, the holy name could not save him when the murderers reached his mouth.

This is amazing indeed. We saw how subtle that defect was. We saw how it vanished on contact with heavenly fire. How could it still have the power to prevent the miracle?

We know that "pronouncing a divine name" can have an effect only if the person involved is himself on the level of revelation expressed by that name. On that level, he may not be subject to the restrictions of the lower world. In this manner, Yesha'ya was able to make himself invisible to human eyes. Even his body was not susceptible to physical attack; he was no longer vulnerable to the forces of the physical world. How then was his mouth still vulnerable?

TESHUVA ON TWO LEVELS

The answer is that on the heavenly level his sin had, indeed, been removed. But however great the *tsaddik*, we know that as long as he is still living in this world, he has a body, and his body is affected. Even if he has conquered all of the defects in his *middot* on the conscious level, there are still vestiges of these defects on the subconscious level of his physical existence. We have called this "body-shadow."[9] The spiritual work of the *tsaddik* is to make his *teshuva* penetrate to this subconscious level. But this is not easy. Since the defect is so subtle, it is very difficult to pinpoint its effect on the physical level and make the necessary correction.

It seems that Yesha'ya's *teshuva* may have been effective on the "heavenly" level. Standing in the Heavenly Temple, he may have grasped with the clarity of prophetic vision the subtlety of his fault and corrected it. However, *teshuva* needs to be done also on the "earthly" level of affecting one's body.[10] Because of this deficiency, the divine name was unable to protect the place of the sin.

THE LESSON FOR US

We can learn from this how futile it is for us to imagine that with our external *teshuva*—either in thought or word alone, or in the transient stirring of the feelings—we can obtain atonement from God, Who is spiritual. We have never succeeded in breaking through to the inner reality of our minds. Our "earthly" dimension—the subconscious roots of our behavior—has not been touched. And our sins are real and substantial; have we really relinquished them?

Now we may comprehend how complete *teshuva* requires such painstaking effort. If we learn the "twenty principles of *teshuva*," set down by Rabbenu Yona in *Sha'arei Teshuva*, we can gain an idea of what is required.

notes

1 *Yesha'ya* 6:5.
2 *Yesha'ya* #406.
3 Ibid.
4 *Parashat Vayishlah* #2.
5 *Avot* 3:18.
6 *Yalkut*, ibid. #407.
7 *Hagiga* 12b.
8 *Yevamot* 49b.
9 See essay of this name in *Strive for Truth!* II, p. 208.
10 Ibid., pp. 212–213.

Yirmeya

[This essay is taken from *Michtav Me-Eliyahu* IV, pp. 164–166.]

Dreams

> A prophet who has a dream—let him relate a dream.
> The one who has My word—let him speak the truth.
> Why mix the straw with the grain? says God.[1]

These words of Yirmeya lead us to consider the significance of dreams. That dreams are indeed significant has always been part of Jewish tradition.

The purpose of a dream is to reveal a person's hidden thoughts—that which is hidden in his subconscious mind. The point is to make a person aware of his true *madrega* and to set about correcting what needs correction. This is how the Zohar puts it: "And so the Holy One, blessed be He, communicates to the soul...these matters, which correspond to the thoughts of his heart, so that a person may accept the path of rebuke."[2] This is a form of heavenly aid to the person. We find in the Talmud that "a person who remains seven days without dreaming is called evil."[3] It is a sign that he is not worthy of being noticed by Heaven and this is why no dreams are given him to awaken him from his moral slumber.

Sometimes a dream may hint at something that is going to happen in the future. The reason for this, too, is to arouse him to repentance.

THE "SUB-SUBCONSCIOUS"

Why do human beings pursue worldly pleasures so avidly? There is a hidden reason for this. They have a subconscious urge to still the pangs of spiritual hunger: the longing of the soul for its state of perfection. Indulgence in physical pleasures is an illusory substitute that stills this hunger. This is why they never satisfy a person.[4]

Beneath the subconscious layer of our mind, which we see as the source of worldly strivings, there is a deeper substratum which is the source of spiritual strivings. [This could be called the "sub-subconscious."] Sometimes a dream may reveal this hidden layer, which the *yetzer ha-ra'* usurps to further its goals. Several dreams are discussed in the Talmud,[5] in which imagery of serious transgressions masks spiritual or intellectual attainments. These dreams represent the pinings of the yetzer ha-ra' to harness a person's spiritual striving in order to get him to pursue physical pleasures. The Talmud gives a number of examples showing how an analysis of the imagery in the dream, based on the metaphors in *Tanach*, can reveal a person's spiritual potential.

WHY "WORTHLESS WORDS"?

"A dream is one-sixtieth of prophecy."[6] This means that dreams, too, come from a high source, as we have seen. The Zohar[7] tells us that they come from the angel Gavriel "who resides in the Palace of Will." Gavriel, from *gevura*, means "the judgment of God." As we saw above, the function of dreams is often to warn us of our moral failings. "The Palace of Will" means the world of free will—*behira*. A person must choose whether to learn from his dreams or not. This is why "there is no dream without words of falsehood...there is no dream without both sides being represented."[8] Similarly, the Talmud says "There is no dream without worthless words."[9] Since the dream comes from the world of *beḥira*, it must contain a mixture of good and bad. The "worthless words" and "words of falsehood" come in order to hide the truth. The *beḥira* of a person is to choose the truth and not the falsehood.

DREAM AND PROPHECY

The Rabbis tells us that "just as there is no grain without straw, so there is no dream without worthless words."[10] This is derived from the quotation from Yirmeya we placed at the beginning of this essay: "A prophet who has a dream..." Rashi explains: "LET HIM RELATE A DREAM.—Let him relate it as nonsense, like other dreams, and not present it as prophecy. WHY MIX THE STRAW WITH THE GRAIN?—What has falsehood to do with truth?"

It would seem that the verse is talking about a false prophet who dreams an ordinary dream and publicizes it as if it were a prophecy. We know that an ordinary dream always contains truth mixed with falsehood, which is not the case with prophecy. A prophecy is absolutely clear to the prophet, beyond any possibility of doubt,[11] and contains no "mixture" whatsoever. [When they said "Dreams are one-sixtieth of prophecy,"[12] they meant that dreams give just a "taste" of prophecy, but there is no true resemblance between them.]

However, the verse may be speaking about a true prophet, but about one who has not yet reached the level of complete clarity in his prophecy. There were some who were called prophets in a broader sense and others who were "students of the prophets,"[13] to whom this might apply. They might have been mistaken about the true level of their prophecy, and it is these students whom the verse warns not to confuse dreams with prophecy.

DREAMS AND INTERPRETATIONS

The Talmud mentions the idea of "amelioration of dreams."[14] "If a person is very troubled about a dream...he should ameliorate it in front of three people. He should bring three people and say to them, 'I saw a good dream.' They should reply: 'It is good and may it be good, and may the All Merciful make it good. May it be decreed from Heaven seven times that it should be good; and it will be good.' And then they should say three verses referring to bad being converted into good, three verses referring to redemption, and three referring to peace."[15]

This idea is connected with the principle "Dreams go after the interpretation."[16] In a similar vein, we find:[17] "If one sees a river in a dream, he should at the first opportunity recite the verse referring to a 'river of peace'[18] before another verse occurs to him referring to a 'river of troubles.'"[19] Many other examples are given.

This is consistent with the dictum we quoted above[20] about both sides being represented in every dream. [Every prophetic warning contains both sides: if you do not repent, such-and-such will happen to you; if you repent, it will be converted into a blessing. Thus Yona's warning "In forty days Nineveh will be overturned" had a double meaning: "Either you will be overturned morally, from bad to good, or you will be overturned physically, by a disaster."[21] Similarly, a dream may contain these two alternatives. Since God is merciful and always prefers the sinner to repent rather than to die for his sins,[22] the person who has been sent the dream should make every effort to seize the good alternative. If his mind grasps the good side, there will be a corresponding reaction from Heaven. The dream will have achieved its purpose.]

notes

1 *Yirmeya* 23:28.

2 I, 183a.

3 *Berachot* 55b.

4 See *Strive for Truth!* II, p. 13.

5 *Berachot* 57a.

6 *Berachot* 57b.

7 I, 149a.

8 Zohar I, 149a.

9 *Berachot* 57a.

10 Ibid.

11 Rabbi M. H. Luzatto, *Derech Hashem* 3:4:1.

12 See note 8, above.

13 *Melachim* II, 2:3 & frequently.

14 *Berachot* 55b.

15 This procedure may be found in the larger prayer books, e.g. *Otzar Ha-tefillot*, pp. 463–464.

16 See note 16, above.

17 *Berachot* 56b.

18 *Yesha'ya* 66:12.

19 Ibid. 59:19.

20 See note 10, above.

21 Rashi, *Yona* 3:4.

22 *Yehezkel* 18:23.

Yeḥezkel

[This essay is taken from *Michtav Me-Eliyahu* IV, pp. 75–77.]

The Narrow Doorway

Our Rabbis have given us two parables to help us picture the concept of *teshuva*. One is in the Midrash as follows:

> A gang of robbers were imprisoned by the king. They dug a tunnel and escaped—all except one. The prison guard came and saw the tunnel and the remaining prisoner still in the cell. He hit him with his stick, saying, "You miserable wretch! Here's the tunnel. Why didn't you escape?" So, too, in the time to come God will say to the wicked: Repentance was available. Why didn't you repent?[1]

The other parable in the Talmud is:

> Why was this world created with a *hey*?[2] Because the world resembles a garden house [*with one side open, like a* hey *which is open at the bottom*] so that whoever wants to leave it can do so [*the ability is given to* resha'im *to follow the evil path if they want to*—Rashi]. Why is the leg of the *hey* hanging [*not attached to the roof*]? Because if he wants to do *teshuva*, he is brought back again [*through the little opening between the leg and the roof*]. Why can he not enter the other way [*by the way he went out*]? This would not be successful. Because...he who wants to purify himself

is given heavenly aid [*such a person needs special help because of the* yetzer ha-ra*, therefore a special path of return is provided* — Rashi].[3]

THE SECRET ACCEPTANCE

Is there a connection between the two parables—the escape tunnel of the Midrash and the little opening in the *hey* of the Gemara? From the words of Rabbi Eliyahu de Vidas in *Reshit Hochma*,[4] it seems that there is. In fact, the escape tunnel and the opening in the *hey* are one and the same thing. He writes that the reason the repentant sinner must return in this way is "so that he may be sheltered from the masters of judgment." This needs explaining, which can be found in another Gemara:[5] "What is the meaning of the verse [*in Yehezkel*] 'And the hands of the man were under their wings [*referring to the Hayyot*]'?[6] This word ["*the hands of*"] is written *yado* [*His hand*] to indicate that the hand of God is stretched out under the wings of the *Hayyot* in order to accept the *baalei teshuva*, because of the attribute of justice." Rashbam comments: "Because of the attribute of justice which accuses and says [*to God*] 'Do not accept them,' therefore He accepts them secretly."[7]

All this seems at first sight extremely puzzling.

THE POINT OF A NEEDLE

There are many levels of *teshuva*, determined by the amount of effort the penitent person expends compared with the amount of heavenly aid he receives.

Normally, according to the spiritual laws of the universe, the first step toward *teshuva* must be taken by the sinner. The spiritual law requires that "arousal from below" must precede "arousal from above."[8] This is in accordance with the verse "Return to Me and I will return to you, says God."[9] Great mercy is required, even for such *teshuva* to be accepted. It is no easy feat to obliterate the past.

There is, however, a type of sinner who does not find within himself the strength to make the first move. His *yetzer ha-ra‘* is too strong; he cannot abandon his sins, however much he would like to. All he can do—and does do—is to cry out to God to help him break the chains of his *yetzer*.

He has failed on all three requirements of *teshuva*: remorse, breaking with the past, and adopting a new lifestyle for the future.[10] He wants God to do everything for him. Such *teshuva* cannot be accepted according to the rules normally governing the spiritual universe. "He is not able to return by the way he came."

But God's mercy is greater than these laws. He counts the cry from the heart of the would-be returnee as sufficient "arousal from below" to warrant a great outpouring of heavenly aid. The Midrash refers to this regarding the verse in *Shir Ha-shirim*, "Open for me, my beloved!"

> God says to Israel: My children! Make for Me one opening of *teshuva* as small as the point of a needle and I will open for you gateways through which wagons and carriages can pass.[11]

That cry from the heart is "the opening as small as the point of a needle." This is the "little opening" of the *hey*. This, too, is the escape tunnel as well as the divine hand which is stretched out under the wings of the *ḥayyot*.

THE POWER OF PRAYER

We see from this that success in all our endeavors depends

on the power of prayer. This does not refer to the reciting of fixed prayers, but rather to a spontaneous cry from the heart. Although after the destruction of the Temple the gates of prayer were said to have closed,[13] my saintly great-grandfather Rabbi Yisrael Salanter assured us that even today there is one prayer which is always answered, every time and in every situation. This is the prayer for heavenly aid in overcoming obstacles in one's spiritual life.[14]

This is the only way to break through the obtuseness of one's own heart. This is the "point of the needle" with which we can approach Hashem. Even though we might only traverse a small part of the journey, Hashem will judge it as if we went equal shares with Him.

notes

1 *Kohelet Rabba* 3:15.

2 See *Bereshit* 2:4, Rashi.

3 *Menahot* 29b.

4 *Sha'arei Teshuva*, Chapter 1.

5 *Pesahim* 119a.

6 *Yehezkel* 1:8.

7 In *Pesahim* ad loc.

8 See above, *parashat Devarim*, "Perspectives of Mercy."

9 *Malachi* 3:7.

10 Rambam, *Mishneh Torah*, "Laws of Repentance" 2:2.

11 *Midrash Rabba*, *Shir Ha-shirim* 5:2.

12 *Midrash Tanhuma*, *Ki-Tissa* #23.

13 *Berachot* 32b.

14 *Or Yisrael*, Letters #14.

Trei 'Asar — Malachi

[For the purpose of the present volume, the essay in *Michtav Me-Eliyahu* II, on the prophet Hoshea', has been replaced by the following essay which is taken from *Michtav Me-Eliyahu* V, pp. 14–15.]

Between Light and Darkness

If one lights one candle after another and there are many candles, one can gradually achieve a respectable degree of light. But switching on a high-powered light bulb is quite another matter. Our future redemption will bring us "from darkness to a great light."[1] Which type of illumination will it be: gradual or sudden?

It seems that the answer can be found in *Malachi*: "Suddenly will He come into His Temple—the Lord whom you are seeking."[2]

IN THE BLINK OF AN EYE

We find a similar concept in the case of Yosef Ha-tzaddik. After the butler had been freed from prison for two years and had not tried to free Yosef, Yosef decided that he must have completely forgotten about him and that there was no longer the slightest hope of his getting out. Even one moment before Pharaoh's messengers arrived, Yosef held no hope of being released through normal, natural means. Suddenly and unexpectedly they knocked on the gates of the prison and took him at top speed.[3]

On the verse "They ran him out of the dungeon,"[4] Seforno comments:

God's salvation is always quick. Compare: "For My salvation is near,"[5] and "If only Israel would listen to Me...in a moment I would subdue their foes."[6] So it was in Egypt: "For they were driven out of Egypt and could not delay,"[7] on which our Rabbis comment: "Our fathers did not even have time for the dough to rise before redemption came."[8] And so we are told it will be in the future: "Suddenly will He enter His Temple—the Lord whom you seek."[9]

AS THE DAWN RISES

On the other hand, we find that God's redemption comes gradually.

Once Rabbi Ḥiyya the Great and Rabbi Shimon ben Ḥalafta were walking in the valley of Arbel at daybreak. They saw the first rays of the dawn breaking through the darkness. Said Rabbi Ḥiyya to Rabbi Shimon ben Ḥalafta: "So is the redemption of Israel. At first it is gradual; the more it proceeds, the stronger it becomes."[10]

This would seem to contradict what we said above. But redemption has two components. There are the deeds of Israel here below and there is the divine action of deliverance when the time is ripe. The merits of Israel accumulate gradually, but when the time comes, God brings the redemption with incredible haste, with no delay whatsoever, as in Egypt.[11]

CONTRASTS

God's acts often contain this element of suddenness because our minds are attuned to sudden changes. We are greatly impressed by dramatic contrasts and diametric opposites. We live in a world of contrasts and deep divisions. "Two people sitting together with no words of Torah exchanged between them are an 'abode of scoffers'...while when two people sit together exchanging words of Torah, the *Shechina* rests between them."[12] Only a word divides a company of scoffers—who, after their death, are unable to enter the presence of the *Shechina*[13]— from the presence of the *Shechina* itself! "A mere word may make all the difference between a *tsaddik* and a *rasha'*."[14]

The Torah declares: "I have set before you a choice: between life and death."[15] There are no compromises. What is not truth is falsehood. A person who is willing to examine himself using the truth perspective[16] can discern this.

HAVDALA

We bless God "Who separates between holy and nonholy, between light and darkness, between Israel and the nations, between the seventh day and the rest of the week."[17] Each of these are opposites—going from one extreme to the other.

Any spiritual change ushers in a completely new situation—a new world. The spiritual is the true essence of everything. And a change in essence creates something completely new. With our limited vision, we may not see much between one spiritual level and another. [The prophet Malachi tells us: "Then you will see the difference between a *tsaddik* and a *rasha'*, between one who serves God and one who does not serve Him."[18] The Talmud asks, "Is not the *tsaddik* identical with 'one who serves God,' and the *rasha'* with 'one who does not serve Him'?"[19] And it replies: "the 'one who serves God' and 'the one who does not' may both be complete *tsaddikim*.

The difference is that one reviews the portion of Torah he is studying a hundred times while the other reviews it a hundred-and-one times." The fact that after completing one hundred reviews he is still not satisfied and makes the great effort required to review it once more puts him in a completely different class. Compared to him, the other has not even begun to serve God!]

*   *   *   *   *

Recognizing contrasts—*havdala*—is important. Recognizing the extreme of evil gives one a great impetus to rise to the opposite—the extreme of good. Avraham rose to the height of greatness because he was brought up in the house of Terah the idol-maker. Ya'akov rose to heights of truth and honesty as a result of the years he spent in the house of Lavan, the swindler. Mosheh came to spiritual greatness just because he was brought up in the palace of Pharaoh; and Israel became the people of God in reaction to the extremes of immorality they encountered in Egypt.[20]

Each rose to heights of greatness by rebelling against the evil environment in which they found themselves. "Out of darkness comes the light!"[21]

notes

1 *Pesaḥ Haggadah*.
2 *Malachi* 3:1.
3 *Bereshit* 41:14.
4 Ibid.
5 *Yesha'ya* 56:1.
6 *Tehillim* 81:14–15.
7 *Shemot* 12:39.
8 *Pesaḥ Haggadah*.
9 See note 2, above.
10 *Yerushalmi Berachot* 1:1.
11 From my friend and colleague Rabbi M. Miller of Gates-head, England.
12 *Avot* 3:2.
13 *Sota* 42a.
14 *Kohelet Rabba* 9:10.
15 *Devarim* 30:19.
16 *Strive for Truth!* I, pp. 161 et seq.
17 Prayer book.
18 *Malachi* 3:18.
19 *Ḥagiga* 9b.
20 See *Strive for Truth!* II, "Light from Darkness," p. 180.
21 See note 1, above.

Tehillim

[This essay is taken from *Michtav Me-Eliyahu* V, pp. 78–79.]

Joy—The Secret of Creation

The question is asked: God is perfect and complete in Himself. Why should He want to create a world? The answer is given: Because God is good, and whoever is good wants to *do* good. But one can do good only for others. Therefore God created others for whom He could do good.[1] Some find this idea reflected in the verse in *Tehillim*: "*'olam ḥessed yibaneh*," which can be understood as: "the world is built on *ḥessed*."[2]

There is a difficulty here, however. Surely God is completely self-sufficient and lacks nothing. Yet the above argument seems to imply that God Himself lacks the opportunity to do *ḥessed* and needs to create a world to fulfill Himself. How are we to understand this?

ḤESSED COMES FROM JOY

In the eighth essay of the "Discourse on Lovingkindness,"[3] we discussed a similar question regarding people who do *ḥessed*. In that essay, we discussed two contrasting types—the giver and the taker. The taker continually feels his material needs, desires, and deficiencies—real or imagined—and spends his life trying to satisfy them—usually without much success. He does this by taking as much as he can from everyone and everything around him. The giver, on the other hand, shuns taking and spends his life giving happiness to as many people as possible.

The question arose in the discourse: What makes the giver want to give? It seems that—like the taker—he feels a need, he experiences a lack; but in his case, what he lacks is an opportunity to do _hessed_. He therefore sets out to satisfy his need and make good his lack by performing _hessed_. What, then, is the essential difference between the taker and the giver?

We answered that the above view of the *ba'al hessed*'s motives is mistaken. The urge to do good for others does not necessarily come from a lack or deficiency. On the contrary, it may come from an overwhelming feeling of happiness. What is the source of this happiness?

The person whose heart prompts him to give rather than to take must feel that spiritual goals are infinitely more important than material goals. This is why he is so happy. As we stated in that essay:

> He is happy because his life is filled with the joys of spiritual pursuits, before whose riches all other interests pale into insignificance. In his happiness, he resembles a river in flood whose life-giving waters overflow all its banks... The heart of one in a state of joy broadens to encompass all who are close to him; the more joyful the person, the greater his desire that all his friends take part in his joy. So it is with the giver. Firmly rooted in the spiritual life, his eyes ever turned towards the heights, he sees in everything great and small "the bounties of Hashem which are unending and His mercies which have no limit." Consequently his joy in these gifts knows no bounds and his life is un-

endingly happy. Out of this fullness of joy and happiness flow giving and love. Thus the urge to do good for others...is an outflow of the ecstatic devotion by which the happy man is attached to Hashem.[3]

CREATION OUT OF JOY

If this can be said about a giver, who tries to emulate God, how much more can be said about the blessed Creator Himself! The question we posed above—"Since God is self-sufficient, how could He *need* to create a world; how could He *need* to do *hessed*?—now seems to be mistaken. If the human urge to do *hessed* can come not from a need but from an overflowing of joy and happiness, we can surely assume this, with infinitely more power and reason, about Hashem Himself!

The infinite bounties of God which led to the creation of the worlds did not come (God forbid) from a need to perfect Himself, for He is all perfect. They came from His perfection itself. If we may be permitted to imagine for a moment that God's perfect Being must encompass a joy which is infinite and forever beyond our grasp, then we can understand the creation of the world for the purpose of *hessed*. It is this joy which overflows and brings in its trail universes of *hessed*. This is the secret of the creation of the universe.

THE JOY OF A MITZVA

In His goodness, God created us in His image. He implanted in us something resembling this joy—the joy of being, the joy of perfection. It emerges that the highest type of human being—the true giver—resembles his Creator in this essential attribute. The source of his giving is something akin to the joy Above.

Some people enjoy performing a mitzva because they feel that they have gained a mitzva. Others perform the mitzva because they enjoy it in and of itself. Similarly with the learning of Torah, some feel a great joy in the Torah learning itself. Their joy, in some sense, partakes of the joy from Above.

Now we have a way of testing the genuineness of the mitzvot we perform. To what extent do they produce "the joy of a mitzva"? We are told in the Torah that punishments come "because you did not serve Hashem your God with joy."[4] Service without joy—without heart—is not service at all. A person should examine the quantity and quality of the joy he experiences from a mitzva and compare them with the quantity and quality of the joy he experiences when he gratifies his material desires. He will then have a clear idea of his true *madrega*.

In the World to Come, we shall "enjoy the splendor of the *Shechina*."[5] This enjoyment includes an element of gaining or having. But as we have discussed at length elsewhere,[6] the main element of spiritual growth pertaining to life in the spiritual world comes from the joy of being.

A person who succeeds in conquering his *yetzer* is happy. On a supremely high level, a person who accepts his sufferings and learns from them may also be happy. He may even come to love the sufferings themselves. [Rabbi Yosef Karo wrote in the *Shulhan Aruch*: "A person must bless God for misfortune with a perfect mind and a willing soul...because for the servants of God misfortune is a joy and a benefit. Since he accepts with love what God has decreed for him, this very acceptance is an act of service, and serving God is a joy for him."[7]]

A person who learns *mussar* sincerely is happy, because he learns to know himself—his true being.

notes

1 Rav Sa'adya Gaon, *Emunot Ve'de'ot*, Part III, beginning. See also Rabbi M. H. Luzatto, *Da'at Tevunot*, beginning.
2 *Tehillim* 89:3.
3 *Strive for Truth!* I, p. 142.
4 *Devarim* 28:47.
5 *Berachot* 17a.
6 See "Being and Having," *Strive for Truth!* III, pp. 185 et seq.
7 *Orah Hayyim* 222:3.

Mishlei

[This essay is taken from *Michtav Me-Eliyahu* III, pp. 121–122.]

For the Sake of Torah

Rabbi Ḥayyim of Volozhyn writes that besides the concept of doing mitzvot and learning Torah *l'shem shamayim* ("for the sake of God"), there is also the concept of learning Torah *lishma shel Torah* ("for the sake of Torah").[1] This means we should love learning and investigating Torah with the goal of obtaining complete clarity in its understanding. When this is done, certain spiritual effects ensue.

This is what he writes:

> ...One has to study Torah with concentrated effort to reach the truth of the Torah's intentions according to one's ability. And the more one learns, the more one will want to continue learning. One will fall in love with the Torah. And if it were possible, one would prefer not to sleep or eat, but to spend his days and nights in its study, toiling and searching and thirstily drinking in its words... Through the illumination he gains at first, he realizes that still greater illumination awaits him, and so on. This will arouse his desire to understand and grasp still more until he grasps the secrets of the world and the fullness thereof... as the verse says [in *Mishlei*]: "So that those who love me may inherit re-

ality."[2] As the Mishna says: "He who learns Torah for its own sake merits many things."

"Merits many things" may also mean that he is given everything, material things—such as wealth and honor—as well as spiritual treasures. And it is right for him to have these things, because one who learns Torah *lishma* is able to use everything as *kelim* for his spiritual advancement.

THREE STEPS

Through Torah learning, a person can raise himself from the lowest level to the highest.

At first his learning will be *she'lo lishma*—not for its own sake, but for ulterior motives, such as money, honor, pride etc. But as he advances in learning and begins to sense the sweetness of Torah, he may proceed to learn "for the love of Torah," as we explained above.

But judging against the highest standards, this is not yet considered complete *lishma*, which means having inner devotion and love for the Giver of the Torah. However, love of Torah can eventually lead to this highest level of all. "God created the *yetzer ha-ra'*, but He created Torah as a condiment."[3] Once a person arrives at the stage where he senses the sweetness of Torah, the power of the *yetzer ha-ra'* is broken. A person whose mind is constantly occupied with thoughts of Torah is likely to arrive at the inner devotion which is the consummation of all our efforts.

But when all is said and done, arrival at this final destination is a gift from God.

Shelomo Ha-melech said in *Mishlei*: "House and fortune are an inheritance from one's fathers; a wise wife is from God."[4] The Vilna Gaon interprets this as follows.

"House and fortune" refer to the other levels of Torah life: all the levels except complete *lishma*. "A wise wife" refers to the soul. The lower levels are attainable by full use of the powers given a person by his heredity. The inner attachment of the soul to its Creator, the ecstatic devotion of complete *lishma*, is "only from Hashem." This is a gift from heaven, given only when a person has completed all his tasks and expanded all the toil and effort required to achieve the lower levels we have previously discussed.

"The Torah joins the lower world with the upper world."[5] The meaning is that love of learning, the *lishma* of Torah, is the middle rung which raises the person from the lowly levels of *she'lo lishma* to the supreme level of complete *le'shem shamayim*.

notes

1 *Ruah Hayyim* 6:1.
2 *Mishlei* 8:21.
3 *Bava Batra* 16a.
4 *Mishlei* 19:14.
5 *Maharal, Derech Ha-hayyim*.

Iyov

[This essay is taken from *Michtav Me-Eliyahu* V, pp. 186–187.]

Iyov and Yisrael

The *Book of Iyov* begins by describing the custom of Iyov's sons and daughters to hold a feast each day at the house of one of the seven brothers. At the close of each cycle, Iyov used to summon his children and offer up burnt offerings "to the number of them all." He was concerned that during the feasting and revelry, they might have entertained thoughts against God.[1]

The Zohar[2] believes that this story reveals one of Iyov's basic faults. On the one hand, he brought offerings to God which were burned completely on the altar—symbolizing the highest form of sacrifice. On the other hand, he allowed his children to enjoy banquets of a completely profane nature. It seems that with the *'olah* offering, which hints at the highest form of service, Iyov wished to cover up the evil of their physical enjoyment that had not the slightest connection with holiness.

The Zohar suggests that instead of this, he should have brought up his children to recognize the offering typical of Yisrael: the *korban shelamim*. [The special characteristic of this peace offering was that part of the meat was burned on the altar, part was given to the priest, and the bulk was eaten by the owner in a special state of purity, as a gift from the table of God. It was called a peace-offering because it made peace between God, the priest, and the owner. It also made peace between man's physical and spiritual strivings. It showed how the pleasures of this world could be brought within the sphere of holiness. Instead of this, however, Iyov preferred to cover up their unredeemed physical indulgence with an outward show of righteousness.]

Later on, the verse also hints that underlying Iyov's overt righteousness was a heart that was by no means on the same level. "In spite of all this, Iyov did not sin *with his lips*."[3] "He did not sin with his lips, but in his heart he sinned."[4]

IYOV AND THE RED SEA

There is an interesting *midrash* in *parashat Beshalaḥ*[5] which is very much in need of elucidation.

> When Israel went out of Egypt, the angel Samael [Satan] rose to accuse them...Lord of the universe! Until now they have been serving idols and now You are going to split the sea for them? A parable: This resembles a shepherd who was taking his flock across a river. A wolf came to attack them. The shepherd, who was an expert, took a large he-goat and set it down in front of the wolf. He said, Let it tackle this one until we cross the river, then I will come back and get him. Similarly, upon hearing Satan's accusation, what did God do? He handed Iyov over to him. Iyov had been one of Pharaoh's advisors and was "a simple and straightforward man."[6] He said to Satan, Here, he is in your hands. God said, While he is busy with Iyov, Israel will be able to enter the sea and leave it. Then I will return and rescue Iyov... Then God said to Mosheh, See I have

handed Iyov over to the Satan. What have you to do?
Speak to the children of Israel and let them go forward!

Maharal has taught us that all the words of our Sages
teach us deep truths. With what we have already discovered about Iyov, it should not be beyond our grasp to reveal the profound truth in this *midrash*.

We saw that Iyov's outwardly perfect behavior hid certain inner failings. With Israel, the situation was reversed.
Israel's outward sins hid a heart full of faith and loyalty to
Hashem. "Their fathers' merits and their own and the
faith they had in Me [when they followed Me into the
desert] are sufficient for the sea to be split for them."[7]
Where overt behavior covers an inwardly pure heart, inwardness will win out in the end.

When Satan accused Israel of misbehavior, it was very
appropriate for God to counter this attack by showing
him Iyov. When Satan saw Iyov's outwardly perfect behavior, he was immediately impelled to question his inner
sincerity. Did his heart match his actions? Thus Satan
himself agreed that if one truly looks at the situation, one
sees that it is inner purity that counts. This, in turn, reveals the true value of Israel.

If the evil is within, hidden by outward good behavior,
the evil will flourish unseen. Hence, disaster is sure to follow.

In the case of Israel however, the inner essence is pure.
Even if it is hidden by much outward evil, eventually the
good will prevail. They will declare "We will do and we
will hear" and become the people of God.

notes

---

1 *Iyov* 1:3–5.
2 II, 34a, 181b.
3 *Iyov* 2:10.
4 Rashi ad loc.
5 *Midrash Rabba, Shemot* 21:7.
6 *Iyov* 1:1.
7 Rashi, *Shemot* 14:15.

Shir Ha-shirim

[This essay is taken from *Michtav Me-Eliyahu* IV, p. 293.]

The Heart of Israel

"I am asleep but my heart is awake."[1]

The Midrash[2] comments: "'I am asleep' for redemption; ['my heart is awake':] the heart of the Holy One blessed be He is awake to redeem us. Rabbi Ḥiyya bar Abba says: Where do we find that the Holy One blessed be He is called 'the heart of Israel'? From this verse: 'The rock of my heart and my portion is God forever.'"[3]

It may seem strange to us that God should be called "the heart of Israel." How can the Creator be called the heart of His creatures?

But it has already been established[4] that whatever we say about God can never refer to His essence. Our thoughts and our language have no possible means of grasping this. We can speak only about His attributes in so far as He reveals them to us.

The language with which we can best grasp His attributes—His love, mercy, justice and so on—is the language of the heart: the language of prayer. While our intellect can never grasp anything at all about God as He is, in the prayer from our hearts we can turn directly to Him. If we cannot speak *about* God in this sense, we can always speak *to* God.

This is what our Rabbis meant when they said: "The Holy One blessed be He [*that is, our awareness of God Himself*] is [*that is, can best be realized in*] the heart of Israel [*for only in our hearts can we make direct contact with Him, when we turn to Him in prayer*]."

notes

1 *Shir Ha-shirim* 5:2.
2 Ad loc.
3 *Tehillim* 73:26.
4 *Michtav Me-Eliyahu* III, p. 269.

Ruth

[This essay is taken from *Michtav Me-Eliyahu* V, p. 175.]

Extracting the Precious
from the Base

It is remarkable that the seed of *Mashiaḥ* seems to have been produced through a series of questionable actions. On the one hand, there is the union of Yehuda and Tamar and that of David and Batsheva. On the other, we have the daughters of Lot who bore sons to their father. And King David traces his lineage back to one of these sons, Moab, through Ruth, the Moabite girl. Also, the union of Ruth and Boaz is preceded by the strange episode at the threshing floor.[1]

REBELLING AGAINST EVIL

At the end of the essay "Between Light and Darkness" (above), we explained that Hashem sometimes places *tsaddikim* in very difficult and morally threatening circumstances. By rebelling against his surroundings, the *tsaddik* can rise to otherwise unattainable heights of greatness. With this concept, we can explain the difficulties raised above.

The union of Yehuda and Tamar brought Tamar to demonstrate that "it is better to allow oneself to be thrown into a fiery furnace rather than put another person to shame in public."[2] On Yehuda's side, this illustrated the first example of a great man publicly confessing to wrongdoing.[3] In the case of David and Batsheva the effectiveness of *teshuva* was demonstrated for all time.[4] And by rebelling against her Moabite antecedents, Ruth earned the title "mother of the kingdom"—of *Mashiah*.[5] But the episode at the threshing floor still needs elucidation. What revelation emerged from this? It was the revelation of the heights of *hessed*, as we shall see.

THE DOUBLE *HESSED*

When Naomi first heard from Ruth the name of the landowner who had treated her so well, she exclaimed "Blessed is he to Hashem, Who has not abandoned His kindness to the living and the dead!"[6] She explained to Ruth that Boaz was their kinsman—a nephew of her husband Elimelech who had died in Moab and a cousin to Mahlon, Ruth's dead husband. The Torah calls such a close relative a *goel*—a "redeemer."[7] It is his duty to redeem the ancestral lands of a family member in trouble.[8]

Naomi realized that by guiding Ruth's footsteps to Boaz's field, Hashem was showing that He was now inclined to once again bestow kindness on them. Boaz would surely redeem their fields. This was Hashem's "kindness to the living." What was His "kindness to the dead"? Naomi expected that Boaz would also marry Ruth. Ruth's husband Mahlon had died childless in Moab. The son who would be born to Boaz and Ruth would eventually take over the ancestral lands and it would be as if Mahlon were still alive. There is no greater gratification to the soul of a dead person who had died childless than to see his divinely appointed task being carried on in this world by someone who is like his own son, "to restore the name of the dead person to his inheritance, so that his name is not cut off from among his brothers and his home town."[9] (The Torah provides for *yibum* among brothers. The people of that time, understanding the purpose of the law, extended some of its provisions to other close relatives.[10])

DRASTIC MEASURES

But the barley and wheat harvests were over and Boaz had not proposed marriage to Ruth. Naomi understood why. Boaz was an elderly man and Ruth was still young. If he proposed to her, Ruth might feel obliged to agree, bearing in mind the mitzva element we discussed above. He did not want to put her under such pressure. After all, she had her own life to live.

Naomi, however, knew that Ruth sincerely and deeply wished to enter into this marriage, not for any selfish reason but purely to do *ḥessed* for her dead husband's soul.[11] (Ruth had indeed received marriage offers from several of the young men of Beit Leḥem, all of which she had rejected.) But how could she convince Boaz of this? Naomi decided that actions speak louder than words. Boaz was sleeping that night at the threshing floor. Naomi sent Ruth to him there, in effect, to ask him to marry her as a *goel*. Boaz realized that she would not have done this if she had not truly and sincerely wanted this marriage.[12]

THE FIRST AND LAST *ḤESSED*

The first words he addressed to her, after he realized who she was, were: "Blessed are you to Hashem, my daughter! This last *ḥessed* of yours is greater than the first—that you did not go after the young men, whether poor or rich."[13] We can now fully understand the meaning of these somewhat enigmatic words.

We see that the "strange episode" of the threshing floor resulted in a great revelation of *ḥessed*—completely unselfish *ḥessed* of a very special kind. Boaz, too, revealed great strength of character during this episode.[14] It is strengths of these kinds which are needed to bring *Mashiaḥ*.

notes

1 *Ruth* 3:1–14.
2 Rashi, *Bereshit* 38:25.
3 *Bereshit* 38:26, 49:8 (Targum).
4 *Avoda Zara* 4b.
5 Rashi, *Melachim* I 2:19.
6 *Ruth* 2:20.
7 *Vayikra* 25:29.
8 Ibid. 25:25.
9 *Ruth* 4:10.
10 Ramban, *Bereshit* 38:8.
11 Ruth's completely unselfish attitude may be hinted at by the omission of the word *elai*—"to me"—in *Ruth* 3:5. Compare also "Eliezer's Mind," *parashat Ḥayyei Sarah*, above. —A.C.
12 Had she not sincerely desired this marriage, she easily could have excused herself from going to the threshing floor. She could have said, without the slightest embarrassment, that she was afraid to go out alone at night. Or she could very plausibly have indicated that she could not bring herself to do what Naomi suggested.—A.C.
13 *Ruth* 3:10.
14 The Rabbis praise Boaz's self-control even more than that of Yosef Ha-tsaddik. See *Sanhedrin* 19b (end).

Eicha

[This essay is taken from *Michtav Me-Eliyahu* IV, pp. 77–78.]

"Bring Us Back!"

"Bring us back to You, O God, and we will return. For if You have utterly rejected us, You have vented Your anger upon us to the limit."[1]

These two final verses of *Eicha* reflect the thoughts of a person in the depths of despair. They reflect a person so far from Hashem, so deeply sunk in sin, that he does not even have the strength to cry out. Nor does he have the ability to break through the obtuseness that surrounds his heart—even a puncture the size of a needle's point.[2] What can a person in that state do?

There is only one ray of light for him: he *wants* things to be different. He can build on this and begin anyway. Let him at least do the little that he *can* do. If he does this without calculations or stipulations, Hashem will help arouse his obtuse heart until he reaches the very doors of *teshuva*.

This is the type of *teshuva* in which a person says to God "You bring me back!"[3] He says "Come back, O God—how long?—change Your mind about Your servants!"[4] A person experiences only a slight spiritual stirring and he hopes that God will do everything else for him. And God, indeed, will look upon him with mercy and count this very slight spiritual stirring as sufficient "arousal from below." From now on he will be guided and assisted until he receives all the heavenly aid needed to bring him to complete repentance. "Before they cry out, I will answer."[5]

This is the type of *teshuva* indicated in the verse that begins this essay.

The secret is hidden in the last two words *'ad me'od*, which we have translated as "to the limit." This means "up to the limit" but not "actually at the limit." Even if Hashem seems to have rejected us utterly because of our sins and has poured his anger over us, the fury has not, God forbid, reached the outermost limit. And since God acts "measure for measure," this means that our sins, too, have not reached the outer limit. One point of holiness is left which has not been affected by the sin. From this point healing can grow.

notes

1 *Eicha* 5:21–22.
2 See essay above "The Narrow Doorway."
3 See note 1, above.
4 *Tehillim* 90:13.
5 *Yesha'ya* 65:24.

Kohelet

[This essay is taken from *Michtav Me-Eliyahu* V, pp. 268–270.]

Values: Illusory and Real

A person values things and people according to their importance for him. Let us compare the way we receive a person whom we happen to need very urgently and the way we receive someone for whom we have no particular need. [But Shammai said: "Receive everyone with a friendly face"![1]]

There are real needs and there are illusory needs. Some people live in a world of illusion. They do not distinguish between "real" existence and imaginary existence. As a result, all their needs are illusory, and similarly all their values. Why do people get so much pleasure from what they see in the movies? Because what they think is "real life" is also actually illusory. As a result, they consider the world of fiction as a real part of their lives, since the distinction between reality and illusion is blurred.

ESSENCE AND PURPOSE

A thing is real if its essence is connected to spiritual values. Without true essence, all that we consider to be "vital needs" are illusory. Without spiritual essence there is no need.

Kohelet stated: "There are riches kept by their owner

for his downfall."[2] This is when the riches serve illusory needs. For such a person, property is only "more worry"[3] and money means only "the desire for more money."[4]

"BREAD OF THE PRESENCE"

When the spiritual essence is present, all needs are real and all values are true. In the Holy Temple, twelve matza-loaves were arranged on the Table from Shabbat to Shabbat "before God."[5] They represented the material sustenance of the twelve tribes of Israel. They were called *leḥem ha-panim*, which should be translated as "Bread of the Presence."[6]

That the bread of Israel was kept "before God" means that our food and all our material needs are meaningful because they were required for the service of God. Everything takes on value and meaning in God's eyes that is associated with a spiritual purpose. And so it should be in our eyes, too.

One who remembers God in all his actions is said to be "standing before God." Such a person is always satisfied. One of the blessings in the Torah is: "You shall eat your bread in satisfaction."[7] Our Rabbis explain: "You will need to eat only a little, but the food will be blessed within you and you will be satisfied."[8] [Satisfaction is largely psychological. "The *tsaddik* eats to satisfy his appetite, but the belly of the *rasha'* is never full."[9]] Only one who has a spiritual essence and whose goals are spiritual is satisfied in this world. Since the affairs of this world have a spiritual import for him, all his values are true.

RAINFALL

We learn in the Talmud[10] that rain is withheld from Israel—and the nation's material existence endangered—because of various spiritual failings. These include: failure to give *teruma* and *ma'aser*, the prevalence of *lashon ha-ra'*, lack of Torah learning, dishonesty, and insincere prayer.

All these endanger the nation's livelihood. Why? Because if the spiritual essence is lacking, the material basis has lost its significance. When the spiritual essence is present, there can be material blessing. Since the material goods are also used for mitzvot, blessing comes and expands the *kelim* of the mitzva. "A mitzva draws another mitzva in its train."[11] If there is no spiritual essence, there can be no blessing derived from the side of holiness.[12] It is only this kind of blessing which grants complete satisfaction, as we have explained above.

In fact, we witness rainfall for the wicked as well. These are not "rains of blessing" and have very little connection with the point of spiritual essence. They do not bring satisfaction even in the physical sense. The rain comes in order to preserve the natural order of the world. "God does not destroy His world because of fools."[13] In other words, the wicked are maintained so that they will produce a future generation which will eventually bring God's spiritual purposes to fruition.[14]

notes

1 *Avot* 1:15.
2 *Kohelet* 5:12.
3 *Avot* 2:8.
4 *Kohelet* 5:9.
5 *Shemot* 25:30.
6 See Ibn Ezra ad loc.
7 *Vayikra* 26:5.
8 Rashi ad loc.
9 *Mishlei* 13:25.
10 *Ta'anit* 7b–8a.
11 *Avot* 4:2.
12 For the meaning of "blessings from the side of holiness" and "blessings from the side of defilement" see *Strive for Truth!* I, "The Attribute of Mercy," pp. 65 and 74, and "The Wisdom of the World" p. 198.
13 *Avoda Zara* 54b.
14 See *Strive for Truth!* I, pp. 67–68.

Esther

[This essay is taken from *Michtav Me-Eliyahu* III, p. 50.]

Revealing the Falsehoods
of the *Yetzer*

How should we deal with the falsehoods of the *yetzer ha-ra'*? The method is hinted at in *Megillat Esther*.

After Haman was eliminated, the king said to Mordechai and Esther: "You write concerning the Jews as is good in your eyes and seal it with the royal seal, because any edict which is written in the king's name and sealed with the royal seal cannot be recalled."[1] This seems difficult to understand. Haman's edict calling for the murder of all the Jews was also sealed with the royal seal. Surely if they wanted to change this effectively, they would have to annul the previous edict?

Rabbi Avraham ibn Ezra[2] solved this puzzle in the following way:

> Mordechai was a great Sage...and wrote in the following manner: "Please be informed as follows: The king commanded Haman...to issue a royal edict which called on the Jews to slay their enemies on the 13th of Adar. However, Haman changed the edict [without the king's knowledge] and made it call for the slaying of the Jews on that day. When the king became aware of

his evil plan, he had him hanged...for daring to attack the Jews, the precise opposite of the king's intention... Therefore the king has commanded that new letters shall be written and sealed by the king, giving effect to the king's original intention." This is what the Megillah means when it states that on Purim everything was reversed.[3]

If we read the Megillah on a deeper level, we find that Haman and Amalek represent the forces of evil in the world, and "the king" means the King of the Universe. Accordingly, we can interpret the narrative as alluding to the battle between the forces of good and the forces of evil in the human soul.

Sometimes it appears that the power that God has given to the Satan (who is the *yetzer ha-ra*[4]) is so great that it is impossible for us to overcome it. "The edict...cannot be rescinded." The obtuseness that has accumulated in our hearts as a result of our sins and failures (the *timtum ha-lev*) may have become so strong that it can no longer be broken.

But if one wants to defeat the *yetzer*, one cannot wait until it has established an impregnable position in our hearts. One has to tackle it from the very beginning, by recognizing the weakness of its arguments and the falsity of its promises. It is not difficult at that stage to realize that all its insinuations are false from beginning to end. We should adopt Mordechai's strategy and insist that *we* have the truth, and it is the *yetzer* which has deliberately perverted the facts. This is the only way to defeat the *yetzer ha-ra*.

A similar strategy is recommended by the Hassidic leader Rabbi Menaḥem Mendel of Vitebsk in his letters from Eretz Yisrael.[5] He states that it is "a tried and tested method" to treat the *yetzer*, when it first comes to tempt us, as someone whose intentions are the precise opposite of what he says. If the *yetzer* says "Do this," understand it to mean "Don't do this," and if it says "Don't do this," read it as an invitation to do it. (There is a game, he mentions, in which two people hold a conversation after having agreed that *yes* shall mean *no* and *no* shall mean *yes*.)

This makes it much easier to defeat the *yetzer*. Once one realizes that whatever the *yetzer* says is wrong, it is possible to recognize the truth by turning the words of the *yetzer* on their head.

notes

1 *Esther* 8:8.
2 Ad loc.
3 Ibid. 9:1.
4 *Bava Batra* 16a.
5 *Pri Ha-aretz* (Warsaw 1878), p. 27a.

Daniel

[This essay is taken from *Michtav Me-Eliyahu* IV, p. 92.]

The Book of Life

Towards the end of the book the angel tells Daniel: "There will be a time of trouble such as there has never been from the beginning of the nation until that time, and at that time your people will escape—all who are found written in the book."[1]

What is this book? And what are the books referred to in our literature: "All your actions are recorded in the book";[2] "the books of the living and the books of the dead are opened";[3] "the signature of every person is in it and it reads itself."?[4] What are they made of? What kind of writing material is used? And how can a book read itself?

The answer is given by Rabbi Yosef Yaavetz. The book God writes in is the human soul, in which all deeds and all thoughts are recorded.[5]

If so, the prayer "Write us in the book of Life" is a prayer for heavenly aid. We are asking for success in our efforts to impress on our innermost soul our desire to live a life of holiness. There are impressions which are related to redemption, and others related to livelihood, forgiveness, merits etc. All these come from a person's innermost state.

THE BOOK OF REMEMBRANCE

"Then those who fear God speak together, one to the other, and it is recorded in the Book of Remembrance before Him, for those who fear Him and think of His name."[6] This refers to people who, in close companionship, discuss together the problems of maintaining a God-fearing attitude in an environment which denies the value of serving God and keeping His mitzvot.[7] The Book of Remembrance is the record of spiritual work carried out by souls who are united in words of reverence and faith.

This lasting impression stands them in good stead, even in times of the greatest trouble. Even in "a time of trouble such as there has never been since the beginning of the nation"—such as that referred to in *Daniel* in the quotation at the beginning of this essay—"those who are recorded in the Book shall escape." What book? The Book of Remembrance referred to above.[8]

The emphasis on "speaking to one another" in the verse in *Malachi* is explained by the *gemara* in *Berachot*. "Wherever we find two people sitting together and discussing Torah—the *Shechina* rests between them,"[9] citing this verse[10] as proof text. Rabbi Menaẖem Meiri explains: "Since they are discussing this together, the words are more deeply engraved on their imagination."[11] This confirms what we cited above: that whatever is engraved on the imagination is recorded on one's soul—and *this* is God's Book of Remembrance.

notes

1 *Daniel* 12:1.

2 *Avot* 2:1.

3 *Rosh Hashana* 16b.

4 High Holy Days prayer book.

5 Quoted by R. Eliyahu de Vidas in *Reshit Hochma*, *Sha'ar Ha-teshuva*.

6 *Malachi* 3:16.

7 Ibid. 14–15.

8 Commentary of Rav Saadya Gaon on *Daniel* 12:1.

9 *Berachot* 6a.

10 See note 6, above.

11 Commentary on *Berachot* ad loc.

Ezra–Nehemya

[This essay is taken from *Michtav Me-Eliyahu* III, pp. 161–163.]

Learning *Emuna*

We are all believers. Each one of us realizes that God created the world and runs it continually. But there are many levels of faith. The Torah says about Avraham: "He had faith in God, and He reckoned this for him as a merit."[1] Even for Avraham Avinu, the founder of all faith, faith was counted as a merit!

This verse is explained in *Nehemya*, in a passage we recite every morning in our prayers, as: "You found his heart faithful before You."[2] This is one of the more advanced levels of *emuna*, as we shall see.

Most of us are equipped with that basic faith we referred to above. But we are commanded to work on expanding and developing that faith. The first mitzva in the ten commandments—"I, Hashem, am your God"[3]—is the mitzva of *emuna*. In practice this means to occupy oneself with *emuna*: to fix it in one's heart and mind continually.[4] A person who does not make a constant effort to clarify *emuna* to himself and to strengthen it in his heart will never really know it. In addition, he will have failed to observe one of the most important mitzvot.

There are four methods by which one can learn to grow in the mitzva of *emuna*.

TRAINING

The first method is by way of training. One can train one-self to be occupied with *emuna*, at least in an external sense. One can get used to saying at every opportunity "Thank God," "If God wills it," "With the help of Hashem," etc. Also, he should be careful to keep the mitzva of *tefilla*. Even if his prayers are not yet with devo-tion or intent, saying the prayers is at least an expression of faith in God. [And as Rambam says, for one's words to count as prayer at all, he must at the very least have in mind that he is standing in front of Hashem. This is im-portant training for growth in *emuna*.[5]]

This applies to all mitzvot that a person performs. Even when inner *kavvana* is missing, at least he should be aware that he is obeying the command of Hashem. This will strengthen his *emuna* at least externally. Since he has gotten into the habit of keeping the mitzvot and avoiding *averot*, this will make it harder for him to deviate from the Torah, even though it is still only outward training and habit.

REFLECTION

The second method has to do with the mind and is closer to inwardness. This is the method of reflection. A person should reflect on the wonders of creation and clarify to himself that all these are the works of God and clear evi-dence of His infinite wisdom. He should teach himself also to see the unity in the diversity of all life and of the whole of creation.

He should also reflect on the inner life of the human being. He should become aware of the *yetzer ha-ra'* and its tricks, the duality in the human heart, and the continual conflict between the forces of good and evil within him.

He will see that the purpose of this conflict is that the forces of good should ultimately overcome the evil. This, too, will teach him the unity of the spiritual world.

HOLINESS

The third method is the way of holiness. We can distinguish three approaches.

The first approach is to cultivate one's sense of truth. One must train oneself to be faithful and trustworthy in one's own heart—to acknowledge the truth about oneself. One must try to be consistent and refuse to accept falsehood as truth. This was the kind of *emuna* which God valued so highly in Avraham Avinu.[1] And as the Levites explained it in their prayer in *Neḥemya*: "You found his heart to be faithful before You,"[2] meaning that his heart remained true to the truth that he recognized.

[The issue there was the ability of Avraham to have children. Avram's scientific knowledge told him that he could not possibly have children. But God assured him that he would be the father of a great nation. God took him, say our Rabbis, outside the vault of heavens and let him look down on the stars, showing him that God can take a person outside the sphere of nature. Avram trusted in God, and that was his merit.]

The second approach is to crush one's *yetzer ha-ra'* and devote oneself to spiritual goals. The less physical desires rule over man, the more one is able to see the light of Hashem.

The third approach is by way of devotion to Torah learning. In deep-level learning there is always novelty to gladden one's heart.

A person whose feelings are numb and is not aroused at all by intellectual or spiritual novelty will remain an ignoramus. He will lack the drive and ambition to succeed in his learning. The excitement of sudden discovery makes the greatest impression on a person, and it is this more than anything that opens the heart to spiritual progress and higher levels of *emuna.*

TRUST

The fourth method of attaining *emuna* is to trust in Hashem in practice in one's everyday life. A person who knows that God can grant him what he needs at any time and that each day has its special bounty from above will never find himself worrying about what will happen tomorrow.

Of course, *emuna* is needed to arrive at this degree of trust. But a person who practices *bitahon* will certainly find his level of *emuna* rising. Once he puts his trust in God, he will experience the direct loving care of Hashem in ways not accessible to other people.

notes

1 *Bereshit* 15:6.

2 *Nehemya* 9:7–8.

3 *Shemot* 20:2.

4 Radbaz, *Ta'amei Ha-mitzvot,* #1.

5 Laws of Prayer 4:16. See *Hiddushei R. Hayyim Ha-Levi,* p. 2.

Divrei Ha-yamim

[This essay is taken from *Michtav Me-Eliyahu* IV, pp. 231–232.]

An Elevated Place

Yehoshafat was one of the good kings of Judah. Of him it is said in *Divrei Ha-yamim*: "His heart was elevated in the ways of God."[1] As a result, he initiated a wide-ranging educational campaign. He organized teams of Levites who visited all the cities of Judah with the *sefer Torah* and taught the populace the word of God.[2]

This "elevation of heart" is true greatness, and it opens all the gates of success. It means that the person raises his sights and strives towards the highest goals. He looks upon them with visions of greatness and not from the viewpoint of humdrum pettiness.

Every level of Torah life has its point of greatness—the highest reach of that particular level. The successful man of spirit raises himself to that height and looks from that vantage point at all that surrounds him. He will look at it with different eyes. He will look at all his affairs with a vision of the ultimate goal and penetrate to their inner essence. The elevated person will see in everything the potential it has for increasing the glory of God. A person who raises himself to the highest point of his own *madrega*—his particular level of purity of heart—will certainly discover that the whole world now looks different to him: completely different from the world to which he was previously accustomed.

A HIGH PLACE IN GEHINNOM

Even on the level which is called Gehinnom—the level of spiritual failure—there is a highest point. At this point, the failure represented by Gehinnom can turn into songs of praise. This secret is revealed to us by the Gemara,[3] referring to the verse "But the sons of Korah did not die."[4] Hazal tell us that when Korah and all his company were swallowed up into the bowels of the earth, "a high place was raised up for them in Gehinnom itself, upon which they sat and uttered a song."[5] Rashi comments on this: "God prepared a high place for them so that they did not sink very deep into Gehinnom and did not die."

The spiritual background of this amazing event is described in the Yalkut.[6]

> What merit did the sons of Korah have that they were saved? When they were sitting with their father Korah, they saw Mosheh approaching. [*Korah and his company refused to rise, since they had rejected his leadership.*] They [*the sons of Korah*] looked down at the ground. They said [*to themselves:*] If we stand before Mosheh Rabbenu, we shall be showing contempt for our father... If we do not, we shall be transgressing the commandment "Rise up before old age." We had better stand up for Mosheh, even though we shall be showing contempt for our father. At that moment, their hearts stirred with *teshuva*. Concerning them David said, "My heart stirred with a good word."[7]

It is clear from this description that the sons of Korah had not completely severed themselves from the rebellion. This was their failure. However, at the last moment they managed, in the midst of their sin, to climb to the highest point of their *madrega*: to realize that the honor due to a father cannot supersede a mitzva from the Torah. This was the "stirring of the heart" which saved them from destruction.

The Yalkut continues:

> This was a foretaste of what God is going to do for the *tsaddikim* in the future, when He will seize the corners of the earth and shake the *resha'im* out of it, while the *tsaddikim* will be suspended at the height of the world.

This refers to the destruction of the physical world after six thousand years.[8] The *tsaddikim* who had always attached themselves to the spiritual aspect of the world—the "high point" of existence—will not be affected by the disappearance of the physical world. The *resha'im*, however, who had always considered the physical to be most important, will fall with the fall of the physical.

> Rabbi Yehuda Ha-nasi said: A kind of pillar was raised up for them [the sons of Korah] in Gehinnom and they stood upon it, in the sight of all Israel.

This was a great *kiddush Hashem*. All Israel recognized the truth of God's judgment, its precision, and the divine mercy shown to the sons because of that very subtle point of merit. The fact that they were the *kelim* for this *kiddush Hashem* increased their merit to a very great degree, and this was their salvation.

> Then they opened their mouths and uttered a song: "As we heard so we saw, in the city of God... May God establish it forever..."[9] This means that in the future

God will build Jerusalem permanently, without inter-
ruption.

A song [*shira*, which comes from the root meaning "to
envision," "to behold"] emerges from complete recognition of the divine in our world. By elevating themselves to
the highest point of *their* level, Hashem enabled them to
reach the highest of all levels—to behold the building of
the eternal, spiritual Jerusalem in the time of *Mashiah*.

[How shall we, the weakest of all generations, be worthy of welcoming the face of the *Mashiah*? Only if we, in
all our lowliness, succeed in raising ourselves to the highest point immediately available to us. God will do the
rest.]

notes

1 *Divrei Ha-yamim* II 17:6.
2 Ibid. 7–9.
3 *Sanhedrin* 110a.
4 *Bemidbar* 26:11.
5 Ibid. 16:32–33.
6 *Parashat Korah* #752.
7 *Tehillim* 45:2, attributed to the sons of Korah.
8 *Sanhedrin* 97a.
9 *Tehillim* 48:9; also "a psalm of the sons of Korah."

Glossary

The following glossary provides a partial explanation of some of the Hebrew words and phrases used in this book. The spellings and explanations reflect the way the specific word is used herein. Often, there are alternate spellings and meanings for the words.

ADAM HA-RISHON: the first man created.

AMORA'IM: the Sages whose opinions comprise the Gemara.

AVEROT: transgressions.

AVODAT HASHEM: service of God.

AVOT: lit., fathers; the Patriarchs.

'AYIN HA-RA': the evil eye.

BA'AL HESSED: one who performs acts of kindness.

BEHIRA: free will; free choice.

BEIT DIN: a court of Jewish law.

BEN TORAH: one devoted to Torah.

BERAITA: a Tannaic compilation, normally expanding on subjects dealt with in the Mishna, to which it is secondary.

BITAHON: faith and trust in God.

'EGEL: the Golden Calf.

EMUNA: faith in God.

GAN 'EDEN: the Garden of Eden.

GEMARA: commentary of the Mishna; together they comprise the Talmud.

GEONIM: Torah geniuses, title given the heads of the Babylonian yeshivas.

GEVURA: strength of character.

HAR SINAI: the mountain at which the Torah was given.

HASHGAHA PRATIT: Divine Providence.

HASSID: pious, righteous man.

HAZAL: an acronym meaning "Our Sages, of blessed memory."

HEKDESH: property consecrated for sacrifice or other Temple use.

HESSED: lovingkindness.

HEY: the fifth letter in the Hebrew alphabet.

HILLUL HASHEM: desecration of the Divine Name.

HORA'AT SHA'AH: a ruling authorized only for a specific time.

HUTZ LA-ARETZ: outside of the Land of Israel.

KABBALA: ancient Jewish mystical philosophy.

KAVVANA: concentration in prayer.

KEDUSHA: holiness.

KELI (-M): instrument(s); implement(s).

KIDDUSH HASHEM: sanctification of the Divine Name.

KLAL YISRAEL: the Nation of Israel.

KOHEN (KOHANIM): priest(s).

KOHEN GADOL: the High Priest.

KORBAN (-OT): sacrifice(s).

LASHON HA-RA': malicious gossip; slander.

LE'SHEM SHAMAYIM: for the sake of Heaven.

LISHMA: "for its own sake"; from unselfish motives.

MA'ASER: a tenth; a tithe of one's income or product set aside to give to a Kohen or Levi.

MADREGA: a spiritual or moral level.

MASHIAH: the Messiah.

MATTAN TORAH: the giving of the Torah.

ME'IL: a coat, one of the priestly garments worn by the High Priest.

METZORA': a person plagued with TZARA'AT.

MIDDA (-DOT): an individual character trait; a positive attribute.

MIDRASH: homiletic teaching of the Sages.

MISHKAN: the Tabernacle.

MISHLEI: the Book of Proverbs.

MISHNA: the codification of the Oral law.

MUSSAR: moral discipline; the ethical movement founded by
R' Yisrael Salanter in the 19th century.

NACH: an acronym for the Books of Prophets and Writings.

NAVI: a prophet.

NAZIR: an ascetic.

NESHAMA: the soul.

OHEL MO'ED: the Tent of Meeting.

'OLAM HA-BA: the World to Come.

RASHA' (RESHA'IM): wicked person(s).

REBBE: a rabbi; a Torah teacher.

SANHEDRIN: the Supreme Court of seventy-one judges in the
time of the Beit Ha-mikdash.

SHECHINA: the Divine Presence.

SUKKA (-KOT): a temporary structure lived in during the holiday of
SUKKOT.

SUKKOT: the Festival of Tabernacles.

TALMID: a student.

TALMID HACHAM: a person learned in the Torah.

TANACH: an acronym for the Bible, comprising the five books of
the Torah, the Prophets, and the Writings.

TERUMA: obligatory offerings to KOHANIM.

TESHUVA: repentance; a return to Jewish practice and observance.

TIKKUN: self perfection.

TORAH SHE-BE'AL PEH: the Oral Tradition given by God to the
Jews at Sinai; Mishna and Gemara.

TSADDIK: a righteous man.

TSADDEKET: a righteous woman.

TUM'A: ritual impurity.

TZARA'AT: a spiritual disease that manifests itself physically as a
   sort of "leprosy" and is brought on by speaking LASHON
   HA-RA'.

YERUSHALMI: the Jerusalem Talmud.

YETZER HA-RA': the evil inclination.

YIR'AT SHAMAYIM: fear of God.

Z"L: Hebrew acronym meaning "may his memory be a blessing."

Available
in regular or
pocket size!

Path of the Just

MESILLAS YESHARIM

R' Moshe Chaim Luzzatto
translated by R' S. Silverstein

The classic text on living a sanctified
life. With depth and a mastery born of
true devotion to God, Ramchal sets
out the path to reaching the highest of
heights. New complete index. 376 pp.

Now available
in compact size!

Challenge

TORAH-VIEWS ON SCIENCE AND ITS PROBLEMS

Edited by Aryeh Carmell and Cyril Domb

*Published in conjunction with the
Association of Orthodox Jewish Scientists*

Challenging many preconceived notions about Orthodox
Judaism and modern science, the 34 articles in this book
show that essentially there is no conflict between the two.
Dealing with the interaction between Torah and science,
Genesis and evolution, "the secular bias," and ethical dilemmas arising out of recent scientific advances, the book portrays the Torah Jew as facing the secular world with assurance,
guided by his age-old tradition. 538 pp.

Now available
in pocket size!

Masterplan

JUDAISM: ITS PROGRAM, MEANINGS, GOALS

Rabbi Aryeh Carmell

Drawing on Talmudic and midrashic sources, the insights of *mussar* and *chassidut* and the writings of S.R. Hirsch, *Masterplan* shows how every mitzva is a building block in the Master Architect's plan for a better world and each is as relevant and applicable today as it was on the day the Torah was given to the People of Israel thousands of years ago.

Rabbi Aryeh Carmell provides explanations for the individual mitzvot but shows how they form a dynamic training program designed to advance the human spirit from selfishness towards selflessness. It emerges that the goal of Judaism is no less than the establishment of a just and caring society which can be a model for all mankind. 424 pp.

מכתב מאליהו

RABBI
ELIYAHU E. DESSLER

Strive for TRUTH!

MICHTAV ME'ELIYAHU

Selected writings of Rabbi E.E.Dessler
rendered into English and annotated by

ARYEH CARMELL

FELDHEIM PUBLISHERS
Jerusalem □ New York

┌─────────────────────────────┐
│ *Transliteration Key*   │
│   h̲ = ח   │
│   a = הָ   │
│   'a, a' = ע   │
└─────────────────────────────┘

Strive for Truth!
PART FIVE

PARTS 5,6:
regular-sized hardcover, gift-boxed set
ISBN 1-58330-354-5
First Published 1999

PARTS 4,5,6:
pocket hardcover, gift-boxed set
ISBN 1-58330-555-6
First Published 2002

Published by permission
of the Committee for Publication
of the Writings of Rabbi E.E. Dessler

Copyright © 2002 by
Aryeh Carmell

FELDHEIM PUBLISHERS
POB 35002 / Jerusalem, Israel

202 Airport Executive Park
Nanuet, NY 10954

www.feldheim.com

10 9 8 7 6 5 4 3 2 1

Printed in Israel

ספר זה מוקדש לזכרו של

ר׳ **יעקב ברויאר** ז״ל

מנהל ישיבת ״הרב שמשון רפאל הירש״
בניו יורק
בן הגאון מוהר״ר לוי יוסף ברייער זצ״ל
רב ואב״ד קהל עדת ישורון, ניו יורק

מורה ומחנך שקירב תלמידיו הרבים
לתורה למצוות ולדרך ארץ

אוהב את המקום

אוהב את הבריות

אוהב את הצדקות

ת נ צ ב ״ ה

contents

Preface

It is with feelings of endless gratitude to Hashem that I present here these two additional volumes in the *Strive for Truth!* series. The previous volume, PART FOUR (*Sanctuaries in Time*), was based on the first half of Volume II of *Michtav Me-Eliyahu*, containing Rabbi Dessler's insights on the special occasions in the Jewish year.

These present two volumes originally began as an adaptation of the latter half of Volume II, comprising essays on most of the weekly Torah readings and many of the other books in *Tanach*. At the suggestion of my son, Reb Avrohom Chaim ד"ג, I incorporated articles from the other three volumes of *Michtav Me-Eliyahu* to create *Strive for Truth!* FOUR and FIVE which now include Rabbi Dessler's thoughts on every one of the weekly portions and each of the remaining books of *Tanach*.

PARTS FOUR and FIVE, entitled *Patriarchs of a Nation*, deal with the giants of spirit whose lives serve as the template for the Jewish concept of greatness. As our Sages teach us, "Every Jew should ask himself, 'When will my deeds resemble the deeds of my forefathers Avraham, Yitzchak and Ya'akov?'" (*Tanna de-Bei Eliyahu Rabba* 1:25).

As in *Strive for Truth!* PART FOUR, some articles have been abbreviated and occasionally simplified for the present work. Since these lectures were given to a variety of audiences, they vary greatly in the depth of the ideas discussed. Many of them presume the reader is familiar with the principles developed by Rabbi Dessler in previous volumes. Cross references are given to other volumes where these ideas are further clarified. (I would strongly suggest that the reader familiarize himself with the section in *Strive for Truth!* PART TWO, "Sins of Great Men" [pp. 190-215] which contains the basic principles of Rabbi Dessler's approach to understanding *Tanach* through the eyes of our Sages.)

I pray to Hashem that He grant me renewed strength and good health to continue making the teachings of my beloved *rebbe* זצ״ל, available to the English reader. Together with my dear wife Gitel, שתח׳, who is a constant fountain of encouragement and loving support, we should merit to see our children and their families continue to follow the path of sincere service of Hashem charted out in these pages.

Aryeh Carmell
Jerusalem
Kislev 5759

Bereshit

Adam's Test and Its Lessons for Us

Nothing is included in the Torah to merely supply information. Every detail holds a lesson. When the Torah recounts the sins of the great ones of old, its purpose can only be to invite us to draw conclusions and apply them to our own lives. However distant from us the events described may be — in time, in circumstances and in spiritual level—we must make the effort to discover what lessons God is trying to teach us. The sin of the first man God created certainly seems far beyond our understanding. But this does not free us from the obligation to exercise our minds to try and discover at least something of what we are meant to learn from it.

ADAM'S SPIRITUAL LEVEL

Adam, formed by God's hand, was created with a tremendously high spiritual level. The Talmud tells us that "the first man extended from earth to sky and from one end of the world to the other,"[1] meaning that the spiritual content of the whole universe was concentrated in him. So overwhelming was his sanctity that the very angels wished to hail him as holy.[2]

Did Adam have free will before his sin? It is clear that he did not have a *yetzer ha-ra'*. This is stressed by the Torah itself. Rashi makes it quite clear: "The *yetzer ha-ra'* entered into him only when he ate of the tree and knew the difference between good and evil."[3] And in one interpretation of the parable of the vineyard of God in *Yesha'ya* 5:2 which compares it with the Garden of Eden, the expression "he cleared it of stones" means "he cleared it of the *yetzer ha-ra'—until Adam ate of the tree*" (Rashi, ad loc.). We must therefore ask: What kind of choice can there be without a *yetzer ha-ra'*?

BEFORE THE SIN

Ramban (*Bereshit* 2:9) goes as far as to say that before the sin, Adam "did what was right naturally...like the heavenly bodies...whose actions involve neither love nor hate. It was the fruit of the tree which produced in him the will and desire to choose...good or evil..."

This seems very puzzling, to say the least. Surely free will is a uniquely human attribute. But how can anyone devoid of any desire to do evil be said to have free will? And under such circumstances, how could Adam ever have committed a sin?

R. Ḥayim of Volozhyn puts it somewhat differently:

Before the sin, Adam was obviously free to go in any direction he wished—toward good or toward the opposite. This was, after all, the purpose of all creation; moreover, we see that he did, in fact, sin. However, the desire for evil was not inside him. Internally, he was completely good...without any admixture of evil or any inclination towards it. The desire for evil stood apart from him, outside him; he was free to make it part of himself if he wished, just as a person is free to walk into fire. The incitement to sin had to come from outside him—from the "serpent." This is very different from our present circumstances, where the *yetzer* which tempts a person to sin is within the person himself, and it seems to him that he himself wants to sin, not that someone outside him is persuading him.[4]

From Rabbi Ḥayim's final sentence it is apparent that the inside and outside referred to here are to be understood in psychological terms. Nowadays—in the era after Adam's sin—the *yetzer ha-raʿ* is inside us, meaning that it presents itself to us in the first person: "*I* want this," "*I* desire that." On the other hand, the *yetzer tov*—the good inclination—presents its demands in the second person: "*You* ought to do this," "*You* must not do that." It speaks to us as if it were another person, outside us. This is something anyone can verify for himself.[5]

In Adam before the sin, the roles were reversed. He was created with an undeviating nature,[6] without any inclination to evil. Adam's "I" desired only the good. So, in what form could sin attract him? Only if it came to him from the outside saying, "You ought to do this." The temptation had to take the form of an invitation to do a mitzva. How this was done is explained later on.

RAMBAM'S SOLUTION

Rambam, near the beginning of his famous *Guide for the Perplexed*, poses almost the same question.[7] From the Torah's narrative (he says), it seems that by sinning, man gained his greatest glory—the faculty of free will. How can this be? In reply, Rambam explains that before the sin, man, with his majestic intellect, could distinguish between truth and falsehood, but morality's concepts of good and bad or proper and improper behavior were meaningless to him. Such ideas entered his consciousness only after his sin.

Perhaps we can interpret this as follows: Since everything exists only by virtue of God's will, it follows that what He rejects has no true existence. Good is what He desires, and therefore only good can be called true and real. Adam, before the sin, saw this so clearly that he saw the whole world only in terms of truth and falsehood. What God wanted was true, and what God did not want was false and unreal.

At a much lower level, we see the world in terms of good and evil. We feel that evil is as real as good. We can imagine ourselves living a life where we reject God, as so many do. We realize that this would be wrong, of course, but we see it could be a successful life in many ways. This is what was meant above by our seeing both good and evil as real.

Before the sin, it would have been impossible to see the world in these terms. It was clear that there was only one reality: a life with God. All else was false, unreal, illusory. Only after the sin could we begin to see the world in terms of two competing realities—good and evil.

It was then that good and evil became inextricably mingled in the human psyche.

ADAM'S TEMPTATION

We have explained elsewhere[8] that each individual is given challenges and tests suited to his current spiritual level. What kind of test would be suitable for Adam's level before the sin, when both good and evil were not yet intermingled in his mind?

His test was not choosing between good and evil as we

understand them, but between two kinds of good.

In the beginning, he was given one mitzva: not to eat from the tree of knowledge of good and evil. This meant that he was not to lower himself to the level of knowing good and evil as realities, but to remain on his unique level, seeing the world purely in terms of truth and falsehood. There was a certain tension inherent in this situation, which we shall soon consider.

At this point, we must realize that all the *kiddush Hashem* which creation was capable of producing was concentrated in this one choice. Had Adam made the right choice, the purpose of creation would have been consummated right then and there. The tension in the situation was that Adam felt he would like to achieve a much higher level of *kiddush Hashem*. He had been placed in *Gan 'Eden* without any direct contact with evil. He believed that if he lowered his *madrega* a little and allowed evil—to a small extent—to enter him, and *then* conquered the evil for the greater glory of God—the resulting *kiddush Hashem* would be incomparably greater. He would be transforming darkness itself into light!

So Adam thought. And it was in this form that temptation came to him. "The woman saw that the tree was...desirable for insight [*le'haskil*]"⁹—the tremendous insight (into the greatness of God) and revelation which would emerge, they thought, from conquering the greater challenges of the lower level. This was the temptation that came from the outside, that is, in the second person in the form of "you ought to do this," "the truth and the love of God *require* you to do this." It might be a sin, they thought, but it would be a sin for the sake of Heaven.

The Snake expressed the temptation it was offering with the words "you shall be like God, knowing good and

evil," on which Rashi comments "you will be like gods
—makers of worlds."[10] Our Rabbis in the Midrash expressed this in the following form: "It was from this tree
that He ate and created the world. He forbids you to eat
of it so that you shall not create other worlds."[11] On the
surface, these are very puzzling statements. But from
what we have learned above, perhaps we can perceive
something of their meaning.

The word 'olam, which we use for the word world,
comes from the root meaning to hide. The creation of the
world is in fact a way of hiding and obscuring the light of
Hashem. This is because any created being necessarily
feels himself separate from God, and this in itself is a form
of darkness. God, in His mercy, decreed that man would
be able to exercise his free will by revealing the hidden
light in the midst of this relative darkness. [This is the
meaning of the puzzling phrase, "He ate from this tree
and created the world." The Hebrew for tree, 'etz, is related to the word 'etza, counsel or idea. "To eat from the
tree" in Midrashic terms means "to conceive of an idea."]
It was this idea—the revealing of the hidden light—which
was the basis of God's creation of the world. God created
Adam in a world of minimum darkness, where there was
not much obstruction between the man and his Creator.
Adam possibly believed that if he deepened the darkness,
he would thus create new worlds of opportunity for kiddush Hashem.

ADAM'S MISTAKE

But with all his good intentions, Adam made a mistake.
Before the sin, before he knew of the meaning or existence of evil, he was unable to imagine its magnitude. He
underestimated the difficulty of the challenge which he

was accepting. He could not conceive that the darkness into which he was throwing himself was a place without God, without spirituality. What he thought would be relatively easy was in fact overwhelmingly difficult.

Nevertheless, what he did was considered a serious sin. What he had considered "a sin for the sake of Heaven" was in fact a sin disguised as a mitzva. This was his temptation, and with all his good intentions, he surrendered to it.

HOW COULD ADAM COME TO SIN?

We cite at the beginning of this essay sources which show that Adam was created with an undeviating nature, without any tendency to sin. How, then, was he able to succumb to temptation? Even if it was a mistake, as we stated above, surely every mistake of this sort must have moral weakness at its base. How could such moral weakness enter "the man without sin"?

To answer this question will require some deep analysis. As we mentioned above, the very fact that a being is created means that the full light of God is in some sense obscured from him. He feels himself separate from God; he has, in a sense, an independent existence. The Rabbis tell us that even the angels have a body, but their soul and their body are both heavenly.[12] They exist only to serve Hashem, but the very fact that they exist means that they feel themselves separate from Hashem. This is their body.

In addition to this, Adam had a body which was formed "from the earth." For him, the light of Hashem was dimmed even more. Although he had no tendency at all to evil, he knew that worlds of good and evil existed, to which he had been forbidden access. This very knowledge very slightly obscured for him the full light of

Hashem.

These worlds held no attraction for him whatsoever, because on his level what God had forbidden had no reality. Nevertheless, he was faced with a test. There were two possible courses before him: (1) he could strive towards the highest point of his *Gan 'Eden* level, in which he would approach with all his being closer and closer to Hashem. Pursuing this path, he would erase from his mind even the possibility of descending to the worlds of good and evil, or (2) he could turn his mind downwards and consider entering those worlds in order to achieve a greater revelation of Hashem—a revelation rising from the midst of greater obscurity. He could feel that he was only taking God's work to its logical conclusion. God had created a world of very little obscurity, and by keeping his one mitzva in that world, he would reveal in some measure the glory of Hashem. Perhaps God had told him not to pursue the path of greater attainment only because He wanted to make things easier for him, but if he on his own accord wished to make things harder and so achieve more, God would approve.

CURIOSITY

A person may be on a spiritual level where a certain type of sin holds no attraction for him. Nevertheless, there is always something within him which wants to know about matters relating to the sin. This "something" is called curiosity. In and of itself, it may be perfectly innocent, but probing things that are hidden from it can often serve as an entrance way to sin. We discussed earlier that Adam's ego was comprised of two factors: (1) the very fact that he was a created being, felt his separateness from God, and wanted to enlarge himself by knowing as much as possi-

ble, and (2) that he knew of the existence of the worlds below him from the very fact that he had been denied access
to them. These two factors combined to create that feeling of curiosity which led him in the direction of sin.[13]

COMPULSION AND FREE WILL

We have before us, therefore, a man who has no tendency
to sin and, in a sense by his very nature, feels compelled to
do the right thing. Awareness of God filled his being, and
he knew no reality other than that of doing the Will of
God for its own sake. Nevertheless, we have seen that
through very subtle influences coming from his own
mind, the situation could change drastically. Something
might happen whereby access to sin would no longer be
closed to him. This is the situation we call "free will."

There is much we can learn from all this, even though
our spiritual level is very different. As we explained elsewhere,[14] the state of free will is only a relatively high-level
state. That is to say, it is above the animals' level because
their actions are completely programmed by instinct, but
it is below a *tsaddik*'s level because sin holds no attraction
for him. Essentially, having free will means that all op-
tions are open. The person is usually in a confused state,
with both good and evil beckoning to him. The person
then must struggle mightily to reach for the good and reject the evil. Success would mean that he brought himself
to a level where evil no longer held any attraction for him.
He managed to achieve the inner compulsion to do good
and only good. In terms of our discussion here, he raised
himself from the world of good and evil to the world of
truth.

We have learned[15] that a person's "free-will point" is
constantly changing. For each person there are things he

is not even tempted to do at that moment; they are below his free-will point. But factors can intervene which lower his spiritual level, and then what was previously inconceivable can become, to him, a genuine possibility. He has descended from the world of truth to the world of good and evil.

Now his task is to pull himself to a higher vantage point from where he can see that the confused world of free will is not for him. By dint of working on himself—doing mitzvot and learning Torah with great intensity—he can reach a higher level, the level of "truth," where evil has lost its attraction and truth prevails. Each person should pray to Hashem to release him from the darkness and confusion of the world of good and evil, and to bring him into the glorious light where he can serve Hashem with joy and devotion.

notes

1 *Ḥagiga* 12a.
2 *Bereshit Rabba* 8.
3 *Bereshit* 2:25.
4 *Nefesh Ha-ḥayyim* 1:6.
5 See also *Strive for Truth!* II, p. 139.
6 *Kohelet* 7:29.
7 *Guide of the Perplexed*, I, 2.
8 *Strive for Truth!* I, pp. 87–90.
9 *Bereshit* 3:6.
10 *Bereshit* 3:5.
11 *Bereshit Rabba* 19:4.
12 *Sifre*, beginning of *parashat Ha'azinu*.
13 Adam realized that he was undergoing a test. He therefore erected for himself and Ḥava what we call "a fence around

the law." He told H̲ava that God's command was not only
to refrain from eating of the tree but even to refrain from
touching it (*Bereshit* 3:3), that is, that they were to have no
mental contact with the sin, even in the utmost corner of
their minds. In most areas, setting boundaries of this sort is
admirable. However, when the sin has to do with egoism,
such action may sometimes be counterproductive. Our
Rabbis tell us (*Avot de-Rabbi Natan* 1) that the fence may
sometimes become more important to the person than the
sin itself. The very fact that he has made the fence increases
his ego. This was another factor enabling Adam to approach the sin, which previously had been inconceivable to
him.

14 See *Strive for Truth!* II, pp. 61–63.
15 Ibid., pp. 52–56.

Adam before the Sin
and the Future World

"The years will come about which you will say, I have no desire for them" (*Kohelet* 12:1): The Talmud explains, "These are the days of the *Mashiah* when there will be neither merit nor guilt."[1]

It seems from these words of the Talmud that after the *Mashiah* comes, there will be no *yetzer ha-ra'*. And so we learn: "In the time to come, God will bring the *yetzer ha-ra'* and slaughter it…"[2]

On the verse in *Devarim*, "Hashem your God will circumcise your heart and the heart of your children to love Hashem…with all your heart and with all your soul…,"[3] Ramban comments:

> In the time of the *Mashiah*, choosing the good will be natural to them; the heart will not desire anything which is not proper and will have no wish for it at all… In that time, man will return to the state in which he was before the sin of Adam.

We know already[4] that Adam indeed had no *yetzer ha-ra'* in the ordinary sense, but he did have a choice and a test according to his spiritual level. Had he withstood his test for that one day, until the entry of Shabbat, he and **Hava** would have entered "the world which is all Shabbat"[5]—the world of everlasting spiritual life. The purpose of the era of the *Mashiah* is to return to the state of Adam in *Gan 'Eden* before the sin. From this state mankind can then progress to the world of everlasting life, which Adam would have attained had he not sinned.

GAN 'EDEN AND THE DAYS OF THE MASHIAH

But there is something here which we must understand. The state of man in the era of the *Mashiah*, in which there is "neither merit nor guilt" would seem to be essentially different from the state of Adam before the sin. Before the sin, Adam had one mitzva. In addition, we find that he was given certain spiritual tasks, since he was put in the Garden "to tend it and to guard it," which the Rabbis say was the practice of positive and negative commandments. (The reference is of course to commandments on the Garden of Eden level. The depth of meaning contained in this statement will be discussed later, with God's help.) So he was assigned a form of service, and therefore his situation contained the concepts of merit and guilt. In the future world, however, where, we are told, there will be "neither merit nor guilt," what room will there be for service?

The solution is this. Everything is measured according to the spiritual state of those who perceive it. For Adam, created directly by God, even the smallest opportunity to exercise free will was a great thing. We would not recognize his situation as having free will at all. We would call his times "years in which there was no desire" and we would not perceive any challenge whatsoever in his test. How one could come to sin through such a low level of *behira* seems a mystery to us.

On the other hand, this spiritual state can serve as a great revelation of the lovingkindness of God, Who reckons the merit of overcoming such an apparently small obstacle as a great achievement—in fact, an achievement upon which all the revelations of all the created worlds depend. And all this is credited to the person who withstands this very small temptation by the exercise of his free will! This revelation of God's lovingkindness could be revealed only by Adam on the level of *Gan 'Eden*.

THE *YETZER* IN THE FUTURE

But if the situation in the future world is to be equal in all respects to the state of Adam before the sin, another question arises. How do we know that the same thing will not recur? Perhaps the *tsaddikim* of the future will also fall into sin, just as Adam did? We know that Israel, when they stood before Mount Sinai, succumbed to temptation and made the Golden Calf, although they too had reached a level equivalent to Adam before the sin.[6]

However, there is a lower limit beyond which the power of evil is not allowed to descend. God made an everlasting covenant with Avraham and his descendants,[7] implying that the people of Israel will never fall below the spiritual level of being the bearers of the covenant. Similarly, God promised the people of Israel that throughout the darkness of their exile "He would never reject them...,"[8] implying that the divine spark would never cease to be active within them.[9] Similarly, we have been promised that in the ultimate future of which we are speaking, evil would not have the power to tempt the *tsaddikim* again. There would never be another "sin of the tree of good and evil," nor would there again be a Golden Calf. Israel would not be allowed to fall below the level of *Gan*

'Eden. Thus, it is said that when God will "slaughter the *yetzer ha-ra'*," this means that the power of the *yetzer* will be limited in this manner.

But *tsaddikim* cannot exist without serving Hashem, and serving Hashem implies progress and the conquest of new worlds. "*Tsaddikim* have no rest, neither in this world nor in the next."[10]

So what will their service be? One choice will always remain: the choice to rise to yet higher levels than the level of *Gan 'Eden*. As we have seen above, Adam had two modes of service in *Gan 'Eden*: "to tend it and to guard it"—positive and negative commands on his level. The negative command was of course not to eat of the fruit of the tree of knowledge, which we have explained[11] as meaning not to probe with his mind in the direction of good and evil. The positive aspect was to raise himself to a still higher level of closeness to Hashem, where even the knowledge of the possibility of good and evil would cease to exist. A positive command always means progress, and in his case, the progress consisted of reaching the realization that this knowledge was part of the world of darkness and illusion, since what the Creator forbids has no existence whatsoever. God's will keeps the whole universe in existence, therefore anything which contradicts His will can have no existence.

Adam knew that only the will of God is true and real and what is not His will is false and nonexistent. This indeed was the level of *Gan 'Eden*. But this realization was only the lowest level of *Gan 'Eden*. Something may be "true," but not "uniquely true." A person may realize that a certain thing is true, but he has not completely eliminated all other possibilities. "Uniquely true" means that all other possibilities have been completely eliminated.

This was the positive service of Adam: to rise above the very possibility of accepting "the knowledge of good and evil" as true.

SERVICE IN THE WORLD TO COME

In the future world, as we have seen, we have been promised that *tsaddikim* will never fall below the level of *Gan 'Eden*. It follows, therefore, that their service will not be in a negative mode, as it was for Adam. The power of evil will be limited and the possibility of *tsaddikim* sinning by entering the world of good and evil, even in thought, will be eliminated. Their service will be in a positive mode: the internal service of raising themselves higher than the level of *Gan 'Eden*. It is in this sense only that the service of the future world is compared to the service of Adam in *Gan 'Eden* before the sin.

This is a very profound concept, and on our level it is almost beyond our grasp to understand. Maybe this is why the future world is described as "what no eye but God's has seen."[12]

CONCLUSION

We are indeed far from such spiritual insights. But we can still learn many great things from the above considerations if we allow a small part of them enter our hearts. We can learn to what extent a person has to flee the path of the *yetzer ha-ra'*. The mere awareness of evil was enough to bring in its trail all the darkness of this world: defilement, death, and suffering. We must summon up all our resources—even on our lowly level—to stay away, at all costs, from evil and sin. We have to fully understand that even our slightest approach to the boundaries of evil, whether it be seeing or hearing or reading forbidden things, can lead to undesirable consequences. We must resist the temptation to catch a glimpse of the world of evil, even without any conscious intention to enter it. On our level, this would be equivalent to the sin of Adam, which was partially caused, as we saw before, by his curiosity. We must concentrate all our powers on Torah and sanctity. Then Hashem will help us to reach higher levels in His service, so that it may be well with us forever.

notes

1 *Shabbat* 151b.
2 *Sukka* 52b.
3 *Devarim* 30:6.
4 See previous essay.
5 *Mishna Tamid*, end.
6 *Shabbat* 146a.
7 *Bereshit* 17:13, 19.
8 *Vayikra* 26:44.
9 See *Strive for Truth!* I, p. 180.
10 *Berachot* 64a.
11 See previous essay.
12 *Yesha'ya* 64:3.

Days of Creation
and Days of History

A person yearns all his life for what he thinks he is lacking. When he acquires the object of his desire, he experiences a novel sensation—that of attaining something new which he previously lacked. The more times he feels this sensation, the more he feels alive.

Everyday pursuits which do not challenge a person's will or desire do not produce the same good feeling. So often, when a person whose main interests lie in material concerns grows old, and he no longer is motivated by his desires, he finds life no longer to be worth living. On the other hand, a person whose main interests lie in spiritual matters finds that his life is still extremely rich and rewarding. The spiritual life is full of moments of novelty no matter what age the person reaches.

Material concerns are limited, but the spiritual life holds continuous challenges. Its goals are vast and varied. A person who has the good fortune to live such a life finds that his mind is like a self-renewing fountain; his "liveliness" never ceases.

We say in the first portion of the *Shema'*: "These words

which I command you today shall be upon your heart."[1]
Our Rabbis explain this to mean that the words of the Torah shall be new to you everyday, as if God had commanded them this very day.[2] In other words, if they are
"on your heart," that is, part of your spiritual life, they
will be constantly new to you. A person who is warmly
attached to Hashem will find that this attachment fills his
life with significance constantly.

THE PERCEPTION OF TIME

We perceive time in relation to the number of new sensations we experience. The more new experiences we undergo in a given period of time, the longer that period
feels. A year of childhood experiences seems, in memory,
a lot longer than a year later in life, because for a child
everything is new and he is constantly experiencing new
sensations.

We have seen that desires and the satisfaction of desires
form the content of a person's life. For a person whose life
is governed by the laws and guidelines of the Torah, each
of these cycles presents a separate opportunity for *beḥira*.[3]
For each occasion, a person has to choose whether, how,
and to what extent to satisfy his desire. For such a person,
whose life is guided by spiritual goals, free will ranges
over a large number of such points. His life, therefore,
contains more novelty and is incomparably richer than
that of the materialist.

This is how things are today, when good and bad are
mingled in our inner life. It is our task, in all our actions
and in all our thoughts, to discern the good from the bad
and to follow the good. This is the essence of *beḥira*,[4] and
our perception of time is determined by these constantly
recurring acts of *beḥira*.

Before Adam's sin, the concept of *beḥira* meant one point only.[5] It was only through this one point that new attainments could be evaluated and registered. Apart from this one point, Adam's life consisted of devotion to truth alone, in the knowledge that the truth was all that existed, as we have explained at length in the two previous essays. We must note that such peaceful attachment and blissful *devekut* had no connection with the concepts of change and novelty. Consequently, Adam's perception of time was meager, looking at it from our point of view. There was room for novelty and change only in his one particular *beḥira* point. It is clear that his experience of time then must have been completely different from our experience of time today. We have no way of really understanding today the joy and bliss Adam felt in his state of complete *devekut*.

CREATION'S DAYS

"...Six days God created heaven and earth..."[6] What is the meaning of "days" or indeed time itself during the process of creation? [Only the Creator was there and He is not subject to time.[7]] But the Torah talks about topics which are far beyond our ken in "human terms," in terms which we can understand in our human framework. "Mosheh brought the Torah down to earth."[8] Also, "the Torah speaks in human language."[9] The Torah speaks to us in our own terms, in the way in which we perceive matter, space, and time.

All that the Torah relates to us concerning the creation process is presented to us in concepts which we can appreciate. If we want to give a person, blind from birth, some concept of the visual world, we have to describe it in terms which make sense to him, by comparison with the senses of hearing and feeling. In a similar way, the Torah reveals to us purely spiritual matters in a physical form, bearing some slight resemblance to the spiritual matter being discussed. This enables us to grasp it insofar as we are able to.

Ramban writes concerning the days of creation:

> ...These were real days composed of hours and min-
> utes, and there were six of them as is the simple mean-
> ing of the passage. The inner meaning of the text is that
> the *sefirot* emanating from the higher world are called
> "days," for every saying which produces existence [i.e.,
> the creation statements of Hashem] is called a day.
> There are six of these, corresponding to the verse "for
> to God belong the greatness, the might, the glory,
> etc."[10] The meaning of the narrative in this sense is
> sublime and hidden from our understanding, we un-
> derstand of it less than a drop from the ocean.[11]

The meaning of Ramban's words is that according to the simple meaning of the verse, that is, the mode which is adjusted to our limited comprehension, we are to understand the days in a literal sense as made up of minutes and hours. But according to the essential meaning, which is the inner meaning, the significance is quite different. The "days" do not refer to periods of time at all, but to six *sefirot*, which are revelations of the ways God conducts the world. It is only out of consideration for our limited understanding that they are presented as days. But the connection between the "six days" and the six revelations is sublime and hidden from us, as Ramban says.

In an ancient kabbalistic work,[12] a question is raised regarding the verse "Six days God made heaven and earth."[13] Why does the Torah say "*Six days* God made, etc." rather than "*In six days* God made, etc."? The answer seems to be that the "six days" are (as Ramban noted) the six *sefirot*, with Shabbat as the seventh, and God "made" these *sefirot* into "heaven and earth." The *sefirot* —— spiritual revelations of God's power and glory—are indeed the building blocks of the universe. The creation narrative actually refers to six interrelated forms of revelation, described in the Torah for our benefit as Day One, Day Two, etc. It is clear, therefore, that the six days are six "powers," six forms of divine revelation, through which and for which heaven and earth were created.

SIX DAYS—SIX THOUSAND YEARS

Ramban goes on to explain that the six days of creation also correspond to the six thousand years of history.[14] The first two days, when all was yet water and nothing had been completed, correspond to the first two thousand years, in which no one had yet called upon the name of God. The third day, on which the continents were revealed and growth started, correspond to the third thousand, in which Avraham and his descendants called upon the name of Hashem, and so on. If one reads his words carefully, one will see that sometimes Ramban writes that such-and-such a day "corresponds to" or "alludes to" such-and-such a thousand year era, yet sometimes he writes that the day *is* the thousand year era. The first form corresponds to our limited mode of comprehension, while the second form, which identifies the "day" with the "era," is based on the inner truth, that is, that the spiritual content of those days and the spiritual revelations contained in those eras are identical.

Along the same lines, the Vilna Gaon writes: "There are three times: the beginning point, the end point, and the present. The creation narrative begins with the word *bereshit* because the six first days were the whole of the six thousand years."[15] The meaning is that all the revelations contained in all the six thousand years were included in the creation days. The souls of all those who were to come into the world were included in the soul of the first man. Through his one test involving free will, he had in his power all that needed to be rectified in the whole of creation. We have already mentioned in the two previous essays that if Adam had not sinned, the world would have endured only for six days and the first Shabbat would have been *'Olam ha-ba*, thus fulfilling the purpose of creation. But when he sinned, all those souls which were contained within him were separated out into individuals, and his one *behira* separated into many. Similarly, the creation days separated out into the six thousand years. The Gaon adds: "Therefore, whoever understands the narrative of creation in every detail of every day will be able to determine what will happen in every moment of all the years." It is said in the name of the Gaon that in this way it would be possible to ascertain the End of Days, but he insisted that anyone who discovered this never reveal it.

THE FUNCTION OF TIME

We have already written[16] that the Festivals of the Torah, and in fact all the moments of our lives, contain divine influences which become available to us as we pass through various points in time. For example, the days of Pesach are open to the same divine influence which was attached to this point of time in the days of the Exodus. We have stated above that throughout the six thousand years those same influences operate that were fixed in the creation days, except that there is an enormous difference in the way we appreciate them.

It is the task of every human being to grasp these opportunities and take the divine influences into his soul. Every moment in his life has the power to influence him in important ways. A person likes to believe that time has nothing to do with his inner self and effects no changes. He thinks his ego is fixed and never changes, and that time simply passes over him. But this concept is wrong. Our Rabbis have stated in the Talmud that during the nine months before someone's birth, he is able to see from one end of the world to the other.[17] The meaning is that he is given the ability to see everything from the perspective of the "end point." From this vantage point he realizes that all the manifold events in the world are one; they all exist for the sole purpose of revealing the glory of Hashem. When a person is born, he enters into the restricted world of space and time. But in fact, this latter state of consciousness reflects only the world of *behira*, in which every moment that passes leaves its imprint on our lives, for good or for bad, according to our reaction to the challenges posed by that moment.

THE MAP

But our experience of moment-to-moment decision making in this world is also limited. To illustrate this, let us imagine a map of a country covered by a sheet of paper which has only one hole in it. If we move the paper so the hole reveals one city, this is all that we see. If we move it to another city, the first city disappears. But we know that in reality there are many cities on the map; they just happen to be covered. And when we remove the sheet of paper, we shall see them all at the same time.

This is our situation. In the world of space and time, the world is revealed to us moment by moment. Each moment that we experience as the present represents one moment of our inner life, while the moments we have already experienced are hidden from us. But, in fact, the moment and its influence and our reaction to it still exist in our soul. They are never obliterated. When the "cover" of this world is removed after our death, we will see our whole life with all its moments coexisting, with its pattern of light and dark corresponding to the good or defective choices that we made during our life.

We can see that time exists in order to give us the opportunity to determine the quality of our own being. We have the opportunity to create ourselves as spiritual beings, close to Hashem; or God forbid, the opposite, to drive ourselves away from the life of the spirit.

"Happy is the man who never forgets You and the person who finds his strength in You."[18] If only we would fully realize the kind of world in which we live and succeed in establishing close contact with Hashem. This would bring us success in this world and in the next.

notes

1 *Devarim* 6:6.

2 See Rashi ad loc.

3 *Strive for Truth!* I, p. 53, II, p. 52.

4 *Strive for Truth!* II, pp. 51–52.

5 Mosheh H. Luzzatto, *Derech Hashem* 1:3:6.

6 *Shemot* 20:11.

7 Rambam, *Yesodei Ha-Torah* 1:11.

8 *Bereshit Rabba* 19:7.

9 *Berachot* 31b.

10 *Divrei Ha-yamim I*, 29:11.

11 *Bereshit* 1:3.

12 *Sefer Ha-bahir* #29. See commentary *Or Ganuz* ad loc. Also #28.

13 *Shemot* 20:11.

14 *Bereshit* 2:3.

15 Selected Writings, end of *Sifra Di-tzeniuta*.

16 *Strive for Truth!* IV, p. 21.

17 *Nidda* 30b.

18 *Musaf* prayer of *Rosh Hashana*.

*Noa_h_*

"Righteous in His Generations"

The fate of the generation of the Flood was stated in these words: "The end of all flesh has come before Me, since the earth is full of the violence they have caused."[1] We see that the purpose of the Flood was to teach us a lesson about the consequences of violence. Violence nullifies and destroys itself. God said: "The end of all flesh has come before Me," i.e., the end did not need to be brought—it came by itself.

Onkelos translates *hamas* (violence) as *hatufin* (snatching, grasping, or seizing). This eloquently defines what we call "the power of taking."[2]

When Noah was saved from the Flood, his deliverance, on a spiritual level, had to be in a form which was the very opposite of taking. It had to be something in the nature of giving and lovingkindness. Let us imagine Noah and his family—eight souls in all—feeding and caring for tens of thousands of living creatures. Each one had to be fed its particular food at a particular time, day or night, all around the clock. And this had to be done continuously throughout the whole year.

Here we have an incomparable example showing supreme love and care. And this lovingkindness was the spiritual essence of the Ark. This was the "precious stone" that shone in the Ark throughout the darkness of the Flood.[3] And this is the same light of the spirit that shines through the darkness of this world.

If once, in the hundreds of thousands of times, Noah was a few minutes late in giving the lion its food, the lion gave him a blow which made him a cripple for life.[4] Considering what was expected of him, even a delay of only a few minutes was counted as a crippling blow to his level of *hessed*. As a result, he became a cripple in fact.

The Ark, made of timber and sealed with pitch, would never have been able to hold its own against the fierce waves and overwhelming waters. But this was the miracle: Noah was kept safe within the wondrous protection of *hessed*.

ERETZ YISRAEL AND THE FLOOD

Noah was in danger of being swept away by the Flood—that is, of being swept away by the spirit of his times—and he was saved by entering the Ark. On another level, the flood posed no danger. This was the level of Eretz Yisrael, over which the Flood had no power at all.[5] This higher level is represented by the type of utter devotion to *hessed* shown by Avraham Avinu, who suffered mental anguish because the heat of the day prevented wayfarers from approaching his tent.[6]

There is a kind of *hessed* which is felt as a duty. A person practices *hessed* when he has to, but he does not feel miserable if no opportunity for *hessed* presents itself. Such a person may be called a *tsaddik*—"Noah was a complete *tsaddik*"[7]—but not a *hassid*. Only Avraham Avinu achieved this supreme form of devotion to *hessed*. It was in merit for this that he was given Eretz Yisrael.

The essence of Eretz Yisrael is the extremely clear vision which comes from receiving divine bounty directly from Hashem. It is said of Eretz Yisrael that this is "the land which Hashem seeks out... His eyes are continually upon it from the beginning of the year to the end of the year."[8] Who is aware of this? Only one on the level of completely selfless ḥessed, for only a person steeped in ḥessed can see the continual ḥessed of Hashem. (A person sees the world only in terms of his own inner being.) On this level, there is no possibility of being overwhelmed by a flood. But Noaḥ, on his level, was not able to gain the refuge of Eretz Yisrael. He needed to be saved by the Ark, that is to say, by an intensive program of training in active ḥessed, as explained above.

NOAḤ, THE RIGHTEOUS MAN

It is stated in the name of the Zohar that a person who commits a sin or fails to observe a positive commandment is considered as one who robbed the *Shechina*.[9] The explanation is as follows. Everything that we observe in our world is, as we know, a *keli* (an instrument given to us to use in the service of Hashem. This is why it was created. For example: the wealth of the rich man is given to him so that he, in turn, can give charity. This charity, in reality, belongs to the poor. If he fails to give it, he is thought to be "robbing the poor." This is what Yeshaʻya meant when he said: "What you have robbed from the poor is in your houses."[10] What you have in your houses was intended for the poor and if you deprive them of it, God counts this as robbery—not only robbery from the poor but robbery, as it were, from God Himself. God entrusts wealth to a person as an instrument for fulfilling the mitzva of *tsedaka*. If a person betrays His trust and takes it for himself and his pleasures, this is robbery.

Similarly, everything which is given to us by Hashem is not given for the purpose of gratifying physical desires, but for serving Hashem. Diverting that gift from its proper purpose leads to our limiting God's bounty. Blessing fails to come to us, because "blessing" means increasing our means of serving Hashem.[11] Such are the consequences of "robbery"; only by repentance can one restore the object to its rightful owner.

ONE'S PORTION IN THIS WORLD

Our Rabbis tell us that before an embryo is formed, an angel brings the fertilized ovum before God and asks: "What shall this drop be: strong or weak, wise or foolish, rich or poor? He does not ask righteous or unrighteous, because this will be the person's own choice."[12] Before a person is created, the instruments which he will be given —his *kelim*—are decided in Heaven in accordance with the task he will be called upon to perform in this world; that is, in accordance with his portion in the service of Hashem. All his gifts, his physical and mental abilities, as well as all the material means at his disposal, are given to him to enable him to fulfill his portion. In addition, say our Rabbis, he is put on oath before his birth "to be a *tsaddik* and not a *rasha*." That is, his task is to use all these instruments justly and fairly. *Tsaddik* means one who is just and fair. One who robs and betrays a person's trust is the opposite of a *tsaddik*.

And so it is with all the instruments we are given. Our eyes are given to us to aid us in doing mitzvot and reading the words of the Torah. Our ears are given to us to listen to the words of the living God. Similarly, all the limbs of our body are given to us to use for the sake of Heaven.

One who wishes "to merit the crown of Torah" is advised to keep to a minimum the material things he wishes to draw upon from this world. "This is the way of Torah: Your food shall be bread and salt, you shall drink water by the measure, sleep on the ground... and labor in Torah. Then you will be happy in this world and the next."[13] We have also learned that if a person wishes to make a success of his life, he should make his Torah learning the fixed point of his life (that is, the focal point of his interest), and his work secondary (on the fringe of his interest).[14]

And what about ourselves? Can we measure the extent of our robberies? And from whom are we robbing? From Hashem Himself!

THE LEVEL OF NOAH

A person is called a *tsaddik* only if he is aware that everything in the world is for the service of Hashem and he diverts nothing from its proper purpose. Such was the level of Noah , of whom it is said: "Noah was a perfect *tsaddik*."[15] "These are the generations of Noah: Noah was..."[16] This verse is explained in the Midrash[17] as follows:

> The repetition of the name Noah means that Noah was the same *tsaddik* in this world and in the next. And when God comes to comfort Jerusalem, it is by Noah the *tsaddik* that He swears not to enslave Israel anymore, as it says: "Just as I swore never to bring the waters of Noah again upon the world, so I have sworn never again to be angry with you or to rebuke you."[18]

What does this verse mean by saying that God swears by Noah the *tsaddik*? How can God swear by the name of a *tsaddik*? The meaning is that as long as righteousness rules in the world and robbery is absent, there will be no drastic changes and no destruction. Disaster threatens only where falsehood and injustice prevail. The future redemption is in essence a redemption from lies and violence. Noah's "name"—his inner essence—was the quality of righteousness. With this quality, God will eventually redeem the world and usher in the era of peace. Each person will rejoice in his portion and strive to fulfill it loyally and honestly. He will have no desire for anything which belongs to his neighbor. By virtue of this quality, Noah was saved from the Flood, which was a result of violence. [God's "swearing by the name of Noah" means that God will adopt Noah's quality of complete honesty as the foundation of the new world order—the Messianic Era.]

PRAISE AND DISGRACE

We seem to find an ambiguity in our Rabbis' evaluation of Noah's character. The words "a perfect *tsaddik* in his generations"[19] is explained by some as praise: "Even in his wicked generation, he was a *tsaddik*; had he lived in a generation of *tsaddikim*, he would have been still greater." But some explain it in the opposite sense: "Compared with his generation, he was a *tsaddik*; had he lived in the generation of Avraham, he would have counted for nothing." This is called "explaining it to Noah's disgrace."[20]

There is no dispute here. Had he lived in Avraham's time, he certainly would have been a greater *tsaddik*. Avraham would have influenced him and raised his righteousness to a higher level. This is praise, for it implies that he had great potential. But it is also true that had he—as he was, with his potential unrealized—lived in the time of Avraham, he would have counted for nothing, compared with Avraham. Regarding the essential character of

Noah, there is no dispute. The disagreement is only with reference to the meaning of the phrase "in his generations."

But there is a different difficulty. In the *Midrash Tanhuma*,[21] a statement appears which seems to contradict what we have just said:

> Why is the name Noah repeated? God replies: To satisfy all those who come into the world [about Noah's true character], so that no one should think that he was a *tsaddik* only in his generation. God [by this repetition] tells us that He considered him the equivalent of Avraham... Just as the Torah repeats the name of Avraham[22] and similarly the name Ya'akov[23] and Mosheh[24] and Shemuel,[25] so does it repeat the name of Noah, in order to equate him with the *tsaddikim*.

It seems clear that the Midrash equates Noah to Avraham, even in his present state. The phrase "to equate him with the *tsaddikim*" is also puzzling. Surely not all *tsaddikim* are on precisely the same level.

THE *TSADDIK* COMPLETES HIS PORTION

To understand in what sense all *tsaddikim* are equal and in what sense they are not, we must realize that *tsidkut*—righteousness—has two aspects.

Each person has his portion in the World to Come, which is the portion that has been allotted to him in the revelation of God's glory. All souls are " 'quarried' from under the Throne of Glory."[26] This means that they are "derived" from the Throne of Glory, since their purpose is the glorification of God's name. (In the language of *Hazal*, the true origin of everything and everyone is the purpose God had in mind when it or he was created.)

Each person has a particular portion in this task.

We have explained above that everyone is given the instruments precisely suited to his individual task. In connection with this task, a man's helpmate is selected, as well as every detail of his physical environment. "Forty days before the embryo is formed, a heavenly voice proclaims: 'The daughter of so-and-so [is destined to marry] so-and-so; the house of so-and-so [is destined to go to] so-and-so; and similarly, the field of so-and-so [will go] to so-and-so'."[27] All of these are instruments a person needs to fulfill his life's purpose according to the portion allotted to his soul. (How foolish are those who query the apparent comparison of the wife to the house and field! They fail to grasp that the whole environment surrounding a person, both personal and material, is fixed in accordance with his spiritual requirements.) This total environment, provided for everyone in keeping with his or her life task, is what our Rabbis refer to as a person's *mazal*.[28]

A person is not called a *tsaddik* if he takes for himself even one tiny bit of all that is given to him. On the contrary, a *tsaddik* returns it all to his Creator by using it—*all of it*—solely for the purpose of glorifying God, which is the purpose of his existence. He does not steal a moment or appropriate one penny of his possessions for his own selfish purposes. He is on a tremendous *madrega* indeed! In this sense all *tsaddikim* are equal.

THE *ḤASSID* ENLARGES HIS PORTION

All that we have said above defines the *madrega* of a *tsaddik*. But a person can change his *mazal*. "One who changes his place, changes his *mazal*."[29] This can be for better or for worse. A person can change his place in a spiritual sense, and consequently, his physical environment and the instruments provided to him may also change correspondingly.

A person may broaden his *mazal* and reach levels beyond those originally envisaged as his allotted portion. A person may "take his portion and the portion of his neighbor in *Gan 'Eden*."[30] "The portion of his neighbor" means the portion allocated to his neighbor, who has failed to use it appropriately. We find this in connection with Avraham, who took the portions of all the ten generations which preceded him.[31]

Originally Avraham's *mazal* was to be Av-ram, the [spiritual] father of the area in the Middle East called Aram. But he broadened his vistas and succeeded in becoming Av-raham, the spiritual father of all the multitudes of humanity.[32] He thus acquired the whole purpose of creation as his portion.

Now the matter is clear. So far as completing their portion in this world is concerned, all *tsaddikim* are equal. If anyone did not fulfill any part of his task, he would not be a *tsaddik*. After all, a *tsaddik* is someone who completes the whole of his allotted task. But there are levels above this. A *tsaddik* can add to his portion, as we have seen above; and it is in this respect that Noah is compared unfavorably to Avraham. If Noah had lived during Avraham's time and had completely fulfilled his task, he still would not have measured up to Avraham. Avraham revealed the glory of Hashem in such a supreme way that his extended portion embraced the portions of all the people in the world over a period of ten generations. However, regarding the completion of his allotted task, Noah was equal to all the other *tsaddikim*.

But can this be called a "disgrace"?[33] Is it a disgrace for

someone not to achieve more than the task which was assigned to him at his creation? We learn from here that it is
indeed a disgrace, for it diminishes the honor of Hashem.
If there is even a possibility we can honor Hashem more,
how can we not do it? This is what the Torah hints at in
its description of Noaḥ. It is indeed demanded of a *tsaddik*
not only to complete his individual task using all of his
abilities, but it is also demanded that he broaden his task
using the additional powers which would be granted to
him from heaven for this new purpose.

To fulfill one's task completely makes a person a *tsaddik*. To strive to do more that his allotted task makes a person a *ḥassid*. It was in this way that Avraham's greatness
exceeded that of Noaḥ's.

notes

1 *Bereshit* 6:13.
2 *Strive for Truth!* I, p. 119.
3 Rashi, *Bereshit* 6:16.
4 Rashi, *Bereshit* 7:23.
5 *Zevaḥim* 113b.
6 Rashi, *Bereshit* 18:1.
7 Ibid. 6:9.
8 *Devarim* 11:12.
9 *Reshit Ḥochma*, ch. 2.
10 *Yesha'ya* 3:14.
11 Rambam, *Hilchot Teshuva* 9:1.
12 *Nidda* 16b.
13 *Avot* 6:4; Rambam, *Hilchot Talmud Torah* 3:6.
14 *Berachot* 35b.
15 See note 7, above.
16 Ibid.

17 *Tanḥuma*, ed. Buber, *Parashat Noaḥ*; sec. 6.

18 *Yesha'ya* 54:9.

19 See note 7, above.

20 *Sanhedrin* 108a; Rashi *ad loc*.

21 See note 17, above.

22 *Bereshit* 22:11.

23 Ibid. 46:2.

24 *Shemot* 3:4.

25 *Shemuel I* 3:10.

26 Zohar III 29b.

27 *Sota* 2a.

28 See at length in *Michtav Me-Eliyahu* IV, pp. 98 et seq.

29 See *Rosh Hashana* 16b.

30 *Hagiga* 15a.

31 *Avot* 5:2. For an explanation of this see *Strive for Truth!* III, p. 101.

32 Rashi, *Bereshit* 17:5.

33 See above, subtitle "Praise and Disgrace."

Lech Lecha

Our Forefathers' Attributes

Our Rabbis say in the Midrash: "The *Avot* were themselves the Divine Chariot."[1] Maharal explains: "[The Forefathers are called the Divine Chariot] because through them the *Shechina* rests on the earth. God's presence is upon them, and therefore they are a throne and a chariot for the *Shechina.*"[2]

This saying certainly possesses depths into which we cannot delve, but the little which we can understand may go something like this: The holy *Avot* merited to attach their whole mind, heart, and being to the Creator. They gave over their whole existence to Hashem, leaving nothing for themselves. All their thoughts and all their deeds, even in matters which seemed to be related to the affairs of everyday life, attested to the holiness of Hashem and the presence of the *Shechina.* By observing them, one could see what God wanted from human beings. They revealed the Divine will, and that is why God is called "the God of Avraham, the God of Yitzhak, and the God of Ya'akov."[3]

It is from this viewpoint that we must examine all that the Torah tells us about the *Avot.* Every single incident of their lives which the Torah relates to us comes to teach us the highest levels of *avodat Hashem*.

Maharal adds that by being three in number, the *Avot* represented the Divine Chariot in all its fullness. Ramban[4] remarks on the same *midrash* that this refers to the fact that Ya'akov represents the height of truth and Avraham that of *hessed*,[5] while Yitzhak represents the fullness of the fear of God.[6] And he adds: "The discerning one will understand," meaning that these three qualities refer to the three *sefirot*: *hessed*, *gevura*, and *tiferet*. This will be explained later in the essay.

Through this gateway we can attain deep insights into the ways of *avodat Hashem* in all its purity. This we will now attempt, with the help of Hashem.

BASIC FORCES

Three basic forces exist in man by means of which he can achieve his spiritual goals. Each one is different in its origin and character.

> (1) *HESSED*. Through the power of lovingkindness, a person turns his efforts towards his fellow beings and tries to make them happy and influence them for good to the best of his ability. Elsewhere[7] we have called this "the power of giving."

> (2) THE FEAR OF GOD. In contrast to *hessed*, in which a person turns his attention chiefly outwards, with the fear and awe of God, a person turns inwards on himself. His chief concern is that his actions will meet the strict criteria of the Divine will.

> (3) TRUTH. Searching for truth clarifies for a person the right way in *avodat Hashem*. This enables him to avoid turning either to the right or to the left. One who is guided by the desire for truth will be less

likely to fall into the extremes of *ḥessed* and *yir'ah* and will thus avoid their negative aspects, as described below under the subtitle "Extremes."

Each one of these three qualities contains within it the potential for the other two. Someone whose dominant quality is *ḥessed* may practice lovingkindness out of a simple desire to bestow good on others – *ḥessed* for the sake of *ḥessed*. But his love for others may develop into love for the supreme Other,[8] and hence he might develop concern about obedience to His commands. Thus love may lead to fear. Or it may lead to truth: A person will want his *ḥessed* to be true *ḥessed* and give real benefit to its recipient.

Similarly, one whose main trait is fear is usually acutely aware of his obligations. This will lead him to *ḥessed*, when he realizes that without *ḥessed* he is not fulfilling his obligations. He will also be concerned that he is failing in his obligations if his words and actions do not reflect the truth.

And one whose basic characteristic is love of truth will eventually find himself drawn to practicing *ḥessed*. He will realize that it is inconsistent and dishonest to demand for himself what he is not prepared to give to others. He will also be concerned that failure to stand in awe of Hashem to the best of his ability would be a deviation from the true path of the Torah.

So we find that each main quality leads to the other two, as we suggested above.

PARALLELS

We mentioned above, when citing the words of Ramban, that these three qualities correspond to the first three of the seven "lower" *sefirot*: *ḥessed* (love), *gevura* (might), and *tiferet* (glory).[9] The process we have described just before, where each quality engenders the other two, corresponds to the idea found in Kabbala that each *sefira* contains within itself all the other *sefirot*. We find this in the Counting of the Omer: the first week is dedicated to *hessed*, the second to *gevura*, etc., while each day of each week is dedicated in turn to one of the seven *sefirot*. Thus the first day is called "*hessed* that is contained within *hessed*," the second day "*gevura* which is contained within *hessed*," the third "*tiferet* which is contained within *hessed*," and so on, and similarly with the other weeks.[10] Thus the first day corresponds to "*hessed* for the sake of *hessed*", the second to "*hessed* leading to *gevura*", the third to "*hessed* leading to truth," and so on.

We can also see that these three qualities correspond to the "three things on which the world stands: Torah, the Temple service, and deeds of love."[11] Torah corresponds to truth (and the *sefira tiferet*); the Temple service corresponds to sacrifice, negation of self; fear of God (the *sefira gevura*) and deeds of love are, of course, *hessed*. The three character traits which "banish man from the world"[12] are the opposite of these. Jealousy is the opposite of *hessed*; lust is the opposite of *gevura* (which, in essence, is the conquest of the *yetzer*), while *kavod* (prestige-seeking) is the opposite of truth, for it is well-known that all the honor and prestige of the world is falsehood and bluff.

Generally a person's character is based mainly on one of the three dominant forces we discussed above. We usually find that all a person's thoughts and deeds are influenced and guided by his particular dominating quality.

When a person decides to devote his life to the service of Hashem, his first act should be to discover and recognize his dominating quality. He should then try to develop it and perfect it and remain true to it to the best of his ability. But he should not be satisfied with this. There are other qualities hidden within him, and to reach his full potential he must try to develop these, too.

THE PERFECTION OF THE *AVOT*: AVRAHAM

In a similar manner, though on an immeasurably higher level than we can comprehend, were the qualities of our holy Forefathers. Each of them reached perfection according to his dominant character trait and then went on to develop the other two qualities as well, bringing them to perfection under the guidance of the dominant quality. By these means, each one succeeded in completing his portion in the creation. As the Zohar states: "Each one of the *Avot* knew the Holy One Blessed be He through his own lens."[13] That is, through the individual dominant quality of his mind.

Before God revealed Himself to Avraham in Haran, he had already reached a very high degree of *hessed* on his own. This is alluded to in the Torah by the words "the souls which they had acquired (literally: made) in Haran,"[14] which refer to the men and women Sara and Avraham had brought near to the service of God.[15] There could be no greater *hessed* than this, since by this they gave those men and women the greatest good in this world and in the next.

Almost all the tests which Avraham had to face after this were in the direction of *gevura*. The command "leave your home" meant to leave his father alone in his old age in order to fulfill God's command. The battle with the four kings was certainly an act of *gevura*. So was *brit mila*, which separated him from the rest of mankind and might have impeded his successful work in bringing the people close to Hashem.

All these tests were extremely difficult for him because they were in opposition to the quality of *ḥessed* which was natural to him. But it was by this opposition and the work entailed in overcoming it that he grew in spiritual status to an incomparable degree. What he had done previously, guided by his own individual quality, he now did out of a much more profound recognition of and trust in the Almighty.

The banishment of Yishmael and Hagar by the command of God went even more against his inborn quality. [Indeed the Midrash describes this as "the worst thing that had happened to Avraham in his whole life until then."[16]] And to crown it all, the hardest of all tests was the test of the *'Akeda*. When he had successfully withstood this test, he was acclaimed by Hashem as "one who fears God."[17]

Thus Avraham, despite his inborn *midda* of *ḥessed*, acquired perfection in the quality of fear, in its highest sense. He had shown himself able and ready to accept the yoke of God's kingdom without any reservations whatsoever. All his possessions, spiritual as well as material, were nothing in his eyes before the divine majesty of Hashem.

YITZḤAK

On the other hand, Yitzḥak's main quality was fear.[18] He was chosen to be an offering to Hashem, as the test of the *'Akeda* teaches us. Let us just consider this for a moment. Here we had a young man being led to the slaughter by the command of God—and he accepted this decree with joy. He obviously valued the glory of God as immeasurably more important than his own life. The negation of himself before the holiness of God's name was complete and absolute. This showed the *midda* of fear in its highest and purest form.

The man of fear turns mainly on himself. In constant awareness of the glory of Hashem, he subjects himself to constant self-criticism regarding every one of his actions. This can bring him to think twice before undertaking any activity, particularly one done in public. He's concerned he will fall into error or that his intentions are not free from selfish interest.

This is why we find that in contrast with his father Avraham, Yitzhak did not at first build an altar "to call upon the name of God."[19] (We recall that this was Avraham's method of attracting people to the service of the one God.[20]) And when God blessed him, He indicated that the blessing would be "for the sake of my servant Avraham."[21] As Seforno points out (on *Bereshit* 26:5), this was a hint to Yitzhak that he was not yet worthy in God's eyes of being blessed in his own merit. He suffered difficulties with the Philistines, who blocked up his wells and eventually banished him from their midst. But all this was before he had aroused himself to call upon the name of God. Finally, he built an altar at Be'er Sheva and called on the name of Hashem, as his father had done.[22] Immediately things changed and the king of the Philistines came to him with his retinue and begged him to make a pact with them.

It seems that the troubles which befell him—such as the famine, the threat to his wife Rivka, and the jealousy of the Philistines—discouraged him from following his father's mode of service, which involved working among the surrounding people. When the Philistines allowed him to keep one of the wells which his servants had dug, he took this as a sign from Hashem.[23] Somewhat encouraged, he went to Be'er Sheva where his father's hospitality had become famous.[24] There he was again encouraged by a prophecy from Hashem saying: "Do not fear for I am with you."[25] He now understood that he need no longer be apprehensive, and he built an altar as his father had done.

His quality of fear having been perfected, it was right and proper for him to go out and spread the word of God. Eventually Yitzhak was tested further in his *midda*, as we shall see later, with the help of Hashem, in the essay entitled "The Blessing of Yitzhak."

YA'AKOV

In the quality of truth, which Ya'akov excelled at, were also intermingled the qualities of *hessed* and *gevura* in a wonderful union. Ya'akov is first described as "a simple man dwelling in tents."[26] What were those tents? "The tent of Shem and the tent of Eiver."[27] The meaning is that, in his simplicity and honesty, he devoted himself from his youngest days to learning Torah from Shem and Eiver, those distinguished ancestors of Avraham. [What they learned was no doubt the Torah of the seven mitzvot given to Noah, and all their ramifications. Our Rabbis say, for example, that the tractate on idolatry in those times comprised no less than four hundred essays.[28]] His love of Torah led him also to teach others what he had learned, and so continue in the tradition of his grandfather.[29] His *gevura*, shown in his iron will and self-discipline, is demonstrated by his diligence in learning. On the verse "he lay down to sleep in that place,"[30] Rashi comments: "In that place he lay down to sleep, but during the fourteen years he served in the house of Eiver, he never lay down to sleep because he was occupied with the Torah." [The meaning is that he did not spend the night on a comfortable bed, but napped on the benches in the *beit ha-midrash*.] Through this combination of the three forces, Ya'akov acquired the quality of truth in an absolute sense. The verse confirms this by saying "you have *given* truth to Ya'akov."[31] When a person has striven to the utmost to acquire a certain *midda*, Hashem may "give" it to him, so that he no longer needs to struggle for it.

EXTREMES

A person whose main quality is *ḥessed* is in danger that, in his yearning to give to others, he may spend more money than he can afford. Then, he will borrow from others and spend it in turn. Eventually it will be found that his excessive desire to do *ḥessed* was counterproductive, for it led him to cause others loss because he could not repay his debts. There is also the possibility that he will eventually "be merciful to the cruel," leading to "cruelty to the merciful," as we find in the example of Shaul Ha-melech.[32] There is also another more insidious danger that, by becoming accustomed to acceding to everyone's requests, he may then come to accede to the demands of the *yetzer ha-ra'*. This is why certain forbidden marriages are referred to as *ḥessed*.[33] (The whole institution of marriage is, of course, a great *ḥessed*. Through it, people bestow a great bounty on mankind by allowing a new generation to emerge. But when this deviates from the bounds set down by Creator, by a person acting simply to gratify his desires or by way of sin, God forbid, then it is called "the *ḥessed* of defilement."[34]) Such is the lot of *ḥessed*, which is not limited by the quality of *gevura*.

Similarly, the quality of *gevura*—even "the *gevura* of holiness"[35]—if taken to extremes is liable to minimize a person's actions, even his good actions, as we saw above.

A person whose main quality is *gevura*, unrestricted by considerations of *ḥessed* and *emet* (truth), is liable to tend to other excesses. By concentrating too much on himself, such a person is likely to minimize the importance of other people. He may then fall under the power of "taking." Or, in addition to controlling himself, he may come to dominate others and fall into the abyss of arrogance and hatred. This is the "*gevura* of uncleanliness"[36] indeed. But this is what is liable to happen to *gevura* when it is not controlled and guided by *ḥessed* and the love of other people.

But the quality of *emet* unites *ḥessed* and *gevura*. When a person seeks the truth—the point of truth in his heart—in every problem and decision, he is freed from the danger of excess in either direction. The desire for truth cannot lead to any unworthy action, as the other qualities can. On the contrary, truth will bring a person to the only correct amalgamation of *ḥessed* and *gevura* in one organic and harmonious whole.

The person of truth strives to find the precise point of truth in every problem and decision. This corresponds to Torah, which is "a Torah of truth."[37] A person who strives for truth will never go wrong. On the contrary, the search for truth will bring a person to the correct balance between *ḥessed* and *gevura*. This is *tiferet*—glory—which is the harmonious union of opposites.

INHERITANCE AND PERSONAL ENDEAVOR

In general, a person passes down to his children his chief characteristics—those which are part of his essential being. The son thus continues to carry out the spiritual task of his father. But in the case of the *Avot*, it was not so. Yitzḥak did not inherit from Avraham the quality of *ḥessed* as his main characteristic. If he had, his service would merely have been a repetition of that of his father. The same applies to Ya'akov. Higher Wisdom decreed that the quality of Yitzhak would be completely different from that of his father, and this would also be the case for Ya'akov regarding his father Yitzhak. In this way, each of the *Avot* would bring into the world a new aspect of *avodat Hashem*. Hence, the three together would establish a complete structure of *avodat Hashem*, based on the three pillars which we referred to above.

We must note, however, that each of the first two *Avot* had a son who did not become a *tsaddik*—Yishmael in the case of Avraham and 'Esav in the case of Yitzhak. Only Ya'akov was distinguished as the one "whose family was complete."[38] The twelve sons born to him were all great *tsaddikim*, who served as the foundation for the House of Israel. The Midrash[39] expresses it in this way:

> When Avraham our Father came into the world, something unworthy was separated from him: Yishmael and the children of Ketura. When Yitzhak came into the world, something unworthy was separated from him too: 'Esav and the princes of Edom. But in Ya'akov nothing was found unworthy, as the verse states: "And Ya'akov was a simple [literally, perfect] man dwelling in tents." To him, God said, "I shall give you the Torah..."

This is a profound matter upon which much is said in Kabbala. If we may presume to interpret it on our level of comprehension, we might suggest the following.

As we explained above, Avraham had one main, inborn characteristic—*hessed*—and secondary *middot* which he acquired through his own effort: *gevura* and *emet*. As usually happens, Yishmael inherited the main characteristic of his father. His task was to develop the *midda* of *ḥessed* and to refine and direct it through *gevura*, as Avraham had done. But Yishmael did not do this. Consequently, his main *midda* turned to immorality—"*ḥessed* of defilement"—the result of the unrestricted expansion of *ḥessed*, as we saw above. Similarly, 'Esav inherited from his father the quality of *gevura*, but instead of refining and directing it by means of *ḥessed* and *emet*, he allowed it to expand to excess. As a result, he sank to the level of arrogance and aggressiveness.

Through these two failures, the greatness of the *Avot* was made clear to all, since they showed how much effort and devoted service were required to perfect a positive and harmonious personality. But Ya'akov was subject to none of this, since the *midda* of truth controls itself, and is never in danger of excess.

There is no doubt that without the solid foundations laid by Avraham and Yitzḥak, Ya'akov would never have arrived at his state of perfection. On the other hand, it was Ya'akov who completed the service of the earlier *Avot* and brought it to its final consummation. The nation of Israel is built upon all three of the aforementioned qualities. Thus Israel became worthy of receiving the Torah, which provides for perfect harmony among the three.

notes

1 *Bereshit Rabba* 47:6.

2 *Gur Aryeh, Bereshit* 17:26.

3 *Shemot* 3:6.

4 On *Bereshit* 17:22.

5 *Micha* 7:20.

6 *Bereshit* 41:32.

7 *Strive for Truth!* I, p. 119.

8 See Rashi, *Shabbat* 31a s.v. "That which is hateful to you"; "Do not abandon your Friend. This refers to God. Do not transgress His words, as you would not like your friend to do this to you..."

9 See *Strive for Truth!* IV, *Sanctuaries in Time*, pp. 140–141.

10 To be found in most prayer books, in the section dealing with the Counting of the Omer.

11 *Avot* 1:2.

12 Ibid. 4:21.

13 Zohar III 302a.

14 *Bereshit* 12:5.

15 *Targum Onkelos* and Rashi *ad loc.*

16 *Pirkei d'R. Eliezer*, Chapter 30.

17 *Bereshit* 22:12.

18 See *Bereshit* 31:42 where God is called "*Pahad Yitzhak*."

19 Compare *Bereshit* 12:8; 13:4; 21:33.

20 "Calling in the name of God" means "gathering many people and explaining to them that there is only one God Who should be served...convincing each according to his understanding and bringing him to the path of truth" (Rambam, *Mishneh Torah*, "Laws of Idolatry," 1:3).

21 See *Bereshit* 26:5, 24.

22 *Bereshit* 26;25.

23 Ibid. 26:22.

24 Ibid. 21:33.

25 Ibid. 26:24.

26 Ibid. 25:27.

27 Rashi *ad loc*.

28 *Avoda Zara* 14b.

29 Seforno, *Bereshit* 26:5.

30 *Bereshit* 27:11.

31 *Micha* 7:20.

32 *Kohelet Rabba* 7:16.

33 *Vayikra* 20:17.

34 *Sefer Ba'al Shem Tov, parashat Kedoshim,* #25.

35 *Michtav Me-Eliyahu* II, p. 204 and *Strive for Truth!* VI, p.167.

36 *Michtav Me-Eliyahu* V, p. 458, note.

37 *Malachi* 2:6.

38 *Shabbat* 146a.

39 *Sifre*, beg. *Parashat V'zot Ha-beracha*.

Avraham and Lot

We find differing opinions in the Midrash regarding Avraham's behavior toward his nephew Lot.

According to Rabbi Yehuda, God was angry with Avraham when he suggested that Lot should part from him. God's criticism was: "Avraham is prepared to welcome everyone and bring them near to him, but not his own nephew?"[1]

Rabbi Nehemya, on the other hand, explains that God was angry with Avraham for apparently adopting his nephew.

> God said: I promised Avraham that I would give this land to his descendants. Now he has taken Lot, his nephew, under his wing, apparently with the intention that he should be his heir. He might as well bring in some waif or stray from the marketplace and make him his heir![2]

Some sources suggest that Avraham was in mortal danger for bringing an unworthy person into his family circle.[3] It is even said that the famine[4] was sent as a result of this act.[5]

LOT'S SPIRITUAL LEVEL

There seems to be a difference of opinion, too, about what Lot was like. According to one source, God said to Ya'akov: "If Avraham refused to be together with Lot, even though he was a *tsaddik* and occupied himself with Torah, you should certainly separate from 'Esav, who is a *rasha'* without any redeeming feature."[6]

On the other hand, we find that "so long as the *rasha'* (Lot) was with him, God did not speak to Avraham."[7] And according to the Midrash, when Lot decided to move away from Avraham, this was considered a complete break with all that Avraham stood for. It was as if he had said, "I want no part in Avraham or his God."[8]

It is clear that these two points of view reflect two aspects of Lot's character. As Rashi puts it, in Lot's own words:

> When I was together with the people of Sodom, God compared my deeds with the deeds of the men of the city and I appeared a *tsaddik* and worthy of being saved; but if I come to stay with the *tsaddik* [Avraham], I shall be like a *rasha'*...[9]

So both aspects are true. In Sodom, Lot was a *tsaddik*. He rebuked the people and tried to teach them how to behave. In spite of the Sodomite laws against hospitality, he insisted on taking two strangers into his house, treated them royally, and braved the townsmen's murderous assault, although he knew they were prepared to carry out their threats. (The girl whom the Sodomites put to death by exposing her to the bees was Lot's daughter.[10])

WAS AVRAHAM RIGHT TO HAVE BEFRIENDED LOT?

On the other hand, the verse states plainly enough what

Lot's motives were in going to Sodom: "Lot... saw all the plain of the Jordan, it was all fertile... like the garden of God, like the land of Egypt... So Lot chose the plain of the Jordan."[11] It is clear: he went there for financial reasons. He should have been able to sense the gravity of his opting for the society of Sodom instead of that of Avraham, but the bias caused by his love of money blinded him. It affected him to such an extent that even after Avraham saved him from captivity, Lot still went back to Sodom.

Greed and love of money was the evil *midda* which, hidden deep in his subconscious, led him to prefer the Sodomites over Avraham, his uncle and teacher, to whom he owed all that was spiritual in his life.[12] His good deeds in Sodom could not protect him; they were not his true *madrega*, as we have explained at length elsewhere.[13]

This explains why Avraham was held accountable for keeping Lot with him for so long. From the point of view of strict justice, it was considered a *hillul hashem** on his part that a man like this was part of his household and even considered to be his prospective heir. And it seems curious that Avraham took no notice of the fact that so long as Lot was with him, Avraham received no prophecy from Hashem.[14]

But God, in His mercy, overruled the harsh verdict against Avraham. God, Who sees the innermost thoughts of a person, saw that the affection Avraham showed to Lot came solely from his great desire to do *hessed*. He was even prepared to forgo the gift of prophecy in the hope

---

* Since Hashem obviously refers to God Himself, it is improper to use the word *hillul* with reference to Him. As it is only His name which can be desecrated, we use *hashem* here in the sense of "the Name."

that he might influence Lot to change his character. (This may perhaps be compared to Avraham's preference for showing kindness to strangers over receiving a communication from Hashem.[15])

SHOULD AVRAHAM HAVE SEPARATED FROM LOT?

There is clearly a dilemma here. From one point of view, as we have seen, Avraham was obliged to bring Lot close to him and influence him as much as possible. He was, after all, his nephew. But on the other hand, it was possible that continued perseverance with Lot could eventually damage Avraham's own *madrega*. Continued association with Lot could also damage his mission of *kiddush Hashem* in the world, as we mentioned above.

It appears, then, that he was obliged to part from Lot. So how could this be held as an accusation against Avraham?

We propose the following solution to this puzzle with much hesitation and much caution. There is no end to the levels of spiritual attainment possible. Maybe if Avraham our Father had elevated himself to a still higher spiritual level, he might have achieved much more. He might have reached a *madrega* on which his association with Lot would not have prevented the spirit of prophecy from coming to him. And still more, he might then have been worthy of supreme heavenly aid in changing Lot completely.

WHAT THIS MEANS FOR US

On our level, we can learn from this the great responsibility we bear when trying to educate our children and our pupils. The more we elevate our own level of *ḥessed*, the better chance we have of influencing others and guiding them in the right direction.

And if we ourselves are the children or the pupils, we must make a great effort to prevent ourselves from making Lot's mistake. We must be careful not to drift away from the environment of our Rabbis and teachers. We must constantly be on the lookout for the uncorrected *midda* in our hearts, such as love of money, which might lead us on a course which we would regret afterwards. God forbid that this would lead us to declare—subconsciously, no doubt—"I want neither Avraham nor..."

We should also beware of good intentions. There is no doubt that when Lot decided to go to Sodom, he thought his intentions were completely for the sake of heaven. On the conscious level, his intention was to teach the people of Sodom to better their ways. He kept hidden—even from himself—his subconscious greed which was his main motivator.

Avraham influenced wayfarers and passersby by inviting them to his tent and using the opportunity to influence them through his acts of kindness and his teachings. He "pitched his tent between two cities,"[16] but he did not take up residence in either of the cities. Lot, on the other hand, went to live among the Sodomites and lost almost his whole family in the process. In our generation, there are many opportunities to bring people closer to Torah. Caution is necessary when deciding which method to choose. [Each of us has to make his own decision according to the lights of the Torah which he has learned and according to the advice of his teachers and masters.] Only in this way will we avoid the dangers presented by our spiritually destitute generation and become the influencers rather than the influenced.

notes

1 *Bereshit Rabba* 41:8.
2 Ibid.
3 *Ba'alei Tosfot al Ha-Torah* on *Bereshit* 13:14.
4 *Bereshit* 12:10.
5 *Yalkut Reuveni, Lech Lecha.*
6 See *Torah Shelema, Lech Lecha* 13, note 34.
7 See Rashi on *Bereshit* 13:14.
8 Cited by Rashi, ibid. 13:11.
9 *Bereshit* 19:19.
10 Zohar, *Vayera.*
11 *Bereshit* 13:10–11.
12 The Rabbis discern an additional subconscious attraction
   which drew Lot to Sodom—the sexual permissiveness pre-
   vailing there (*Horiot* 10b). This is referred to briefly by
   Rashi on note 11.
13 *Strive for Truth!* II, pp. 59–60.
14 See note 7, above.
15 *Shabbat* 127a.
16 *Bereshit* 12:8.

Avraham and the King of Sodom

After Avraham had conquered the four kings and restored all the captives and the wealth of Sodom, the king of Sodom came out to meet him. By right of conquest, Avraham was entitled to keep both the captives and the wealth. However, the king of Sodom tried to bargain with him. "Keep the wealth, but return the people to me." Whereupon Avraham "raised his hands to God" and swore an oath "to Hashem, the Supreme God, Owner of heaven and earth," that he would take nothing whatsoever from the wealth of Sodom, "not even a thread or a shoelace; I do not want you to say that you made Avraham rich."[1]

To see God as "Owner of heaven and earth" is to recognize that the whole of creation contains nothing but the means (*kelim*) for serving God and carrying out His will. The fact that He provides us with such ample means with which to serve Him makes Him *El Elyon*—the God of supreme *hessed*.

MAKING AND BREAKING *KELIM*

There are many types of *kelim* which a person can use to

further his spiritual progress. *Kelim* may be external things, such as property, environment, teachers, and pupils. Or they may be internal things, such as talents, abilities, character traits and so on. External *kelim* are apt to change according to the changing level of a person's service. They may also be removed if the person reaches a level where he no longer has need of them.

A child may be induced to learn by offering him candies or a small coin. These are his *kelim* for progress at his level. An older boy may be encouraged to study by offering more valuable prizes or honors which distinguish him from his peers. What was an inducement when he was younger has now lost its significance; it is no longer a *keli* for him. When a person reaches the level of learning for its own sake—*lishma*—all the inducements of *she'lo lishma*, including honor and distinction, no longer hold any attraction. This "breaking of the *kelim*" simply means that the *kelim* have served their purpose, which was to help a person in his spiritual progress until they are no longer necessary.

KELIM BELONG TO GOD

When Avraham said "I raise my hands to God," this implied that all he had—all his *kelim*, both external and internal—were devoted solely to the service of Hashem. *Hazal* have told us that "Avraham had made peace with his *yetzer*."[2] This means that the suggestions of the *yetzer* no longer had the power to tempt him. He saw in them only an opportunity to serve Hashem. The suggestions of the *yetzer* only provided him with an opportunity to reject them for the glory of Hashem.

Now perhaps we can understand why Avraham added: "I do not want you to say that you made Avraham rich."

At first, this might seem unworthy of Avraham. He seems to be saying: "I do not want to be obliged to you; I cannot stand your boasting that you made me rich." But such a thought was very far from Avraham's intention. This is why he prefaced his remarks by saying "I have raised my hands to God," meaning that these words themselves were part of his service to Hashem, as we shall see.

THE TYPICAL SODOMITE

From the way the Torah relates this episode, we see very clearly the corrupt and selfish character of the king of Sodom. Let us just consider: Avraham had risked his life to do battle with the four kings from the north, who were stronger than all the mighty warriors of the Land of Canaan. With his small band of men, he had defeated these kings and saved the king of Sodom and his fellow kings from a hopeless situation. Surely any normal person would have felt obliged to go down on his knees to thank his savior! Malkitzedek, the king of Jerusalem, who is identified with Shem the son of Noah, and who had not been personally affected by the invasion, took it upon himself to offer Avraham blessings and praise and to greet him with bread and wine. But the Sodomite king did not learn from this. No word of thanks escaped his lips. Instead, he coldly proposed a bargain: "Give me the captives and keep the property," meaning: "I know you are entitled to everything, but I'm asking you to return the people." Is this the way to speak to someone who has just risked his life to rescue you from a hopeless situation?

Here we can recognize the dominant characteristics of Sodom: rampant selfishness and ingratitude. Avraham replies: " I shall take nothing from you, because if I were to keep even the smallest part of what I am fully entitled to keep, you would claim that you had done me a favor and made me rich." Avraham was trying to teach the Sodomite king a lesson. He was deeply grieved to see the Sodomite king sunk in his evil *middot* and therefore tried, by example, to lead him in the direction of giving. The whole of his speech to the king proceeded solely from *ḥessed* and pity. This is how a person behaves whose personal qualities are devoted to Hashem, and to Him alone.

ANOTHER WAY IN WHICH *KELIM* MAY BE BROKEN

As we have seen, *kelim* may be broken and become useless because a person's spiritual progress makes them unnecessary. However, they may also be broken because a person failed to progress and indeed descended the spiritual ladder. He may have fallen under the influence of the *yetzer ha-ra'* to such an extent that he no longer uses his *kelim*—both external and internal—for progress. They are no longer useful to him, therefore they become broken and useless. If we look carefully at the words "darkness on the face of the deep (*ve-ḥoshech al penei tehom*)" at the beginning of the Torah,[3] we see that the last letters of these words spell the word *kelim*. The Torah is hinting that if a person, God forbid, descends to the *tehom* of darkness and materialism, his *kelim*, too, return to *tohu va'vohu*—chaos.

In our generation, we find that this type of "breaking of the vessels" is a frequent occurrence. Our generation is a part of what is called in the Talmud "the footsteps of *Mashiaḥ*."[4] Rulership is in the hands of "the mixed multitude": men for whom only external appearances count.[5] Torah no longer commands respect, and those who devote themselves to its study can expect no honor or affluence in this world.

The instruments of *she'lo lishma* have been broken. Why

should this be so? The people of our generation are on such a low level that they cannot be trusted to use *she'lo lishma* as a means of spiritual progress. If they were given the *keli* of *she'lo lishma*, they would stay with it and make no progress whatsoever. For example, if such people were paid well to learn Torah, they would learn just to the extent needed to enable them to collect the money. It would never occur to them to delve into Torah to such depth that it would engage their whole being and they would come to learn it for its own sake—the level of *lishma*. Therefore, Hashem has removed the *kelim* of *she'lo lishma*. Progress will be made only by those who possess the inner yearning and utter sincerity to propel them towards closeness to Hashem.[6]

THE WAY TO TRANSCEND THE DARKNESS

What method can we suggest which might enable us to leave the confused world of vessels that have been broken because they no longer serve for spiritual ascent? Rav Naḥman of Bretzlav cites the verse: "The people stood at a distance and Mosheh approached the darkness where God was."[7] He explains that a person can feel himself so far from Hashem that he sees no possible way of ever coming close to Him. But, says Rav Naḥman, a person who has a yearning to come close to Hashem at all costs must approach the darkness—enter that part of his mind where Hashem is most hidden—and he will find that "God is there."[8] God hides within the darkness and this is where He may be found.

A person who is so far mired in sin that it is impossible for him to emerge through *kelim* and *she'lo lishma*, has these aids taken away from him. There is no point in his having them. He is left with his broken *kelim* until he reaches the extreme of despair. Then, if there is still a spark of sense left in him, he will realize that he can no longer continue on this path which only leads to desolation and destruction. He will see that his only chance is to gather the remnants of his strength and smash all the apparent obstacles in his path in an extreme form of *teshuva*.

This repentance will change him completely in every detail. Nothing in his life today will resemble his behavior of yesterday. He will rise in rebellion against the *yetzer ha-raʿ* on all fronts. This is what Rav Naḥman meant when he said that a sensible person will recognize his Creator in the midst of all the obstacles and difficulties. He will understand that they were all given to him to assist him to return to Hashem with tremendous impetus. "God is there in the darkness—for the one who is determined will come near."[9]

In the course of Avraham's battle against the four kings, the Torah relates: "And he divided against them by night,"[10] on which the Midrash states: "The night was divided by itself"; others say: "Its Creator divided it."[11] Night alludes to the spiritual darkness of utter confusion. The first opinion tells us that the person who is determined to emerge from this darkness into the light of *teshuva* will find that the darkness divides and is torn apart by itself. This is its nature. The second opinion states that only heavenly aid can enable a person to emerge from the darkness of despair. "His Creator divides it." The point of the second comment is that it is absolutely essential for a person to pray for heavenly aid at every stage of his endeavor. His own powers are not sufficient. His success will not be permanent without heavenly aid, and heavenly aid is available only through prayer.

notes

1 *Bereshit* 14:21–23.
2 *Nedarim* 32b.
3 *Bereshit* 1:2.
4 *Mishna Sotah*, end.
5 Zohar III, *Raya Mehemna*, 279a.
6 Compare *Strive for Truth!* I, p. 109.
7 See *Shemot* 20:18.
8 Ibid.
9 See note 7, above.
10 *Bereshit* 14:15.
11 *Bereshit Rabba* 43:3.

Causes of the Egyptian Exile

From the Torah's account of the Covenant between the Pieces[1], it appears that the exile of his descendants to "a country which is not theirs"[2] is a punishment for Avraham for something he had done or failed to do.

In the Talmud the question is asked, "Why was Avraham our Father punished and his children enslaved in Egypt for two hundred and ten years?"[3] Amoraim propose three different reasons for this:

(1) When he set out to rescue Lot from the invading kings, he enlisted the men of his household, who should have been studying Torah. The verse states, "He emptied the house of his pupils who were born in his home."[4]

(2) He took the liberty of asking God: "How do I know that I will inherit the land?"[5]

(3) He denied people the opportunity of entering into the service of the Almighty. When the king of Sodom proposed that he would give back the captured Sodomites,[6] he should have refused. He should have brought them into his household and introduced them to the service of the Most High.

Each of these reasons presents great difficulties. Ma-haral of Prague discusses this matter in *Gevurot Hashem*, his book on the redemption from Egypt.[7] He explains that each one of these acts or omissions attributed to Avraham our Father represents an extremely subtle failure in *emu-nah*. The exile in Egypt was not so much a punishment as a means of rectifying these failings.

Before we delve into this matter, we must understand that our holy *Avot*, of blessed memory, served God to the full extent of their power every single moment of their lives. As a result, they merited to become the "Chariot of the *Shechina*."[8] Nevertheless, the holy Torah finds occa-sion to weigh their deeds on the scales of Torah justice and sometimes reveals to us faults so fine and so subtle that they are scarcely discernible to our minds. It is clear that these faults cannot be real faults as we understand them, but rather in the nature of "shadow faults," as we have explained at length elsewhere.[9]

We explained there that even after a *tsaddik* has com-pletely conquered his *yetzer* and attained perfection in his *middot*, he still has work to do in what we call "the shadow of the *middot*." Even though his motives may be for the sake of heaven to a degree which is beyond our imagina-tion, these motives may nevertheless be accompanied in the subconscious region of the mind by something which is not a bad *midda*, but which in some sense resembles one. Thus, there is still much work left for the *tsaddik* who has refined all of his *middot*. This is to work on his subcon-scious and to refine more and more of these shadowy resi-dues of *middot*.

QUESTIONS OF FAITH

Maharal explains that in all the above three reasons a

question of faith in Hashem was involved—on Avraham's level, of course. As a result, a certain weakness of this sort was carried over to the subconscious minds of his descendants. Hence, the exile in Egypt and the tremendous miracles of the redemption were required to strengthen the people's faith and rectify this weakness.

[Avraham was justified in taking some fighting men with him to do battle with the kings, says Maharal. After all, one should not rely on miracles. But the fact that he took not only men suited to this task, but also those who were studying Torah, showed, on his level—in some "shadowy" sense—a lack of faith. With pure faith, he would have realized that Hashem helps those who love Him and that victory does not depend on numbers.]

"HOW SHALL I KNOW...?"

Avraham's question was completely innocent. His intention was to ask: How can I be sure that my children will inherit the Holy Land and their sins will not prevent it? On a deeper level, our Rabbis teach that when Ya'akov sent Yosef to his brothers, thus setting in motion the events that led to the Egyptian exile, he was following "the profound thought of the *tsaddik* who is buried in Hevron [Avraham]."[10] The profound thought was that, by his question, Avraham elicited the divine response: "You shall know that your children shall be strangers..."[11] Avraham learned that only exile for his children would serve as atonement for their sins and ensure that their ownership of the Holy Land would be eternal.[12] What fault can there be in this?

There was indeed no fault. But the words "How do I know..." *sounded* like a lack of faith in God's promise. There was the appearance of a sin, and appearances can be dangerous. An appearance of wrongdoing can not only affect a person's surroundings, but it can also affect the person himself. A person's subconscious may be adversely touched by something that he does in all innocence, but has the appearance of a wrongdoing.

It was this "shadow fault" for which Avraham was made responsible. The slight lack of faith which it signified had to be corrected in his descendants through the exile and the redemption.

AVRAHAM'S REPLY TO THE KING OF SODOM

[Maharal attaches serious weight to the statement above that Avraham should have restored to the king of Sodom his wealth, but kept the people. By returning the people to Sodom, he lost a unique opportunity to bring a large number of people to faith in the Almighty. By not being eager enough to bring these people to faith, he showed, in a sense, a certain lack of faith.]

However, it is possible that Avraham's decision was the right one. As we saw in the previous essay, Avraham's motive was to teach the evil king a lesson in *ḥessed*. But maybe this righteous motive was accompanied by a slight feeling of personal dislike for the men of Sodom, who had shown themselves to be in direct opposition to his *ḥessed* ideal. On Avraham's level, this very hint of a feeling might have counted as a sin.

"SHADOW FAULTS" AND THEIR CORRECTION

We can learn from all this the extremely high level at which the *Avot* conducted their lives. Their service of Hashem was so constant and so intense that whatever they did, felt, or thought had tremendous consequences on their future generations. Because Avraham brought the bread to his visitors himself, God Himself brought the manna to Israel in the desert.[13] Because Avraham indicated that the water would be brought by a servant, water was provided for Israel in the desert by indirect means.[14] When _Hazal_ say that the descendants were punished for slight, shadowy lapses on the part of the _Avot_, we must remember that punishment here means education. Future generations had to be taught to make good the spiritual gaps exposed by these shadowy faults.

Similarly, the Rabbis tell us that one of the causes of the Egyptian exile was the special coat which Ya'akov gave to Yosef, thus distinguishing him from his other sons. The jealousy which this caused set in motion the events which led to Israel's descent into Egypt.[15] We should not think that Ya'akov our Father acted thoughtlessly, God forbid. He no doubt decided, for good reasons, that it was necessary for him to show special honor to Yosef.[16] But accompanying his proper motives, there might have been a slight inclination to favor Yosef simply for personal reasons. It was these personal reasons which aroused the brothers' jealousy and led to the exile. Had Ya'akov eliminated this almost imperceptible personal motive, the lessons that could have been learned from this tremendous achievement might have made unnecessary all the lessons which were to be learned in the future from the exile and redemption.

AVRAHAM'S DESCENT INTO EGYPT

Avraham had hardly arrived in the Holy Land, bearing God's blessing and promise of a great destiny, when he was faced with a severe famine. He was forced to go to Egypt, where his wife faced great dangers from which she was miraculously saved, and then he and his family returned to Eretz Yisrael with great wealth.[17]

There are different interpretations of this episode. Ramban cites a *midrash* in which this descent into Egypt is seen as a forerunner of the future Egyptian exile.[18] Just as happened with Avraham and Sara, Israel was miraculously delivered and left Egypt with great wealth.

But Ramban also states it as his opinion that Avraham unintentionally committed a great sin by going to Egypt instead of relying on Hashem to help him in Eretz Yisrael, and also by endangering his wife. He gives this as a reason for the exile.[19]

When Ya'akov, having learned that Yosef was alive, decided to go down to Egypt, our Rabbis state that this was not of his own accord; he was compelled to do so by the word of God.[20] This is an amazing statement. Although there was a famine in the Land of Canaan, and although he had just received the news that Yosef—his beloved son whom he had thought dead for twenty years—was alive, in spite of all this, *Hazal* tell us that he felt not the slightest desire to go to Egypt. He felt compelled by the word of God.

When God said to him in Be'er Sheva, "Ya'akov, Ya'akov... do not be afraid of going down to Egypt..." our Rabbis comment, "One says 'don't be afraid' only to one who is afraid."[21] He was afraid of leaving the holiness of the Holy Land. By comparison, it appears that Avraham did not feel this strong reluctance to leave the land. On his level and almost imperceptibly, he seems to have lacked the feeling of hesitancy experienced by Ya'akov. Consciously, all his thoughts were directed to the purpose of blazing a trail in a spiritual sense for his children to follow. In addition, his actions did much to soften the hard shell of Egyptian defilement. However, Avraham was not acting completely under Hashem's compulsion. He might have felt, in some "shadowy" sense, that going to Egypt was an economic necessity. And because he had not achieved the final step of eliminating this slightly residual attachment to the world of nature, this task was left to his future generations, and hence the necessity of the exile.

THE GREATNESS OF THE *AVOT*

As we have seen, punishment often means education and rectification. It is therefore possible for one punishment to rectify many sins. Thus, there is no contradiction between what was said in the Talmud[22] about the reasons for the exile and what Ramban and others wrote about this. Ramban is simply citing an additional lapse which the exile rectified. It is also possible that the three causes mentioned in the Gemara are all linked, one being the cause of the other.[23]

It may well be that had Avraham our Father, of blessed memory, achieved the final victory of feeling himself utterly compelled to go down to Egypt, this might have eliminated the possibility of the other slight lapses which came later. As it stands, this fine point of a "shadow" feeling concerning his own personal needs might have been counted on his level as a slight failing in faith. And this could have led to the other lapses we discussed, which as we have seen, all involve questions of *emuna*.

How great are our holy *Avot* of blessed memory! All the great revelations connected with the enslavement in Egypt and our subsequent deliverance through the world-shaking miracles which are described in the Torah, came to fix in our souls the realization—the pure faith—that God rules the world. And to think that if our *Avot* had undertaken one more fine point in their spiritual service, it might have taken the place of all those tremendous revelations!

notes

1 *Bereshit* 15.
2 Ibid. 15:13.
3 *Nedarim* 32a.
4 *Bereshit* 14:14.
5 Ibid. 15:8.
6 Ibid. 14:21.
7 Chapter 9.
8 See above in the essay, "The Quality of Our Forefathers."
9 See *Strive for Truth!* II, pp. 190–216.
10 *Bereshit* 37:13–14.
11 Ibid. 15:17.
12 *Sotah* 11a; *Bereshit Rabba* 44:21.
13 *Bereshit Rabba* 48:10.
14 Ibid.
15 *Shabbat* 10b.
16 See the essay, "Ya'akov and Yosef," later in this volume.
17 *Bereshit* 12:10–13:2.
18 *Bereshit Rabba* 40:8.
19 Ramban on *Bereshit* 12:10. See also Zohar (*Bereshit* 81b), where the same two apparently contradictory comments are made.
20 Sifre on *Devarim* 26:5; see also *Haggada shel Pesach*.
21 Zohar II 53a.
22 See note 15, above.
23 See Rosh, *Nedarim* 32a.

Vayera

Avraham's Service and the Bestowal of _Hessed_

Rabbenu Behai tells us that a person who is good to some-one else because he feels pity is, in a sense, being good to himself. He cannot bear to see the other person in pain, so by helping him, he is at the same time helping himself.[1]

Of course, feeling another person's loss as our own is a great quality—and we might wish we felt it more strongly. But still, it is not the quality of _hessed_, but rather of pity. What's the difference? One who feels pity is moti-vated by external circumstances. When he sees a destitute person, he feels obliged to help him—and indeed helps him to the best of his ability. His pity usually evaporates when he no longer sees the person in need. The _ba'al hessed_, however, pursues _hessed_ with all his might. If he fails to see anyone in need, he uses his imagination and goes around looking for someone. What motivates him is the quality of _hessed_ itself which he possesses. He does not need external motivation. _Hessed_ fills his whole being and flows from him continuously. Indeed, he views his whole life as an opportunity for doing _hessed_.

Avot de-Rabbi Natan graphically describes the superior-ity of Avraham's type of _hessed_:

> "The poor should be the members of your house-
> hold."³ Iyov, too, was a very hospitable person... How-
> ever, God said to him: Iyov, you have not even reached
> one half of the level of Avraham. You sit in your house
> and wayfarers enter. If one is used to eating meat, you
> give him meat; if one is used to drinking wine, you give
> him wine. Avraham does not act in this way; he goes
> around the world [looking for guests] and when he
> finds them, he brings them into his house. Even to one
> who is not used to eating meat he serves meat, and even
> to one who is not used to drinking wine he serves wine.
> Moreover, he built a large house by the crossroads and
> laid out in it food and drink, and whoever wanted
> would enter, partake of the food, and bless God in
> heaven. This is what gave Avraham pleasure. And
> whatever anybody asked for was available in Avra-
> ham's house.²

Here we see the difference between _hessed_ and mercy.
Iyov supplied only what the wayfarers lacked. Avraham
gave even what they did not lack, because _hessed_ means to
love the act of giving for its own sake. He not only had
pity on the needy people who came before him, but he
searched for opportunities to do _hessed_. When, out of consideration for Avraham's weakened condition after his *brit
mila*, Hashem made the sun extremely hot so that no wayfarers would disturb him, Avraham still felt great distress
at not being able to do _hessed_.³

AVRAHAM AND NOAH

Herein also lies the difference between Avraham and
Noah. Noah was a *tsaddik*, while Avraham was a man of

hessed. It goes without saying that Noah also did an enormous amount of *hessed.* His exemplary service in looking after all the animals in the ark for an entire year is well known.[4] And we may be sure that he did it out of love. No one could have labored so long and so faithfully without love. Nevertheless, in all this he was doing *tzedek*—he was fulfilling his obligation. Love, too, is included in one's obligation to others. It is *tzedek,* but it is not yet *hessed.* As we have said, *hessed* is only that which flows from one's very being, without the need for external motivation—even the imperative of fulfilling one's obligations.

This distinction is also important regarding mitzvot between man and God. Service of God, too, can be performed either in response to externals, such as the need to fulfill one's obligations, or as an act of *hessed,* superseding all obligations and other factors. The person becomes, so to speak, a giver—even to the Almighty—and strives to "do *hessed* to his Creator."[5]

HIGHER THAN *DEVEKUT*

"Noah walked with God: he needed God's aid and support. Avraham walked before [in front of] God: he produced his righteousness from his own resources."[6] What was this aid which Noah needed, but Avraham did not need? Maharal explains that this was *devekut*—having God in one's mind continually.[7] This certainly guards a person from sin. But Avraham was able to act on his own, without necessarily having God continually in his consciousness. We see this from the fact that Avraham was tested on many occasions, and during a test God is, in a certain sense, inaccessible.

From here we can derive a surprising conclusion. It seems that *devekut* is not the highest achievement. What is beyond *devekut*? The service of *hessed*! This is the pure service which, as we saw above, flows from the depth of one's being, requiring no external or other type of aid whatsoever.

A person who has reached this level need no longer fear tests and trials. Even though every test involves a certain withdrawal, in that Hashem deprives the person of His normal aid and support, the *ba'al hessed* does not require support. He has inner resources. His love and giving overflow from the deep happiness which fills his heart.[8]

THE INNER WORLD OF *HESSED*

We learn from the first verses of *Vayera* that Avraham's three guests arrived while God was about to bestow upon him a prophecy. Whereupon Avraham said to God: "Please do not leave Your servant." He was, in effect, asking God to wait while he attended to his guests.[9] We learn from this an important principle: "Hospitality to strangers is greater than receiving the presence of the *Shechina*."[10]

But this is surely puzzling. It seems discourteous to ask God to wait, so to speak. Is this not, in a sense, a *hillul hashem*? But there is a very profound thought here.

Avraham's guests appeared as three idolatrous strangers who prostrated themselves before the dust of their feet.[11] *Hessed* to such people is the purest and most elevated form of it, [for the lower the level of the recipient, the greater is the giving]. This world of pure *hessed* is higher even than the world of prophecy, which is the world of closeness to Hashem. From the viewpoint of this higher world, there is no *hillul*. In that world, only the inner reality counts.

GUARDING THE SPARKS

In every member of *Klal Yisrael*, sparks from the level of Avraham our Father are present.[12] It is possible to arouse points of *ḥessed* in every Jew—points of giving without any calculation of receiving something in return, points of pure giving not mediated by feelings of obligation or pity. In this way, we are still connected with Avraham Avinu.

One spark of true *ḥessed* can save a person from jealousy, arrogance, and sometimes even from lust. A person who is ready to give of himself to others has thereby abolished the causes of hatred, and similarly, of arrogance. Lust, too, is often centered on egoism, since such a person feels that all pleasures belong to him. This, too, may be cured by the power of *ḥessed*.

Mitzvot relating to the Almighty can and should also be performed as acts of *ḥessed*; that is, out of gratitude to Hashem for all His amazing goodness to us.[13] "There is no greater giver than the one who gives to his Creator."[14] Such giving is without hope of benefit or reward; it is a service higher than all external factors. May we merit to guard these sparks and to ignite them in our hearts; then our service will be beyond all boundaries and limitations.

notes

1 _Hovot Ha-levavot_, section III, introduction.

2 Chapter 7, # 1.

3 Rashi, _Bereshit_ 18:1.

4 See _Michtav Me-Eliyahu_ II, p. 155.

5 See _Strive for Truth!_ I, pp. 153–155.

6 See Rashi on _Bereshit_ 6:9.

7 _Gur Aryeh ad loc._

8 See _Strive for Truth!_ I, p. 142.

9 See Rashi _Bereshit_ 18:3, second explanation.

10 _Shabbat_ 127a.

11 Rashi, _Bereshit_ 18:4.

12 Compare _Strive for Truth!_ I, pp. 54–58.

13 See note 5, above.

14 Zohar III 281a.

Avraham's Prayer for Sodom

Our holy forefathers taught us the concept of prayer, as our Rabbis say, "Prayers were instituted by the *Avot*."[1] In fact, if we reflect on this matter we shall see that the *Avot* taught us the meaning of prayer in all its depth and scope.

The Torah introduces Avraham's prayer for Sodom with the words, "He drew near and said, 'Will you even sweep away the *tsaddik* with the *rasha*'?' "[2] The Rabbis comment, "The expression 'drawing near' is used for battle, appeasement, and prayer."[3] Rashi adds, "Avraham prepared himself for all three: for strong speaking, for appeasement, and for prayer."[4] Maharal explains that all three are forms of prayer. Avraham had three ideas in mind in his prayer.

> Some of the things which Avraham said were somewhat strong ["...Shall the Judge of the World not do justice?"; this is what the Rabbis call "doing battle"]. Nevertheless, they included words of appeasement, "Perhaps there are fifty *tsaddikim*..."; this is a form of appeasement. He is asking God to act because of the *tsaddikim*. Thirdly, he asked God to act by way of

prayer. [Maharal then adds the following:] In this *midrash*, our Rabbis hinted at a very profound matter. Avraham directed his prayer towards the three names of God: *El, Elohim,* and *Hashem.* To *Elohim,* representing the quality of justice, he spoke strong words... Corresponding to *El,* which is the attitude of kindness, he spoke words of appeasement. And towards the Unique Name, he directed a prayer of mercy... This is what we mean by "the way of prayer." This needs to be understood.[5]

There is indeed much that still needs to be understood in the words of Maharal. How is it at all possible to pray to God by, so to speak, "doing battle"? Is there not a hint of *hillul hashem* here? And what is the meaning of "praying by way of prayer"?

THREE TYPES OF PRAYER

The explanation is as follows. There is a form of prayer in which a person requests God to make good a certain deficiency which he feels—whether his own or another person's. He recognizes that only God the All Powerful can fulfill his needs, and by this very recognition, he may merit God making good his deficiency. Maybe God deprived him of this thing he feels he needs so much in order for him to approach God in prayer. When the person in fact does this, the deficiency has served its purpose and can now be removed. In this way, God has answered his prayer. This is the type of prayer which our Rabbis called "prayer *per se*"—prayer without any qualifications, and this is what Maharal meant by praying "by way of prayer."

The type of prayer which is called "appeasement" refers to a situation where sins have broken man's connection with Hashem and heavenly aid is withdrawn. When the person returns in repentance and wishes to renew his closeness to Hashem, he may ask God to renew His aid and grant him new *kelim* to enable him to resume his service of Hashem. This is an appeal which God rarely refuses.

Both these forms occur in Avraham's prayer. Prayer *per se* may be found in his request to God to spare the people of Sodom. This flowed from his pity for them as God's creatures and was rooted in his profound recognition of Hashem as the Source of all life and the only Power capable of granting his request. We can find here also the prayer of appeasement. This is seen in his emphasis on the *tsaddikim* who might be found in the city. The point here is that if there are still *tsaddikim* in the city—active *tsaddikim*, as implied by the oft-repeated words "in the midst of the city"—there is still a chance that they might induce the people to do *teshuva* and thus merit a renewal of life, as explained above.

HOW *TSADDIKIM* "DO BATTLE" IN THEIR PRAYER

There is a third form of prayer in which the *tsaddik* argues that one of God's decisions is causing him great suffering. It is disturbing the clarity of his perception of God's justice or lovingkindness. He might find in this a kind of *ḥillul hashem*—a desecration, so to speak, of his own innermost sanctum. His service suffers. For these reasons, he begs God to change His decision.

There are some *tsaddikim* who are referred to as "the stout-hearted ones, far from charity."[6] This means that they, in their personal lives, are able to stand up to the scrutiny of strict justice. Unlike most people, they have no need to ask God for charity and mercy in forgiving their sins.[7]

This type of *tsaddik* might call on the attribute of justice to fulfill his request. He might appeal to God's promise to *tsaddikim* that they will not lack the *kelim* essential for their service. In the new situation which thus arises, the decision might well be changed so that the *tsaddik* can pursue his service undisturbed. This is what is meant by the *tsaddik* "doing battle" in his prayer. He summons up his own resources and puts his own merits on the scale so that justice may not only be done, but may be <u>seen</u>.

There is no doubt that Avraham our Father had absolute faith that the acts of God were just and fair and that justice informed all His ways, even if he was not yet able to understand them.[8] He was not, God forbid, arguing against the righteousness of God's actions. His argument was that the utter destruction of Sodom, together with any *tsaddikim* it might contain, would perforce disturb—at least to some small extent—the clarity of his vision of the Almighty. His request was that God not let this occur.

When we consider these three categories of prayer, we may begin to understand what Maharal meant when he said (as we cited above) that "strong speech" corresponds to the attribute of justice, "appeasement"—to the attribute of *ḥessed*, and "prayer *per se*"—to the attribute of mercy. "Strong speech" applies only when the *tsaddik* is able to rally strict justice to his cause. "Prayer *per se*" asks for the giving of heavenly aid to one who is trying to maintain his service of God; he appeals to God's attribute of mercy. "Appeasement" applies to the person who stands far from God and has lost everything through sin. He begs to be given back *kelim* to enable him to resume his service. This is addressed to the attribute of God's unlimited *ḥessed*.

PURE PRAYER PREVAILS

As we saw, the form of prayer which is called "strong speech" is possible only for a *tsaddik* who stands at the highest point of perfection. It is clear that in his request there is not the slightest hint of complaint concerning God's running of the world. There is only a deep yearning to be able to appreciate the holiness of God to the fullest. There is no desecration in this prayer; to the contrary, it is itself a great *kiddush Hashem*—a profound appeal for the removal of misunderstanding.

There is, however, great danger in this type of prayer. If any of the conditions we described above are lacking, it would indeed become a *ḥillul hashem*. This is what the Rabbis meant when they contrasted this prayer of Avraham with the complaints of Iyov.

> Rabbi Levi said: Two people said apparently the same thing: Avraham and Iyov. Avraham said: "Far be it from You to do a thing like this, to kill the *tsaddik* with the *rasha'*." Iyov said: "It is all one; that's why I say He destroys the innocent with the guilty."[9] Avraham was rewarded, but Iyov was punished. Why? For Avraham it was a mature statement; for Iyov it was immature.[10]

Avraham and Iyov apparently said the same thing. But there was a world of difference in the intention behind their words. Avraham was not personally involved; on the contrary, those doomed to destruction were people who opposed to the utmost all that he stood for. His "strong speech" came from the purest intentions, as we explained above. His approach was "mature." Iyov, on the other hand, was complaining about what God had done to him personally. He was not yet able to raise himself above his personal plight and see it in the context of the whole of creation. This approach the Rabbis called immature."

GOD DECREES, THE *TSADDIK* REVOKES

Perhaps we can now understand the difficult dictum of our Sages: "God decrees, and the *tsaddik* revokes the decree."[11] There are some *tsaddikim* through whose merit the whole world exists. Whatever happens in the world is something that they learn from and use for their sublime *'avoda*; and it is their learning opportunities which sustain the whole generation, including lowly people such as ourselves. All are, in a sense, *kelim* for the *tsaddik*, who sees the tremendous *hessed* of God sustaining all the people who have no merits of their own.

If such a *tsaddik* observes something which obscures the glory of Hashem, he is justified in asking Hashem to remove it, even though this may involve a change in God's management of the world. This is what the Rabbis mean when they say that a *tsaddik* can revoke God's decree.

Of course, if a person who is not on that sublime level were to attempt such a thing, this would be considered a sin. So we are taught in the Midrash:[12]

> God says: People should not think that they can speak to Me the same way as Avraham did and I will overlook it. God says: "I will not be silent at his words."[13] It was only at Avraham's words that I remained silent. Why? Because he remained silent to Me. I said to him: "Through Yitzhak will your descendants be named."[14] Then I said to him: "Take your son...Yitzhak...and offer him...";[15] and he remained silent at my words. Therefore I will remain silent for him, even though he expressed himself rather strongly...by saying: "Will You even sweep away the righteous with the wicked?"[16] Avraham's intention was that the nations of

the world should not misinterpret God's actions and say that [God forbid] God destroys indiscriminately...God said [to Iyov]: I will pass all the generations before you and please tell me if you consider that I acted unjustly on any occasion.

Only Avraham, in his greatness, could pray this way. He felt with all the depth of his being that the nations of the world might err and misinterpret God's actions, and through this, God's _ḥessed_ would be obscured. Avraham loved God so much that he could not bear this. His complaint was purely for the sake of God Himself. But at the 'Akeda, in which he was so personally involved, he remained silent. This shows that all his arguments were, so to speak, to preserve God's good name in the world.

MOSHEH'S COMPLAINT

In the same manner, we can understand Mosheh Rabbenu's complaint, when he said to God, "Why have You dealt badly with these people...?"[17] [This was when Pharaoh had reacted harshly to Mosheh's request, and greatly increased the burdens of the people.] But the tone of Mosheh's complaint to God is rather startling. As the Rabbis comment:[18]

How could Mosheh have spoken in this manner to the Almighty? In the normal way of the world, if a person says to his fellow, "Why did you do such a thing?" he would be annoyed with him. Yet Mosheh said such a thing to God? But this was Mosheh's argument: "I have taken the _Book of Bereshit_ and read it, and I saw what happened to the generation of the Flood...and what happened to the generation of Dispersion, and to the Sodomites...and one could see the justice of Your actions. But what have these people done to deserve all this?" ...At that moment, the attribute of justice wanted to strike Mosheh down. But when God saw that he was speaking only for the sake of Israel, the attribute of justice could not affect him.

It was evident to God that Mosheh was speaking only "for the sake of Israel." He could not stand the thought of his people suffering any more harsh persecution.

In a similar manner, we must understand Mosheh's great prayer after the episode of the Golden Calf: "Why should Egypt say that He took them out with an evil intent...to kill them in the desert?"[19] as we explained elsewhere.[20] How do we know that this prayer was said only because of Mosheh's love of God? Because when speaking to Israel, he does not spare any words in rebuking them for their sin. As the Rabbis said, "Mosheh (so to speak) rebuked Me for the sake of Israel, but he also rebuked Israel for My sake. To Israel he said, 'You have sinned a great sin,'[21] but to Me he said, 'Why are You so angry with Your people?'"[22] When speaking for the good of Israel, his arguments are counted as a great mitzva. He wanted nothing but the elevation of God's glory and the sanctification of His name throughout the world. This is the battle the *tsaddikim* wage in their prayers to their Creator.

notes

---

1 *Berachot* 26b.
2 *Bereshit* 18:23.
3 See *Bereshit Rabba* 49:8.
4 *Bereshit ad loc.*
5 *Gur Aryeh ad loc.*
6 *Yesha'ya* 46:12.
7 *Berachot* 17b.
8 See *Devarim* 32:4.
9 *Iyov* 9:22.
10 *Bereshit Rabba* 49:9.
11 *Moed Katan* 16b.
12 *Yalkut Shim'oni, Iyov* #927.
13 *Iyov* 41:4.
14 *Bereshit* 21:12.
15 Ibid. 22:2.
16 See note 2, above.
17 *Shemot* 5:22–23.
18 *Shemot Rabba* 5:22.
19 Ibid. 32:12.
20 *Michtav Me-Eliyahu* II, p. 89.
21 *Shemot* 32:30.
22 Ibid. 32:11.

The Banishment of
Hagar and Yishmael

Avraham's ninth test—the last before his final and greatest test, the *'Akeda*—was when Hashem told him to listen to Sara and send his maidservant Hagar and her son "away from me and from my son Yitzhak, from this world and from the next."[1] The Midrash adds: "And of all the misfortunes that had befallen Avraham in his lifetime, this was for him the worst."[2]

God gave our Father Avraham, the greatest *ba'al hessed* in all creation, many tests dealing with the quality of *gevura* [see "Our Forefathers' Attributes"]. He bore a great love for his son Yishmael; and even after Yitzhak was born, his affection for Yishmael did not lessen. The command to banish him from his house was a great blow to Avraham, as we saw in the *midrash* quoted above. His quality of *gevura* was clearly demonstrated by the manner in which he performed this task. [See *Bereshit* 21:14.]

First, "He rose early in the morning": with alacrity, without the slightest hesitation. Second: "He took bread and a flask of water." Contrast this with the meal he served the three strangers! Then: "He put it on her shoulder, together with the child." The boy was sick[3] but God's command was carried out immediately. And then: "She wandered in the desert." He did not provide a servant to help her or guide her.

He proved himself to be in complete control of his emotions. Where apparent severity was demanded, he was perfectly able to provide it. If the mitzva is "banishment," then banishment it must be, in the full sense of the word. In this way, he fulfilled Hashem's will in these particular circumstances and passed his tests completely. [A lesson was being taught. Even *ḥessed* has its limitations. It is not true *ḥessed* to tolerate an evil influence in one's household. But even so, the severity with which Avraham sent them away was only apparent. Avraham had already been told that he need not be unduly concerned about Yishmael; he would become a great nation.[4] In this situation, miracles would be provided for their preservation.[5]]

THE COVENANT WITH AVIMELECH

After the banishment of Hagar and Yishmael, the Torah begins a new *parasha*. "At that time, Avimelech...said to Avraham, 'God is with you in all that you do' ...and the two of them made a covenant."[6] Why does the Torah tell us that the covenant with Avimelech occurred just "at that time"?

The significance is this. Avraham, the master of *ḥessed*, certainly loved peace and pursued it in all his relationships. But particularly at that time—when he was obliged to act with apparent severity in turning Hagar and Yishmael out of his house—at that time particularly, he rejoiced in the opportunity to make a peace pact with Avimelech, the king of the Philistines.

However, we find that *Hazal* advance some criticism of Avraham's action. Rashbam[7] quotes a *midrash* which teaches the following:

> God said to him: You gave [Avimelech] seven ewe lambs.[8] By your life, [I swear to you] that his descendants will wage seven wars against your descendants and defeat them... By your life, his descendants will kill seven righteous men of your descendants: Shimshon,[9] Hofni and Pinhas,[10] Shaul and his three sons...[11] By your life, his descendants will destroy seven temples: the Tabernacle, Gilgal, Nov, Shiloh, Giv'on, and the First and Second Temples. Also: The Ark of the Covenant was in captivity for seven months in the land of the Philistines.[12]

Our Rabbis, with access to *ruah ha-kodesh*—the holy spirit—tell us that, according to the judgment of absolute truth, Avraham might have displayed a very slight excess of *hessed* in this connection. Avimelech was, after all, an idolatrous king who was occupying part of the territory promised to Avraham. Perhaps by making such a pact, not only for himself, but also for future generations,[13] he was prejudicing future battles which might be required in the process of conquering the land. Those future disasters, hint our Rabbis, may have been needed to atone for this very slight defect in Avraham Avinu's *middot*.[14]

Immediately after the account of the pact with Avimelech, the Torah introduces the *parasha* of the 'Akeda. This is prefaced by the words "After these things."[15] Again we can ask, What is the connection between these two *parshiyot*? Rashbam explains that one of the factors leading to the test of the 'Akeda was the need to correct the very slight excess of *hessed* which *Hazal* detected in Avraham's eagerness to conclude the peace pact with Avimelech.

notes

1 *Pirkei d'R. Eliezer* 30.
2 Ibid. See above, "Our Forefathers' Attributes," paragraph "The Perfection of the Avot: Avraham.
3 See Rashi, *Bereshit* 21:14.
4 Ibid., v. 12–13.
5 Ibid., v. 17–19.
6 *Bereshit* 21:22–34.
7 On *Bereshit* 22:1.
8 *Bereshit* 21:28–30.
9 *Shoftim* 16:30.
10 *Shemuel I* 4:11.
11 Ibid. 31:6.
12 Ibid. 6:1.
13 *Bereshit* 21:23.
14 Compare earlier essay, "Causes of the Egyptian Exile."
15 Ibid. 22:1.

The Test of the 'Akeda

We all know that the 'Akeda was the most momentous and decisive test of Avraham's life, and the merit of the 'Akeda continues to stand Israel in good stead throughout the generations. In the simplest sense, the 'Akeda demonstrated Avraham's readiness to carry out God's will, even to the extent of giving up his beloved, only son. As God Himself said: "You did not withhold your only son from Me."[1]

From another viewpoint, the 'Akeda showed Avraham's willing self-sacrifice even in the spiritual sphere. Avraham had been eminently successful in bringing people close to God and showing them "the way of Hashem: to practice charity and justice."[2] He had taught them the quality of ḥessed and fought against the horrible practice of sacrificing one's children to some idol. And now he was being commanded, apparently, to do that very thing for God! Would this not destroy the wonderful structure of service which he had built up for over more than a century? But Avraham, in his great simplicity, took no account of all this. His only desire was to fulfill the will of the Creator, blessed be His Name. And since it had been revealed to him beyond any shadow of a doubt [as he thought] that this was the will of Hashem, nothing else mattered.

This act would not only cause darkness and confusion in the outside world, but also within Avraham's heart. Through this one command, all God's conduct of the world and all that He stood for became an impenetrable mystery. Hashem had promised Avraham that he would become a great nation, which would descend from his son Yitzhak.[3] However, the command of the 'Akeda stood in direct contradiction to that promise. Surely one would expect Avraham to pray to God to enlighten his eyes and explain the apparent contradiction. But he did not do so. He did not say a word, but instead "rose up early in the morning" to carry out God's command without questioning and without having any answers. This seems amazing.

At the conclusion of the 'Akeda, we are told that "Avraham called the name of the place Hashem Yireh [may God see]."[4] Our Rabbis comment on this:

> Avraham spoke before God: Lord of all the worlds, when You said to me, "Please take your only son...," I could have answered You: Yesterday You told me that all my descendants would come from Yitzhak, and now You tell me to offer him up...! But...I did not do so. I suppressed my mercy in order to do Your will. So may it be Your will, O God, that if, in times to come, the children of Yitzhak will fall into sin and unworthy deeds, please remember this 'Akeda and act towards them with mercy.[5]

In another midrash, the Rabbis put the same idea in slightly different terms:

> He said to Him: Lord of the universe, You know very

well that when You told me to offer up Yitzhak, I could have challenged this command... But I did not do so. I pretended to be deaf and dumb... Similarly, when in times to come, Yitzhak's children will be judged and You will have unanswerable questions about their behavior, please do the same to them and be deaf to the words of the accuser.[6]

THE ESSENCE OF THE TEST

From this we see that the essence of the test of the 'Akeda lay in not demanding from God that He resolve the open contradiction between His promise and His command. We have already explained in a previous essay[7] that it was in Avraham's power to demand a resolution which would remove the confusion and hillul hashem (in his mind) resulting from his inability to understand the ways of God. He made such a demand when he was pleading for the people of Sodom, but here he said nothing. Why not?

Here we see our forefather's wondrous purity of heart. He was afraid that if he were to ask God to clear up the difficulty, his request would contain a slight element of opposition to God's will. Some hint of his great love for Yitzhak might have motivated the question. Therefore he preferred not to approach God with any prayer or any question whatsoever—even one word. He accepted the command totally, with all the difficulties and questions it entailed. This is the deeper meaning of God's words: "Now I know that you fear God and you did not withhold your son..." Avraham's desire to withhold his son had not the slightest power over him. This was the clearest sign of his greatness regarding the service of Hashem.

After he withstood his tests, Avraham prayed that the power to break one's personal will would remain with Israel throughout the generations in order to silence the voice of the accuser. This is why he called the place *Hashem Yireh*; it was a prayer for the future—that God would see a vestige of that spiritual power in every Jew's heart. This would ensure that God would listen to their prayers and forgive their sins.

The inner point with which one merits this spiritual power is the ability to recognize the truth. There is an inner point in the Jewish heart which is ready to suppress personal desires in favor of God's will. Even though the person may not understand the reasons why God did something and His qualities of goodness and *hessed* are completely hidden, he nevertheless rejoices at fulfilling God's will. This inner point, which is present in every Jewish heart, is often deeply hidden and fails to break out into the open. But it is still alive, and in special circumstances, it may be activated.

Our Rabbis have said that if a Jew gives money to charity, hoping that the merit of the mitzva will help his son recover from a serious illness, such a person is a *tsaddik gamur*—a completely righteous person.[8] On the other hand, the Gemara tells us that when the king of Persia sent an offering to Jerusalem "for the life of the king and his sons,"[9] this did not count to his merit since it was *she'lo lishma*—from selfish, personal motives. What is the difference between his offering and the donation to *tzedaka* which we mentioned above? The difference emerges if, God forbid, the hoped for result is not forthcoming: for example, if the son does not live. The nonJew normally treats the whole matter as a kind of premium he is paying in order to get results. If he does not get what he wanted, he considers his donation to have been a waste of money. In similar circumstances, the Jew will say to himself: God knows best, but at least I have done a mitzva.[10]

Here we see the Jew's readiness to submit to God's will, even though he may not understand it. This point of truth in the Jewish heart is a result of Avraham Avinu's great achievement in this sphere.[11]

*　　　*　　　*

The essence of prayer lies in the person's devotion—*kavvana*. "God is close to all who call to Him—all who call to Him in truth."[12] The point of truth which we referred to above must accompany all our prayers if they are to be worthy of acceptance. We are obliged to pray at the appointed times, even if true devotion is lacking. This is to insure that the institution of prayer will not disappear from Israel. (This is similar to the *din* that if a person cannot obtain a *tallit katan* of the proper size, he should wear one anyway "so that the law of *tzitzit* should not be forgotten."[13]) But such prayer will not bring a person much closer to God. Happy is the person who prays with full intention and devotion. Such prayer will certainly be worthy of acceptance. Much heavenly aid depends on this.

notes

---

1 *Bereshit* 22:12.

2 Ibid. 18:19.

3 Ibid. 21:12.

4 Ibid. 22:14.

5 *Bereshit Rabba* 56:10.

6 *Pesikta Rabbati* #42.

7 *Avraham's Prayer for Sodom*.

8 *Bava Batra* 10b.

9 *Ezra* 6:10.

10 *Bava Batra* 10b, Rashi s.v. *kan*.

11 See *Strive for Truth!* I, p. 54 et seq., especially pp. 59–60.

12 *Tehillim* 145:18.

13 *Ora__h Hayyim* #16, *Mishna Berurah* #4.

The Command of the 'Akeda

The 'Akeda—the supreme test of all time—presents many
difficulties. When Ḥazal discuss the arguments which
Avraham might have presented to God, they usually
mention the fact that this command seemed in direct contradiction to the promise previously made by God that
Avraham would have descendants through his Yitzḥak.[1]
But upon reflection, it would seem that Avraham could
have presented a much more fundamental argument. He
could have asked God how he was expected to transgress
the command against murder. And was not the sacrifice of
children one of the "abominations of the Canaanites"?[2]

Furthermore, the angel said to Avraham, "Do not
stretch out your hand towards the lad and do not do *anything* to him."[3] What is the meaning of *anything*? Rashi explains: "Avraham replied: Does that mean that I have
come all this way for nothing? Let me at least wound him
slightly and shed a little blood. He replied: Do not do
anything (*me'ooma*) to him—do not cause him the slightest
blemish (*moom*)." This is very difficult. Since it is now revealed that there never was any intention for him to sacrifice his son, surely it is obvious that God did not want
him to be harmed in any way.

There is another *midrash* which tells us that when Avraham learned that the '*Akeda* would not proceed, his reaction was: "Why, have you found some defect in me or in my son which disqualifies me from carrying out this sacrifice?"[4] According to our ordinary understanding of this matter, how could Avraham even pose such a question?

THE MEANING OF SACRIFICE

Maharal, in his book *Gevurot Hashem*, reveals a very profound insight.[5] God's existence is awesome, unique, and absolute. All human life, and the existence of the universe itself, pales into utter insignificance by comparison. The offerings in the Temple—the *korbanot*—according to Maharal, symbolize this idea. The offering of the animal teaches that all physical existence has no significance compared with the absolute existence of God.

It would be completely wrong, however, for a person to think that it would be the supreme form of service to demonstrate this idea in practice. He would be terribly mistaken to think that he could, for this reason, take his own life or that of his children. An animal is created to be a *keli* for man. This is its portion in creation. If it can serve as a *keli* for man's physical needs, it can certainly serve as a *keli* for his spiritual needs, by being used to portray profound spiritual truths, such as the one referred to above. But the value of a human life normally lies in the sum of all the free choices a person makes (or causes[6]) during his lifetime. Depriving a human being of life would be to destroy or curtail his portion in creation, which is built upon those free choices which he is offered during his lifetime. This is the basis of the Torah's prohibition against murder.

PROPHETIC REVELATION AND THE 'AKEDA

There is, in theory, a remote possibility that a person could be born whose sole purpose—whose whole portion in creation—would be to serve as a *keli* for his father. By conquering his own emotions in deference to God's will, the father could reveal something of God's glory. If the son reached adulthood, he also could share in his father's achievement by choosing to accept the divine decree with joy. Of course, no one on his own can possibly know the ultimate purpose of anyone's life. Only a person who is accustomed to receiving prophecies from God and who, so to speak, "knows the voice of God"[7]—only such a person can act on such a prophecy if he receives it. (The Torah allows a known prophet to temporarily rescind a Torah law if the circumstances demand it and if he is given a prophecy to do so.[8])

Now perhaps we can understand how it was possible for Avraham to interpret God's command in the literal sense. He must have thought that God was telling him that the whole purpose of Yitzhak's life was to bring both of them to this supreme test. The only question that remained, but he did not ask, was how this was consistent with God's previous promise regarding Yitzhak's great future.

Avraham was well-practiced in prophecy and there was not the slightest doubt in his mind that this was what God wanted. The Midrash[9] tells us that during the journey to Mount Moria, the Satan came to Avraham and said to him (among other things): "Maybe the voice which told you to kill your son came from the Tempter. Will you listen to the Tempter and destroy a human life?" Whereupon Avraham answered him very emphatically: "This was not from any Tempter; this was the voice of God."

THE IMPORTANCE OF ACTION

We can now also understand why Avraham asked for permission to wound or draw blood from Yitzḥak in some way, and also why his first reaction was that maybe a defect (that is, a spiritual defect) in himself or Yitzḥak stopped the ʿAkeda. Since, in theory at least, carrying out the ʿAkeda make sense, Avraham feared that maybe some flaw in his or his son's *madrega* prevented the ʿAkeda from being carried out in practice. When he was told that this was not the case, he asked for permission to do something which would at least fix the concept of absolute sacrifice in the world of action.[10] When this, too, was denied him, Avraham saw the ram, which our Rabbis say was destined from the beginning of creation for this moment. He then understood that the ultimate sacrifice was to be symbolized by offering this ram in place of his son.

We can learn from this the importance of action. All the tremendous struggles which had been going on in Avraham's mind during the three days which had passed since the command of the ʿAkeda would have come to nothing had they not been fixed in his subconscious mind through some symbolic act of sacrifice. The revelations of God's glory which resulted from the ʿAkeda went a long way in fulfilling the purpose of creation. In a sense, all creation had been waiting for this moment.[11] In order for the sacrifice to have its full effect, Avraham imagined that every act he performed on the ram was being done to his son. As our Rabbis say in the Midrash:[12]

> He said before God: Lord of the world, please look upon the blood of this ram as if it were the blood of my

son Yitzhak; the inward parts of this ram as if they were the inward parts of my son Yitzhak; as the Mishna states: To effect an exchange between one sacrifice and another one would have to say: This is instead of that, this is in exchange for that, this is a replacement for that.

In fact, this is how every offering operates—symbolically, the person offers up himself.[13] When the Rabbis say that "Yitzhak's ashes were heaped up before Hashem,"[14] note that they say "Yitzhak's ashes" and not "the ram's ashes." This is because in heaven it was counted as though Yitzhak himself had been sacrificed. When Avraham imagined Yitzhak burning as the ram burned, this became a spiritual reality in the eyes of God. We learn from this that even though a physical act is needed to "fix" the revelation and make it "real," the revelation itself does not come from the act but from the innermost intention of the heart.

Another thing we learn from the 'Akeda is that when a person breaks his own will and sacrifices his imagined future to Hashem, it is counted for him as though he sacrificed something real and not just something imaginary. For example, if it seems likely that a person could eventually live a life of ease and affluence and he abandons this path in order to dedicate his life to Torah and the service of Hashem, he is credited as if he were already, in fact, living a life of comfort and affluence, and had given it all up in order to serve Hashem and live without all these things. And, if he chooses to give up his materialistic hopes and dreams for this purpose, and it turns out afterwards that he is blessed with both worlds, he is rewarded in the same way as if he had in fact sacrificed everything—on one condition: that he takes one step or performs one act of sacrifice to "fix" his thoughts and translate them into reality. "Hashem joins a good thought to a good deed."[15]

notes

1 See previous essay, near the beginning.
2 *Devarim* 12:31.
3 *Bereshit* 22:12.
4 *Kohelet Rabba* 9:7.
5 Chapters 40 and 69.
6 See *Strive for Truth!* I, p. 90.
7 *Tanḥuma, parashat Vayera.*
8 *Yevamot* 90b. Examples: (*a*) Eliyahu bringing a sacrifice outside the Temple of Jerusalem (*Melachim I* 18:32–33) and (*b*) the prophet who commanded a soldier to wound him with his sword (*Melachim I* 20:35–38).
9 See note 7, above.
10 See the essay in *Vayetzei* entitled "Inwardness and Outwardness," paragraph "Actions 'Fix' Thoughts."
11 See *Strive for Truth!* III, p. 231.
12 *Bereshit Rabba* 56:14 and Rashi on *Bereshit* 22:13.
13 See *Midrash Aggadat Bereshit, parashat Vayera.*
14 Rashi on *Vayikra* 26:42.
15 *Kiddushin* 14a.

Avraham's Ram

In the previous essay we explained that Avraham's sacrificing of the ram was the act by which he gave reality to all the tremendous revelations of Hashem's glory which were included in the '*Akeda*. Our Rabbis comment:[1]

> Rabbi Ḥanina ben Dosa says: That ram which was created in the twilight [between the sixth and seventh day of creation] was fully used; none of it was wasted. The sinews of the ram became the ten strings of David's harp. The skin of the ram became the leather girdle around Eliyahu's waist. The left horn of the ram was the shofar blown at Har Sinai. And its right horn, which was larger than the left, will one day be used to usher in the era of the *Mashiaḥ*, as the verse says: "On that day the great shofar will be blown."[2]

"THE RAM WHICH WAS CREATED IN THE TWILIGHT ." The twilight between the sixth and seventh days of creation represents the realm between this world and the supernatural. Avraham's spiritual attainment through the test of the '*Akeda* was the highest possible in this world.

"ITS SINEWS BECAME THE TEN STRINGS, ETC. " That revelation embraced all the spiritual attainments of King

David, of blessed memory—even those represented by "the harp of ten strings" which reflected the World to Come.

"ITS SKIN BECAME ELIYAHU'S LEATHER GIRDLE. " Eliyahu's girdle represents his power—his zeal in ridding Israel of idolatry. This came from the same root as the spiritual attainment of our Father Avraham in the test of the 'Akeda. Subduing one's will is like destroying idolatry, because one's own will is the idol one sets up in place of God.

"ITS LEFT HORN BECAME THE SHOFAR AT HAR SINAI. " All the revelations of the giving of the Torah were included in Avraham's attainments. These are derived from the left horn because the great excitement and publicity which attended the giving of the first Tablets provided an opportunity for the Satan (symbolized by the "left") to accuse. "The first Tablets were given with great publicity and therefore they were subject to the evil eye and were broken."[3]

"THE RIGHT HORN...THE GREAT SHOFAR OF THE FUTURE." The shofar of Mashiaḥ, which announces the end of the era of the yetzer ha-ra‘, will indeed create great publicity and tremendous revelations, but over these the yetzer ha-ra‘ will have no power, for it will have been removed from the world.

We can learn from this that by withstanding the test of the 'Akeda, our Father Avraham reached the highest level of self-abnegation that is possible in this world. And this high point served as the root of all of Israel's subsequent spiritual developments, including Mattan Torah and the era of the Mashiaḥ.

HIGH POINT OF THE 'AKEDA

One question remains. The verse states:[4] "And Avraham raised his eyes and saw one ram, afterwards, caught in the bushes by its horns." On this, Rashi comments (in some versions): "*Afterwards* means after all the words of the angel and of God and after all of Avraham's arguments." The question can be raised: Considering the importance of this sacrificial ram, why didn't God allow Avraham to see it until then?

Avraham's argument with the angel concerning his wish to make a small wound on his son, and also his statement to God concerning His promise that Yitzhak would be the bearer of the future[5]—all these were fine, subtle points contained within the test of the 'Akeda. Through them, as we have explained, Avraham's self-sacrifice and love of God became crystal clear. This, in fact, was the high point of the 'Akeda. This was why God arranged for the appearance of the ram to be delayed until all these points had been brought into being, so that all of them could be made a reality by the sacrifice of the ram.

And why did the ram have to be "caught in the bushes by its horns"? Rashi states: "It was running towards Avraham, but the Satan entangled it among the trees." We know that everything Satan does is for the sake of Heaven, in order to make the test greater and thereby increase the revelation. So what was the point of this delay? The point was that after Avraham's incredible struggles, self-sacrifice, and unlimited love—after all these, one further small effort was required of him. The ram was on the fringe of his vision; he had to strain his eyes and notice the ram and walk over to the place where the ram was entangled in the bush. Without this additional effort, the "fixing" of these wonderful spiritual attainments would have been lacking! We can learn from this the supreme value of labor and effort—physical effort. This may seem of small importance to us, but in fact its value is very great, and only through it can we attain the highest levels of serving Hashem.

notes

1 *Yalkut Shimoni, Vayera* #101.
2 *Yesha'ya* 27:13.
3 *Tanḥuma, Ki Tissa* #31.
4 *Bereshit* 22:13.
5 See above in the essay entitled "The Test of the *'Akeda*."

<u>H</u>ayyei Sara

Eliezer's Mind

"The conversation of the *Avot*'s servants seems more valuable than the Torah of their later descendants. Eliezer's narrative takes up two or three columns in the *sefer Torah*, whereas certain important laws are derived from a single letter."[1]

It is clear that many important lessons can be derived from Eliezer's narrative. Let us study it carefully and perhaps a little of the wealth it contains will be revealed to us.

If we compare the manner in which Eliezer relates his experiences and actions to Lavan and Betuel (*Bereshit* 24:34–48) with the way in which the Torah records them in the first instance (24:2–27), we notice several discrepancies. For example, when Eliezer recounts his conversation with Avraham, he mentions his question to his master: "Perhaps the woman will not follow me?" (v. 39), but he omits the rest of the sentence: "Shall I return your son to the land from which you came?" (v. 5). Letters are significant and it should be noted that the word *ulai* —"perhaps" [in v. 5] is spelled *malei*, with a *vav*—while in Eliezer's account [in v. 39], the same word is spelled without a *vav*, so that it could possibly be read as *elai*—"to me." The significance of this is, as Rashi tells us:[2] "The possible reading *elai*—"to me"—hints at the fact that Eliezer had a daughter who, he thought, would be a suitable wife for Yitzhak and he hoped that Avraham would agree to this match." But in this case, we could ask why the Torah introduced this hint only in Eliezer's own report of his question [v. 39] and not in the Torah's account of the same question [v. 5]. Again, in Eliezer's account, he first inquired about the girl's family and only then gave her the jewelry, while in the Torah's account he gave her the jewelry first and asked about her family afterwards. Rashi explains: "He changed the order of events...so that they would not object: 'How could you have given it to her if you didn't know yet who she was?'"

We have discussed elsewhere at length[3] how the mind is subject to prejudice and bias. Everyone has a field of vision which is determined by the strength of his eyesight. The same principle operates in the spiritual world. A person can only see the truth to the extent that his spiritual level permits. Beyond this horizon, he can see nothing. A person on a lower level cannot possibly grasp matters which belong to a higher spiritual level. For example, a person who has not modified his natural selfishness cannot possibly grasp the unselfish actions of the giving personality.[4] He will inevitably attribute them to selfish motives; his mental horizon does not allow him to "see" *hessed* done for its own sake.

The sins of great personalities are often interpreted by *Hazal* as actions which hardly seem to us to be wrong at all. We are told that God punishes *tsaddikim* even for sins which are "like a hair's breadth."[5] This means that things which seem to us to be as light and insignificant as a hair may—for the *tsaddik* with his vastly expanded spiritual horizon—be considered serious sins.

In this way we can understand why Eliezer changed the order of events when he was telling his narrative to Lavan and Betuel. Eliezer's deep faith and his joy at the miracle that had happened for him caused him to put the bracelets on Rivka's hands even before he asked her about her family. He was absolutely sure what her answer would be. But when it was time to recount the events to people like Betuel and Lavan, he recognized, in his wisdom, that with their limited mental horizon they would not be able to accept that a sensible person could act like that. For them, such an act was merely foolhardy and his credibility would have suffered. A person whose vision is limited by the materialistic will never be able to grasp the truth as seen on a higher level.

Anyone who has prejudices and whose perceptions are colored by self-interest will never see the truth in any area in which his bias operates. Only when his bias is removed will he be able to understand the truth. When Avraham sent Eliezer on his mission, warning him not to take a wife for Yitzhak from the daughters of Canaan, Eliezer replied: "Perhaps the woman will not want to follow me... Shall I return your son...?"—and there, the *ulai* is spelled with a *vav* and cannot possibly mean "to me." At that time, he still entertained the hope that his daughter would turn out to be the one. He expected Avraham's reply to be, "If there is no possibility of finding anyone from my family who is willing to come here, then you may take even a girl of Canaanite origin, provided that she is very exceptional in character," which would have left his daughter as a suitable candidate.

Eliezer was not conscious of his personal bias. These motivations and imaginings were all on a subconscious level, the hint of his self-interest—the *ulai* spelled as *elai*—does not appear in the Torah at this stage. But when he was speaking to Betuel and Lavan, he understood that Yitzhak's mate had already been chosen by heaven. There was no possibility that his hopes would ever be realized and he now became aware of his bias. At this point the Torah introduced the hint of "*ulai – elai*," because the bias was now in the open. Eliezer was now aware of the hidden motive behind the question "Shall I return your son Yitzhak...?" and therefore he omitted it in his account.

Happy is the person who can discover his hidden motives! He will be able to see the truth.

notes

1 Rashi on *Bereshit* 24:42 from *Bereshit Rabba* 60:11.
2 On *Bereshit* 24:39 from *Yalkut Shimoni, Hoshea* #12 and *Bereshit Rabba* 59:9.
3 *Strive for Truth!* I, pp. 161–172.
4 Ibid., p. 119 et seq.
5 *Yevamot* 121b.

Toldot

Yitzḥak's Service

"And God saw that all He had made, and see!—It was very good."[1] On this our Rabbis comment: "'Good' means the *yetzer tov*; 'very good' means the *yetzer ha-ra'*."[2]

The evil inclination is called "very good" because the whole purpose of creation depends on it. The world was created for the *kiddush Hashem* which emerges from people choosing to act correctly, and choice is only possible because of the existence of the *yetzer ha-ra'*. A human being battles against the evil within him in order to do Hashem's will. He chooses good and thereby creates a *kiddush Hashem*. But even if a person, God forbid, follows the advice of the *yetzer ha-ra'*—although at first sight this may seem to be a *ḥillul hashem*—ultimately it, too, will lead to *kiddush Hashem*. The evil will be punished according to God's judgment, and from this punishment people will eventually learn the depth of evil which lies in sin. This will be a revelation of the truth of God's justice, which is another form of *kiddush Hashem*. So God's great name is sanctified in all events; either by the good choice of the *tsaddik* or by the punishment of the *rasha'*.[3]

THE ATTRIBUTE OF JUSTICE

We have already discussed the reason why Avraham's chief *midda* of *ḥessed* had to be succeeded by Yitzḥak's chief *midda* of *gevura*.[4] *Gevura*, as we know, corresponds to the attribute of strict justice. *Middat ha-din*, the attribute of justice, is the basis of all the obscurity in the world. As we have just explained, the obscurity and evil in the world make possible the *kiddush Hashem* which proceeds from human choices. And it is *middat ha-din* which insists that a person must take responsibility for his choices. After Avraham opened the gates of lovingkindness, the world was flooded with great *ḥessed*. As a result, the power of justice was weakened and the obscurity in the world was reduced and in need of reinforcement.

This is the deeper reason underlying 'Esav's birth to our Father Yitzḥak. Through 'Esav, the power of obscurity and *middat ha-din* would be strengthened. This does not mean that 'Esav was predestined to be a *rasha'*. We certainly find many instances of his connection with obscurity and evil. There is the hint residing in the fact that he was "all red, like a mantle of hair."[5] Again: "When Rivka passed a temple of idolatry, 'Esav struggled to emerge."[6] But all these things indicate only the intensity of service which was demanded of him.

There is no doubt that 'Esav was given powers for good corresponding to his powers for evil. Had he summoned up all his powers for good, he could have conquered the evil. He could have used his attribute of *gevura* for good, and thus approached the level of Yitzḥak our Father.

This is why Yitzḥak showed him so much affection. He wanted to encourage him to follow in this path of service, which was also his own. This is also the meaning of the blessing Yitzhak wanted to give him, as we shall explain, with God's help, in the next essay.

To sum up: The service of God consists of continually overcoming difficulties and obstacles—a constant struggle with the *yetzer ha-ra'*. As Rabbi Yeruham Levovitz so dramatically put it:[7]

> The essence of the service of God lies precisely in the *yetzer ha-ra'*—in situations where one has lost the will [to do good] or where the very "taste" of doing good is lacking. "With all your life—even if He takes your life" refers to situations of the utmost difficulty. "With all your might—with all your property" means even a person who normally would refuse to give up a penny will give up all his property for the love of God. Indeed, the love of God emerges from just such a situation... Without overcoming obstacles there can be no love of God.

notes

1 *Bereshit* 1:31.
2 *Bereshit Rabba* 9:7.
3 See *Michtav Me-Eliyahu* III, p. 230.
4 See essay, "The Qualities of Our Forefathers."
5 *Bereshit* 25:25.
6 Ibid. 25:22, Rashi.
7 *Da'at Hochma U-mussar* #96 [5695].

Yitzhak's Blessing

Understanding Torah requires deep reflection, particularly when studying the deeds and lives of the *Avot*, of blessed memory. Every detail of their actions involves tremendous acts of service and elevated levels of spirituality. The Rabbis use an extraordinary but graphic metaphor to describe the intensity of their service: "The *Avot* ran before Me like horses."[1] There are great difficulties, to be sure, in these narratives. We must abandon the superficial ideas we formed in our childhood and try to examine their profundity with the aid of the words of our holy Sages. We shall then see that even their simple meaning contains sublime truths. The *parasha* of Yitzhak's blessing is one of these. It is indeed obscure, but with proper consideration we may merit, with God's help, to remove some of the difficulties and to clarify the issues involved.

First we have to understand how a blessing can possibly be won by a trick. Surely the blessing depends on the intention of the person who is giving it? And even if we succeed in overcoming this difficulty, we must still ask why it was decided in heaven that Ya'akov should obtain the blessing by deceit rather than in a straightforward manner. And how could Yitzhak prefer 'Esav to Ya'akov?

Are we to understand that he knew nothing whatsoever of 'Esav's character?

This last question is raised by the Zohar, which asks: Surely our Father Yitzhak was a prophet and the *Shechina* was constantly with him; how could he not notice 'Esav's true character? The answer given is that Hashem hid the truth from him so that Ya'akov would be blessed "not according to Yitzhak's ideas, but according to Hashem's ideas."[2] This obviously needs further elucidation.

There is another difficulty. In one *midrash* we are told that the word *begadav* [his garments] is to be read as *bogedav* [his traitors]. The *midrash* explains that Yitzhak saw in a prophetic vision that from this person standing before him there would descend *resha'im* who would be traitors to God and to the Jewish people, and when he saw the final outcome, he blessed him. Two such traitors are mentioned, Yosef Meshitta and Yakum of Tzereidot, who, on two separate occasions in a time of persecution of the Jewish people, joined the enemies of Israel, but by hearing a few words which went straight to their hearts, each made full repentance and gave up their lives in the process.[3] Why should this have induced Yitzhak to give the blessing?

On the other hand, in a comment on the words "He smelled the odor of his garments and said: 'See! The odor of my son is like the odor of a field blessed by God,'"[4] the *midrash* tells us that when Ya'akov entered, the odor of *Gan 'Eden* entered with him, whereupon Yitzhak blessed him.[5] From this it would seem that it was not a vision of evildoers but a vision of the highest purity that moved Yitzhak to give his blessing.

We know that apparently conflicting *midrashim* often can reveal to us different aspects of the truth. We shall have to try and understand the deeper meaning behind these two *midrashim*.

THE CONCEPT OF BLESSING

We must, of course, realize that a blessing, which is, in effect, like a prayer for someone else, can never affect the other person's essential act of *beḥira*, as we have explained in "The Discourse on Free Will."[6] Education, upbringing, and genetic endowment, as well as the heavenly aid which may come by way of a blessing, can affect only the outward aspects of our lives. As we put it in that discourse, all these can affect only the position of a person's *beḥira*-point. They can never affect the essential, inward act of *beḥira* itself. A blessing, too, can affect only these external factors.

As we know, Yitzḥak's main *midda* was *gevura*—strict judgment. From the point of view of strict judgment (*middat ha-din*), external aids should be given only to the person who needs them, that is, the person who has not yet reached inwardness, but whose service of God is still, to a considerable extent, on the external level. (See above in the essay entitled "Avraham's Service: The Bestowal of *Ḥessed*," in which we discussed why Noaḥ needed heavenly aid and Avraham did not.) A person whose service has reached the level of complete inwardness does not need such external aids and, according to the viewpoint of strict justice, should do without them.

Yitzḥak was aware beyond all possible doubt that his son Ya'akov was a *tsaddik* of complete inwardness. Such a *tsaddik* should be able to win on the basis of justice alone, by the force of his own unaided *beḥira*, without external aids which are in the nature of mercy and charity. If deprivation of such aids makes his path very hard in this world, what of it? Let him suffer pain, exile, and persecution. All these will serve as challenges, to draw out of him the fullest merits of inwardness. According to this viewpoint, only the most "outward" person should receive blessings. These enable him to continue on his path so that he may eventually do complete *teshuva* and reach the level of complete "inwardness".

YITZHAK'S LOVE FOR 'ESAV

Yitzhak knew that 'Esav was very different from Ya'akov. He knew that 'Esav was an "outward" person. He believed, however, that 'Esav, like Yitzhak himself, was engaged in a continual battle with the lower, external aspects of his character. What he did not know was that 'Esav had, of his own free will, virtually extinguished the spark of good in his heart.

This explains why Yitzhak wanted to bless his son 'Esav, and not Ya'akov. He loved 'Esav, that is, he lavished upon him attention and affection in order to help him win the battle which Yitzhak thought he was waging against his baser nature. In his idealized vision, he saw in 'Esav a duplicate of his struggles with *gevura* which he personally had undergone years earlier. As the Zohar[7] puts it: "Like loves like."

YITZHAK'S TEST

A blessing, like prayer, involves great spiritual struggle on the part of the *tsaddik*. The blessing of Yitzhak our Father, which was to have repercussions throughout the generations, could not come to pass without tremendous acts of spiritual service. It had to involve a test—possibly the greatest test of Yitzhak's life.

When Ya'akov came into his father's presence and

Yitzḥak heard his voice and felt his hands, which were covered by the goatskins, Yitzḥak uttered the famous words: "The voice is the voice of Ya'akov and the hands are the hands of 'Esav."[8] The hands represent the external actions of a person, while the voice represents a person's inner essence. This served only to confirm Yitzḥak's belief that 'Esav was essentially an inwardly-oriented person who was struggling to insure that his inward truth would gain ascendancy over his outward actions. It also reinforced his conviction that the blessing most appropriately belonged to 'Esav—to help him in his ongoing struggle. Thus the Torah says: "He did not recognize him... and he blessed him."[9]

This view was even further reinforced by the vision of the two traitors [as cited above from the Midrash] who were led by the "spark of inner truth" to abandon their evil ways and die honorably as true Jews. This, too, represented to Yitzḥak the final triumph of good over evil in the struggle he believed was going on in 'Esav's soul. Whereupon the Torah again says "And he blessed him."[10] This means he wished to bless him, since this seemed to confirm his view that a blessing should be given only to a person engaged in this struggle, and not to the "inner" *tsaddik* whose struggle already lay behind him.

However, the odor of 'Esav's garments also had another interpretation, as we saw above. The odor Yitzḥak smelled was that of *Gan 'Eden*. He said: "See! The odor of my son is like the odor of the field which God has blessed," whereupon he proceeded to give the blessing. The odor of *Gan 'Eden*—which represents a level of complete inwardness in which the *yetzer ha-ra'* hardly exists —came to him as a complete surprise, even a shock. To whom did he say "'See!'? He said it to his own heart."[11] This was a challenge to his personal viewpoint which we have stated above, and was a hint that blessings should be directed not only to the person struggling with his outer shell but also to the *tsaddik* who is above the struggle. The *ḥessed* of God recognizes that there is no person in the world who can do without *ḥessed*. This is what is meant by our Rabbis' statement that God wanted the blessing to be given according to His views (that is, according to the quality of *ḥessed*), and not according to Yitzhak's views (that is the attribute of *gevura*).

This was perhaps the greatest test in Yitzhak's life. He could not understand the logic of the hint (the odor) which was given to him, but he nevertheless succeeded in subduing his own *gevura* and accepting that the inward person—the *Gan 'Eden* person—also needs blessing. This is why Yitzhak, after experiencing inner turmoil upon realizing that he had given the *beracha* to Ya'akov, immediately pronounced the words: "He, too, shall be blessed."[12] Now everything fell into place in his mind and he wholeheartedly accepted God's decision. Thus he passed his greatest test.

The truth is that the blessing was given not only to Ya'akov, but also to all his descendants throughout the generations. Among his descendants there would certainly be those in whom the inner spark was fighting to assert itself, as with the two traitors we mentioned earlier. Here the blessing operated in accordance with Yitzhak's original intention. But principally, the blessing took effect "in accordance with the viewpoint of Hashem."[13] This means that even the greatest *tsaddik* needs to be blessed continually with heavenly aid regarding his service. No one, not even the holy *Avot*, can do without *ḥessed*.

notes

1 *Sanhedrin* 96a.
2 I, 139a.
3 *Bereshit Rabba* 65:22.
4 *Bereshit* 27:27.
5 See note 3, above.
6 See *Strive for Truth!* II, pp. 49 et seq.
7 I, 137b.
8 *Bereshit* 27:22.
9 Ibid., v. 23.
10 Ibid., v. 27.
11 Ibn Ezra ad loc.
12 *Bereshit* 27:33.
13 See note 2, above.

Vayetzei

[For the purposes of the present volume, the essay in *Michtav Me-Eliyahu* II under this heading ("The Perfection of Ya'akov") has been replaced by the following, which is taken from *Michtav Me-Eliyahu* III, pp. 127–131.]

Inwardness and Outwardness

We have explained many times in this work that the main purpose of our life in this world is to reach the level of inward service. Our Rabbis say: "God requires the heart."[1] This being so, we have to clarify the value and purpose of external action. The Torah requires us to continually practice the outward actions of the mitzvot; we have to increase their number as much as possible and pay attention to their finest details. We shall find that actions of this sort have three functions.

ACTIONS AROUSE THE HEART

Rabbi M. H. Luzatto, of blessed memory, teaches us in his masterly work *Mesillat Yesharim* the following important principle: Outward actions elicit inward emotions.

> Outward movements arouse inwardness. It is easier to act than to acquire inward levels of perception. But if a person makes use of what comes to hand, he will acquire, in the course of time, levels which are not now within his reach. [Alacrity in outward actions] engenders in a person inward joy, will, and desire. This will happen if his actions are done with good will and with excitement.[2]

The author of *Sefer Ha-Ḥinnuch* emphasizes on many occasions that "a person is influenced by his actions and his emotions and all his thoughts always follow the actions in which he is involved."[3] This means that even actions which are carried out without inward intention nevertheless exert an influence over our hearts, provided that we practice them continuously and exert ourselves to perform them with precision. Eventually they will penetrate into our inward recesses. This is the first function of outward actions.

ACTIONS "FIX" THOUGHTS

We also find that one of the special properties of outward actions is that they have the power to fix in our subconscious mind the spiritual awakenings which we may experience from time to time. If a person fails to fix these experiences by means of action, they are liable to remain unproductive.[4] And not only this, there is a danger that increased knowledge can be harmful if it is not fixed in the heart with actions. We are reminded of the saying of our Rabbis: "One whose wisdom is greater than his actions resembles a tree whose foliage is greater than its roots. A wind will come and uproot it and turn it on its face."[5]

Rabbi Menaḥem Mendel of Vitebsk expresses this idea very graphically:

> The important thing is not the learning but the doing... If a person's wisdom is greater than his actions, not only does it not improve him, but on the contrary, it overthrows him completely... As it is said: "The greater a person is [in knowledge], the greater is his *yetzer*..." Even if he increases his ethical knowledge and studies

ways to avoid some particular desire without at the same time increasing his performance of the practical mitzvot related to that same matter, this will also be extremely harmful... "Why was the *parasha* of *Sota* put next to the *parasha* of *Nazir*? Because whoever sees the *Sota* in her disgrace should make a Nazirite vow to refrain from wine." [It seems to be saying that] a person who did not see a *Sota* in her disgrace, and therefore has less knowledge about the evils of adultery, does not need to refrain from wine. Surely, one would think, it should be the other way around? ...But this confirms what we have been saying. The more a person sees and understands the evils of a certain situation... the more he needs to be on his guard against falling into the same sin. *He has not yet performed the practical actions which would prevent the knowledge from turning itself on its face...* Torah and knowledge take up a different form in a person, good or bad, in accordance with his character.[6]

We learn from his words the absolute necessity of multiplying good actions to the best of one's ability. Without this, learning *mussar* and even learning Torah are dangerous. Our Rabbis say of Torah itself: "If he has merit, the Torah becomes for him an elixir of life; if he has no merit, it becomes a deadly poison."[7] "If he has merit" means if he has purified himself with practical mitzva acts. This is the second function of these actions.

ACTIONS PRESERVE THOUGHTS

Actions can also serve to preserve the inward achievements of a person. "The shell preserves the fruit." Even if the spiritual perception is fixed in his heart, actions are still needed to preserve the clarity of his vision. Forgetfulness operates in the spiritual sphere just as it does in the intellectual. The mind sometimes remembers things by casual, external memory aids which may have nothing to do with the content of the memory. We read in the Talmud: "Does the Rav remember what Shemuel said to us when he was standing with one foot on the quay and one foot on the ferry? And he immediately remembered the statement which Shemuel had then made."[8]

As in the intellectual sphere, the inner insights experienced by a person easily fade. They can, however, be preserved by attaching them to externals. Thus our Rabbis say: "Whoever fixes a place for his prayers will be assisted by the God of Avraham."[9] It was Avraham who taught us this principle, as the verse states: "And Avraham rose early in the morning [and went] to the place where he had previously stood [in prayer] before the presence of God."[10] All the thoughts and feelings comprised in a person's prayers over a long period are concentrated in this one place, and all these associations are available to him when he stands at that place again. This considerably aids the level of inwardness of his present prayer and serves to guard it from the fading which we referred to above.

THE POWER OF ASSOCIATION

We also find Yitzhak making use of the associations connected with a holy place for the purpose of spiritual elevation. Yitzhak was especially attracted to the place called *Be'er Lahai Ro'ee* ["the well of the Living One Who sees me"]. When Rivka arrived with Eliezer from Padan Aram, they met Yitzhak, who had just come "from spending some time at *Be'er Lahai Ro'ee*."[11] This name was given by Hagar to the well, marking the place where the angel appeared to her after she ran away from her mistress Sara.[12] Ramban remarks on this: "It may well be... that

Yitzhak used to visit this place frequently. It served him as a place of prayer because it was there that the angel had appeared."[13] Later too we find that after the death of his father, "Yitzhak dwelled near *Be'er Lahai Ro'ee*,"[14] which *Targum Yonatan* translates as: "And Yitzhak dwelled near the well where the glory of the living and enduring One Who sees and is not seen had been revealed." He loved this place because of the intense spiritual elevation he derived from it. By standing there, he could visualize the great mercies Hashem showed all His creatures, even Hagar the Egyptian maidservant on her flight from Sara. He derived encouragement from this for his own situation, which—because of his self-critical attitude—he considered to be much lower than Hagar's.

Ya'akov, too, made a great effort to pray at the place which was sanctified by the prayers of his father and grandfather—Har Moria, the site of the '*Akeda*. The Rabbis tell us that on his journey to Harran, he passed by Har Moria without praying there. However, when he reached Harran, he said to himself: "How can I have passed by the place where my parents prayed without praying myself?" As soon as he set his mind to return—he immediately found himself at the place.[15]

We need to consider why, on the way to Harran, Ya'akov passed by that holy place—the site of the future Temple—without making use of the holiness of the place to elevate his prayers, while after he had arrived in Harran, he suddenly remembered to do this. To answer "it just happened like that" is unsatisfactory. Nothing happens by accident and we know that all the actions of our Fathers, as described in the Torah and all the words of *Hazal*, come to teach us fundamental principles.

THE IMPORTANCE OF EXTERNAL FACTORS

The solution is this. We know that the main attribute of
Ya'akov was the quality of truth. As a result, his desire
was to acquire his spiritual standing through the applica-
tion of the standard of strict justice. If a person needs
God's mercies to help him along the way, the level he has
attained is, in a sense, not truly his. Ya'akov therefore
wanted to minimize the external aids he received as much
as possible. This is the meaning of his declaration to
God:[16] "If God will be with me... and I return in peace to
my father's house, then *Hashem* shall be to me as *Elohim*."
That is to say, what others obtain only through the attribute of mercy [*Hashem*] I want to merit through the attribute of strict justice [*Elohim*]. As long as he was in Eretz
Yisrael, which is particularly conducive to the attainment
of high spiritual levels, he was able to realize this wish.
Therefore, he deliberately did not turn aside to spend
time at Har Moria; he felt he could do without external
associations.

However, when he reached Ḥarran, which is outside
Eretz Yisrael, he found that the spiritual atmosphere was
anything but conducive to inwardness. On the contrary,
the emphasis there was on external things and he saw that
he would have to expend extraordinary effort in order to
preserve his spiritual attainments. He therefore decided
that he needed all the help he could get. Now bitterly re-
gretting that he had not stopped at "the place where his
father and grandfather had prayed," he made up his mind
to return immediately, without even giving himself time
to rest from the arduous journey which he had just completed. (What would we have done if we had found ourselves in a similar situation? Say we had been visiting

Eretz Yisrael and had forgotten to stand in prayer at the spot nearest the site of the holy Temple—the *Kotel Ha-Ma'aravi*. Say we remembered this only after we had left Eretz Yisrael and arrived at our destination in *ḥutz la-aretz*. Which of us would immediately return to Eretz Yisrael to make good our failure to pray at the Kotel? And what if in the meantime it had become dangerous to visit Eretz Yisrael? But this is precisely what Ya'akov our Father did. He returned to Eretz Yisrael in spite of the danger awaiting him from his angry brother 'Esav.) Ya'akov's determination to return at once teaches us the utmost importance of seeking ways and means to preserve our spiritual level and the clarity of our spiritual insights. Nothing is more important than this. And it was the strength of his determination which created the miraculous shortening of his journey.

We should learn from this, in our lowliness, how much we need to struggle to make sure that all our interests are devoted to the holy Torah. We must insure that all our daily activities are bound up intimately with Torah and the service of Hashem. If we imprint upon them insights from the Torah, they may turn into important aids in preserving our inner spiritual values from the inroads of forgetfulness.

notes

---

1 *Sanhedrin* 106b.
2 Chapter 7, end.
3 Mitzva 16.
4 See above in "The Command of the '*Akeda*," paragraph "The Importance of Action."
5 *Avot* 3:16.
6 *Pri Ha-aretz, Naso.*
7 *Yoma* 72b.
8 *Kiddushin* 70b.
9 *Berachot* 6b.
10 *Bereshit* 19:27.
11 Ibid. 24:62.
12 Ibid. 16:14.
13 See note 11, above.
14 Ibid. 25:11.
15 *Hullin* 91b.
16 *Bereshit* 28:21.

Vayishlah

[This essay is taken from *Michtav Me-Eliyahu* III, pp.155–157.]

Ya'akov's Tests

Every *midda* comes to its perfection only when the person passes tests and trials which involve the opposite of that *midda*, as we saw in the case of Avraham Avinu.[1] If a person is working on abstention from unnecessary pleasures, he may be tested on whether he can eat a good meal "for the sake of heaven." Perfection in the *midda* of trust in God is tested by being put in a situation in which one has to work hard for his livelihood. These are the greatest tests of all. They clarify the true level of even the greatest *tsaddik*.

With this knowledge we can gain insight into some of Ya'akov Avinu's trials and tests. We are often puzzled by the fact that Ya'akov, whose *midda* was truth, was so often involved in situations in which he had to act in a manner which seemed to be the opposite of truth. As 'Esav exclaimed: "Is this why he is called Ya'akov, because he cheated me twice—once with the birthright and once with the blessing?"[2] Also, when Ya'akov entered Lavan's house and Raḥel said to him: "My father is a deceiver; you will not be able to get the better of him," he replied: "I am his equal in deception." She said: "Is it permitted for *tsaddikim* to practice deception?" He answered: "Yes, with a crooked person one must act crookedly."[3] And indeed, in the episode of the peeled sticks which he set up at the watering troughs,[4] it seems that he did adopt what appeared to be a questionable method.

But when we consider the principle we referred to above, it will be seen that our Father Ya'akov could reach the perfection of his *midda* of truth only by being given tests which would involve him in actions which were apparently false. His task was to carry out these actions with absolutely pure motives—solely for the sake of truth. This need to battle against falsehood would draw out of him the full power of truth. This no doubt involved a great struggle, but he emerged from his tests with his *midda* of truth greatly strengthened.

[Even when a test of this sort has been successfully passed, there is always the danger that the external action will leave some slightly adverse affect on the character. To counteract this, the *tsaddik* will use the first opportunity to go to the other extreme. Thus, if the test was in deception *le'shem Shamayim*, the *tsaddik* will perform a series of actions involving utmost honesty. When Ya'akov was overtaken by Lavan on his journey home and accused of "stealing his gods," Ya'akov reminded Lavan in no uncertain terms of the extremely honest and devoted service he had given him—something Lavan was unable to deny. "I have been twenty years in your service," Ya'akov declared, "and your ewe lambs never once lost their young... If an animal was torn by a wild beast, I paid for it out of my own pocket, [even though legally I did not need to]... In the day I was consumed by heat and in the night by frost; my sleep was driven from my eyes [when I got up in the night to tend to ewes in distress]."[5] It should be noted that the "twenty years" to which Ya'akov referred include the second seven years which Lavan tricked Ya'akov into serving without wages, by giving him Leah as a wife instead of Raḥel.[6] Lavan stole all the labor of those second seven years from him. Another person would have been tempted, in response, to lessen the devotion of his service, but Ya'akov had a task to fulfill. In the equally devoted service he gave Lavan during those stolen years, we see the tremendous honesty of Ya'akov Avinu. It may well be that by passing this prolonged test, he acquired the name of "the man of truth."[7]]

DID YA'AKOV PROSTRATE HIMSELF BEFORE 'ESAV?

The meeting between Ya'akov and 'Esav at the beginning of *parashat Vayishlaḥ*[8] also constituted a test of the type we have described above. Ya'akov behaved in an extremely subservient manner towards 'Esav. He called him "my lord" and himself "your servant," and at their meeting "he passed before them and he prostrated himself to the ground seven times until he had approached his brother."[9]

The Zohar[10] queries this apparent self-abasement. "How could Ya'akov, the most perfect of our Fathers, so prostrate himself before 'Esav, who represented idolatry and the power of evil?" The Zohar answers that the words "and he passed before them"[11] refer to the high and holy presence of God which was passing at that moment before them. "Ya'akov said: Now is the time to bow down before God... And so he did seven times until he approached his brother. Nowhere does it say that he prostrated himself to 'Esav. In fact, when he saw that God was passing before him, it was to God that he prostrated himself. Ya'akov would give such honor only to God."

Here again, Ya'akov seems to be acting dishonestly. Everybody thinks he is prostrating himself before 'Esav, but in fact he is prostrating himself before God. However, there is a deeper meaning in this. Every event can be seen in two ways: from the lower, external viewpoint and from the higher, spiritual viewpoint. Externally this was merely a case of the weaker party abasing himself before the stronger. As our Rabbis say: "When a fox has his hour, bow down to him."[12] But the Zohar shows us a different insight. From that very ordinary human situation Ya'akov elevated himself to a higher vantage point. He saw through the enemy with his military might; behind all this he saw the presence of God, Who decrees the facts of history. Behind all human actions stands God, Who uses everything to conform to His plan. It was no accident that the presence of God passed at that moment. With his heightened vision, Ya'akov beheld the hand of God behind all worldly power. Thus, when bowing down to 'Esav, he was in fact bowing down to the One behind him.

This was one of the typical tests which Ya'akov had to undergo, as we explained above. What is common to them all is that Ya'akov had to find the spiritual strength to transcend the external situation and attach himself to the spiritual truth beyond it and within it. Only when he emerged successfully from all these tests was his name changed from Ya'akov to Yisrael, which comes from the root *sara*, meaning "overcoming."[13]

TWO VIEWPOINTS ON *GALUT*

In this insight resides the secret of why the long, drawn out exile of the Jewish people never affected their collective soul or spirit. Even when they were compelled to submit to those who had power over them, it did not affect their spirit in the slightest. In their hearts, they saw their situation as Hashem's decree and nothing more.

They considered their enemies, with all their power, to be lowly and despicable. The humiliations which their enemies showered upon them, the Jews considered to be no more than the acts of wild beasts. Never did our enemies succeed even once in diminishing a Jew's sense of pride in what he was—his own inner worth.

So it was in earlier times. In later times, however, when our sense of our inner worth diminished, the value and significance of our enemies correspondingly increased in our eyes. We began to feel their contempt as something significant. We tried to ape our masters and follow in their ways. It was at this point that some felt the yoke of exile too hard to bear. Some wrongly saw in this an awakening of Jewish secular nationalism. But the truth is the precise opposite of this.

Jews in earlier generations were on a high spiritual level and the contempt of their enemies meant nothing to them. Only when they lost their spiritual pride did their enemies become great in their eyes. Instead of looking upon themselves from a spiritual vantage point, Jews began to see themselves through their enemies' eyes. True Jewish pride was lost.

We need to rediscover the greatness of our ancestors' spirit, to see events from a truly spiritual viewpoint. We must follow in the footsteps of our father Ya'akov and overcome our tests as he did. Then we will be elevated by them and change the darkness into light.

notes

1 See essay above, "Our Forefathers' Attributes."
2 *Bereshit* 27:36.
3 *Megillah* 13b, cited by Rashi, *Bereshit* 29:12.
4 *Bereshit* 30:37–42.
5 Ibid. 31:38–40.
6 Ibid. 29:26–27.
7 Micha 7:20.
8 *Bereshit* 32:3–33:16.
9 Ibid. 33:3.
10 I, 171b.
11 Ibid.
12 *Megillah* 16b.
13 *Bereshit* 32:29.

Vayeshev

Ya'akov and Yosef

Parashat Vayeshev begins with the words: "These are the generations of Ya'akov—Yosef..."[1] Rashi cites three reasons for the singling out of Yosef:

(1) Ya'akov's purpose in serving Lavan was to marry Rahel, Yosef's mother.

(2) Yosef's features and appearance resembled those of Ya'akov.

(3) Everything that happened to Ya'akov also happened to Yosef: both were hated; each had a brother who planned to kill him, etc.

The Midrash[2] finds many other resemblances, such as: "The mother of each was barren, bore two sons, and had difficulties during birth; both were shepherds; both were blessed with riches; both spent much time outside Eretz Yisrael; both died and were embalmed in Egypt; both asked to be buried in Eretz Yisrael, etc." We shall now try to explain this connection and the reasons for it.

YOSEF—A CONTINUATION OF YA'AKOV'S PORTION

It is well known that each person who comes into the world has a unique task to perform, which is his "portion" in the service of Hashem.[3] He is given all the means—*kelim*—which he will need in order to fulfill this purpose. These include both his mental characteristics and abilities and his property, environment, state of health and all the events which will occur in his lifetime. All these together provide the special tests and trials which he will endure during his life; the manner in which he reacts to these tests will constitute his spiritual portion in creation.

A person's children continue the service of their parents. This is why, in the majority of cases, children resemble their parents, both in their mental characteristics and their external appearance, since from these the tests which constitute their portion are woven. For the same reason, children inherit their parents' property. Since the portion of the children resembles that of the parents, it is only right that the residue of the parents' *kelim* should pass to the children.

The events of Ya'akov's and Yosef's lives are so alike because their portions in creation are closely linked.

RAHEL AND LEAH

"Ya'akov's purpose in serving Lavan was to marry Rahel."

In the first essay in this book, we described the mode of serving God that was applicable before Adam's sin and the different mode that was applicable after the sin. Before the sin, all service was on a much higher level, in which everything was seen in terms of truth and falsehood, and evil was seen as a mere illusion. After the sin, however, the world was seen in terms of two realities: good and evil. In that essay, we tried to explain in some depth the meaning of these two types of perceptions.

Before Ya'akov conquered the mysterious "man" who struggled with him in the night[4]—the guardian angel of

'Esav[5]—he was called Ya'akov; after this conquest, he was given the name Yisrael. The two names correspond to two different levels of service. Ya'akov's mode of service after his conquest of the angel corresponded to the mode of service before Adam's sin; his mode of service before that event corresponded to the level after Adam's sin. One could say that Ya'akov had two different "portions"—one on the lower level, corresponding to the name Ya'akov and one on the higher level, corresponding to the name Yisrael.

Rahel and Leah, too, represent two different spiritual goals. The portion of Rahel, who was distinguished by her beauty, corresponded to the lower portion, which the Zohar calls "the revealed world." On the other hand, Leah, who was not so beautiful, reflected the higher portion—"the hidden world."

A man and a woman have separate portions in creation. When they marry, these portions complement one another. Rahel and Leah corresponded to the two different modes of Ya'akov's service—Rahel to the level of "Ya'akov," and Leah to the level of "Yisrael."

[Ya'akov's entry into the mode of service called "Yisrael" coincided with his return to Eretz Yisrael, and this, in turn, coincided with the death of Rahel. Thus Leah was his sole helpmate during the period of his Yisrael-service, which included many of the years that he thought his beloved son Yosef was dead. During this time, Ya'akov was inconsolable, thinking that his life had been an utter failure.[6] This was service in the "hidden" world indeed. From the point of view of the lower, visible world, he had lost everything; there was nothing to hope for, neither in this world nor the next. This was Ya'akov's greatest test.

It should be noted that Rahel, whose task lay in "the re-

vealed world," had progeny who were eminently successful in making a *kiddush Hashem* in the visible world. Yosef
became viceroy of Egypt, sustained the family in famine,
and settled them in Egypt. Yehoshua, his descendant, led
the conquest of the Land of Israel. Leah, on the other
hand, whose task lay in "the hidden world," produced
Levi (Mosheh and Aharon) and Yehuda (David), through
whom God gave to Israel, respectively, the spiritual gifts
of Torah, priesthood, and the seed of *Mashiah*.]

TRUTH IS "GIVEN" TO YA'AKOV

Ya'akov reached perfection on the lower level through his
faithful service to Lavan, as we explained in the previous
essay. He acquired perfection in the quality of truth as a
heavenly gift, as the verse says: "You *give* truth to
Ya'akov."[7] In reward for his tremendous effort, this quality became a permanent part of his character, as well as
one of the main characteristics of his descendants: "For
the remnant of Israel do no injustice, nor do they speak
falsehood."[8] This was the crowning achievement in the
lower world represented by the name Ya'akov. As we saw
above, Ya'akov recognized that his most appropriate help
in this task would come from Rahel. This is why "Ya'akov's purpose in serving Lavan was to marry Rahel."

The task of Yosef, the son of Ya'akov and Rahel, was to
continue Ya'akov's portion. Indeed, Ya'akov's and Yosef's
portion together constituted one unified task. Ya'akov's
main characteristic, as we know, was truth—the perfection of truth—which corresponds to the *sefira* of *tiferet*. In
the state of perfection there are no inner contradictions.
The perfected personality unites and harmonizes all contradictions. *Tiferet* stands for harmony.[9]

The main quality of Yosef Ha-tsaddik corresponds to

the *sefira* of *yesod*, as the verse says: "The *tsaddik* is the foundation [*yesod*] of the world."[10] He, too, earned his *midda* with his outstanding loyalty and devotion in the service of his master, above all in his refusal to succumb to the temptations of his master's wife.[11] The quality of *yesod*, which is also the quality of righteousness and just behavior, includes everything within its scope, for justice is the foundation of everything. (In the verse from which the names of the *sefirot* are taken, *yesod* is referred to as "all that is in heaven and earth."[12]) Righteousness and justice have their source in truth. The *sefira* of *yesod* is a continuation of *tiferet*. It represents the active element which brings truth to bear on the affairs of everyday life. In this sense it can be said—as we mentioned above—that Yosef's task was a continuation of his father's.

YOSEF AS THE CHIEF PROGENY OF YA'AKOV

"Yosef resembled his father in facial characteristics."

This corresponds to what we wrote about the continuation of a person's portion into the next generation. Facial characteristics are part of the *kelim* a person receives in this world, and as we know, *kelim* correspond to the person's particular portion in creation. (You may refer here to the essay, "Avraham and the King of Sodom," where the concept of *kelim* is explained.) Maharal has some very insightful things to say about this matter as follows:

> Facial characteristics, when mentioned by *Hazal*, have a very deep import. Ya'akov was different from all other people in his facial characteristics... "The beauty of Ya'akov resembled the beauty of Adam,"[13] who was in the image of God. And Yosef merited the same distinction... because Ya'akov transferred all his own wis-

dom to him. He was able to absorb this because he was the main progeny of Yaakov... ["*The wisdom of a person shines in his face.*"[14]] This means that Ya'akov had a very elevated spiritual character. ["*The beauty of Adam*" refers to his spiritual level in Gan 'Eden *before the sin.*] None of these descriptions refer to physical matters. What *Hazal* are saying is that Yosef's qualities were of an extremely spiritual nature.[15]

We have quoted Maharal's language here (with some inserts) so that we can learn to what extent Maharal valued the clear and profound understanding of the Torah interpretations of *Hazal*.

HATRED BECAUSE OF VIRTUE

"Everything that happened to Ya'akov also happened to Yosef: both were hated..." A person may hate someone because he has done him harm. But there is also what is called "causeless hatred," which is the product of jealousy. "It has been established that 'Esav hates Ya'akov."[16] Even though in certain circumstances this may not be apparent to us, we should be aware of this and never forget it. In their heart of hearts, the children of 'Esav know that the purpose of creation and the ultimate redemption of mankind belong to us, *and this is why they hate us.*

In a similar sense, though obviously in a much attenuated form, Yosef's brothers hated him because in their heart of hearts they were aware of his special qualities. As Maharal said: "Ya'akov was hated by his brother because of his virtue... and for the same reason Yosef was hated by his brothers. What Ya'akov and Yosef had in common was that their high degree of spiritual refinement set them apart from the normal run of mankind, and for this reason they were hated and their lives were threatened. Just as

Ya'akov was set apart from 'Esav, so Yosef was set apart from his brothers because he was destined for kingship."[17]

Maharal's mention of kingship in connection with Yosef is very significant. Kingship has two aspects. First, the social aspect: kingship means government, and it is only the fear of government that deters people from "eating each other alive."[18] But there is also an inner aspect. From the honor and pomp surrounding royalty we can gain an inkling of the glory of the kingship of God. Our Rabbis tell us to take every opportunity to observe a king—even a nonJewish king. If we merit it, one day we will be able to see the difference between the gentile and the Jewish king—the *melech ha-Mashiah*.[19]

We see that when Yosef rose to the status of what can be termed royalty, he used his power to increase *kiddush Hashem* in Egypt—a process which would reach fulfillment in the exodus.

YOSEF'S KINGSHIP

Yosef used his power solely to teach the Egyptians about the absolute power of Hashem. Even when he was a slave in the house of Potifar, and later when he was in prison and very much dependent on the mercies of other people, the Torah states repeatedly that "God was with him,"[20] meaning that "the name of God was frequently on his lips."[21] He did not hide his allegiance to the God of Israel; on the contrary, he went out of his way to show everyone that his allegiance was not to the gods of Egypt, but to the Almighty. Even as a slave he showed kingship, showing independence and refusing to be daunted by his surroundings. He saw it as his task to teach the Egyptians about the true God.

Afterwards, when he stood before Pharaoh, a prisoner

seized from his dungeon to appear before the great king, he did not take advantage of this unique opportunity to obtain his release by guarding his speech so as not to say anything which might offend Pharaoh. Instead, when Pharaoh said: "I've heard that you are able to interpret dreams," Yosef answered: "It is not in my power; it is God who will attend to the welfare of Pharaoh."[22] Reckless of his own personal interest, Yosef found it necessary to use this opportunity to emphasize to the Egyptian king the absolute power of Hashem.

It was because of his independence of spirit and the intimations of kingship which he evinced that his brothers were jealous of him. As Maharal revealed to us, the deeper reason for their jealousy and hatred was the spiritual greatness which they discerned in him.

We see that the fates of Ya'akov and Yosef and the tests they had to undergo were closely related, reflecting their united portion in the creation.

YA'AKOV'S AND YOSEF'S SUFFERING

"Ya'akov wanted to dwell in peace. God said: 'Is the reward of the righteous in the World to Come not enough for them that they desire to live in peace in this world too?' Whereupon the fury of [the loss of] Yosef pounced upon him."[23]

We may be puzzled by the seeming harshness of this decree. Why indeed should the *tsaddikim* not be allowed to carry on their service in peace and quiet in this world after all the suffering and struggles they endured in the earlier part of their lives? But there is a deeper aspect to this.

In the prophecy of Malachi, God declares: "I will open for you the windows of heaven and shower upon you blessing until there is no more 'Enough!'"[24] The Gemara explains this as: "Until your lips wither away through saying 'Enough!'"[25] A very profound insight is contained in these words.

Some people do not want to take anything from their friends for the wrong reason: they simply do not want to be obliged to show gratitude. But there may be another reason. If a person feels that the gift is so wonderful that he will never be equal to the task of responding adequately, then his refusing the gift comes from a lofty motive. This is the reason why a *tsaddik* may feel compelled to say "Enough!" to the bounties of Hashem. He may feel himself so lowly and insignificant compared with the greatness of Hashem that he finds himself unable to thank God adequately for all His lovingkindness. He feels his own nothingness when he realizes his obligation to Hashem for the immeasurable bounties which Hashem has showered upon him. This thought is eloquently expressed in the *Nishmat* poem which we say in our Shabbat morning prayers:

> ...If our mouths were as full of song as the ocean, and our tongues exulted like the thundering of its waves, and our lips were as full of praise as the vastness of the sky, and our eyes as luminous as the sun and the moon, and our arms outstretched like the eagles of heaven, and our feet as fleet as antelopes—we would not be able to praise You, God, our God and God of our fathers, and to bless Your Name for even one million millionth part of all the bounties which You have bestowed upon our fathers and ourselves.

Hence, we can understand how a person might come to feel in the depth of his heart that God is bestowing upon him too much.

But this is still not the highest level. How does a person reach a level where he totally turns himself over to God's will? What is complete *devekut*? When a person comes to the point of feeling "Who am I not to want to be obligated for something which I cannot perform? I am so insignificant that it is not for me even to want or not to want anything. How can I, a lowly creature, have any will which is different from the will of my Creator? If it is His will that I should receive, how can I refuse?" This is what the Gemara means by "Until your lips wither away from saying 'Enough!'" There are no more lips, there is no longer any possibility of saying "Enough!" This is the highest blessing of all.

A *tsaddik* is judged by extremely high standards. For him, even a suspicion that he is exercising his own will instead of the will of his Creator—even for the highest motives—may be considered a sin. The attribute of strict justice asks "Is what they have in the next world not enough for them that they *want* to have peace and quiet in this world too?" The very wanting may, on their level, be considered a sin which requires expiation—"the fury of Yosef."

"SUFFERINGS OF LOVE"

Many people have great difficulty in understanding the concept of "sufferings of love" mentioned in the Gemara. "If a person sees that sufferings come upon him, he should examine his actions. If he has examined them and found nothing, he should attribute them to *bittul Torah* (not using his time to the fullest for learning Torah). If he still did not find anything wrong, he should know that they are 'sufferings of love'."[26] If a person is a *tsaddik* and fit for a higher *madrega*, but there is something in him—some attachment to the physical—which makes it impossible for him to attain that *madrega*, sufferings are bestowed upon him which cleanse his soul of that physical attachment. He is then purified and can reach the higher level. This is why they are called sufferings of love; they are a sign that Hashem loves him and wishes to bring him closer to Himself. But this applies only when the person accepts them with love. If he does not, this shows that he is not attached to Hashem and therefore they cannot be sufferings of love.[27]

This was the nature of the sufferings of Ya'akov and Yosef.

YOSEF'S TEST

Hazal tell us that when Ya'akov said of Yosef, "A wild animal has devoured him,"[28] a spark of the holy spirit spoke in him. Unknowingly, he was referring to the wife of Potiphar.[29] And when the two of them were left alone in the house and the verse says that Yosef "came into the house to do his work," *Hazal* tell us that Yosef was very close to succumbing to temptation, but the vision of his father's face appeared to him.[30]

It is difficult for us to understand how a *tsaddik* of Yosef's caliber—whose destiny was united with that of his father and who was so close to Hashem that his sufferings were "sufferings of love"—could even entertain the thought of such a sin.

We have found in our holy books that a *tsaddik* such as Yosef could indeed never have entertained the idea of such a sin in normal terms. We must remember that *Hazal* tell us that the wife of Potiphar—like Tamar, the daughter-in-law of Yehuda—had sincere motives for what she did; both their actions were "for the sake of heaven." The wife of Potiphar saw that her destiny was linked with that of Yosef. She was going to bear children from him, but she did not know whether they were to be from herself or from her daughter.[31] Yosef knew about this linking of their destinies and there was room for him to think that it was God's will that in these special circumstances he could override the normal *din*. He was about to act on this decision and it was very difficult for him to discover the error which lay behind it. In a similar situation, Yehudah and Tamar had brought forth the seed of the *Mashiah*,[32] and David made a similar mistake regarding Batsheva.[33] In such circumstances the hidden *yetzer* is extremely difficult to discern. Even Yosef Ha-tsaddik, who was so close to Hashem, thought for a moment that this might indeed be a holy act. But the vision of his father's face—Ya'akov the man of truth—helped him to realize the truth at the last moment, and he conquered his *yetzer*.

notes

1 *Bereshit* 37:2.
2 *Bereshit Rabba* 84:6.
3 See *Michtav Me-Eliyahu*, p. 155.
4 *Bereshit* 32:24.
5 Rashi ad loc.
6 *Bereshit* 37:35, Rashi.
7 *Micha* 7:20.
8 *Tzefania* 3:13.
9 See essay above "Our Forefathers' Attributes," subhead "Ya'akov."
10 *Mishlei* 10:25.
11 *Bereshit* 39:4–6.

12 *Divrei Ha-yamim I* 29:11. See also *Michtav Me-Eliyahu* V, p. 476.

13 *Bava Metzia* 84a.

14 *Kohelet* 8:1.

15 *Gur Aryeh* on *Bereshit* 37:2.

16 *Sifre Bemidbar* 9:10, cited by Rashi on *Bereshit* 33:4.

17 See note 13, above.

18 *Avot* 3:2.

19 *Berachot* 9b.

20 Ibid. 39:3, 23.

21 Rashi on *Bereshit* 39:3.

22 *Bereshit* 41:16.

23 Rashi, beginning of *Vayeshev*.

24 *Malachi* 3:10.

25 *Shabbat* 32b, end.

26 *Berachot* 5a.

27 *Netiv Ha-yesurim*, Chapter 1.

28 *Bereshit* 37:33.

29 *Bereshit Rabba* 84:19.

30 *Sota* 36b.

31 Rashi, *Bereshit* 39:1. *Hazal* tell us that Yosef's wife, Osnat, was in fact the daughter of the wife of Potiphar (*Bereshit* 41:45). Some say she was the adopted daughter of Potiphar's wife, being in fact the daughter of Dina by the Canaanite. (See *Da'at Zekenim Mi-Ba'alei Ha-Tosefot* on *Bereshit* 41:45.)

32 *Bereshit Rabba* 85:10.

33 *Sanhedrin* 107a.

Miketz

Preparations for the
Egyptian Exile, I

Many of Yosef's actions, which might seem puzzling at first sight, were undertaken in order to lighten the burden of the Egyptian exile, which he knew was coming, for the children of Israel.

Yosef saw his rise to power over the Egyptians as a God-given means of helping his brethren. By supplying the needs of the Egyptians during the famine, he was building up a store of good will towards himself and his people. He hoped that this would make it more difficult for the Egyptians to enslave his people, and we know this was effective for a while.

Yosef's rise to quasi-regal status was, as we said, a divine gift. It was an "awakening from above," which could not take place without a prior "awakening from below."[1] Yosef had to supply this a "awakening from below" through the tests and sufferings which preceded his quasi-royal appointment. He had to be sold as a slave—and by his own brothers—and in the worst possible location. Egypt was known as the country from which no slave could escape, and it treated its slaves with extreme harshness. Once his situation eased because his master noticed he was successfuly running his estate, Yosef had to face the extremely difficult test posed by his master's wife. After this, instead of being rewarded for passing the test, he was thrown into prison, from which there was no foreseeable chance of escape. In spite of all this, he maintained his faith in God to the full. This formed the awakening from below which, so to speak, enabled Hashem to bestow upon him the gift of rulership which was an essential prerequisite for the Egyptian exile and the emergence of Israel as the people of God.

In one very difficult passage in this *parasha*, we learn that Yosef ordered the Egyptians to circumcise themselves. When they complained to Pharaoh about this, he told them to obey Yosef without question.[2] We might well ask, What was the purpose of this? Circumcision was not one of the mitzvot which applied to Egyptians. It meant nothing to them, as Pharaoh said, "Even if he tells you to cut off parts of your flesh and feed them to the birds, you had better listen to him."[3] Is there any virtue to a mitzva performed in such a manner?

Maharal discloses to us a profound thought behind Yosef's action. It is impossible, he tells us, for anyone to benefit from the merit of a *tsaddik* unless he, the recipient, bears some resemblance—even outwardly—to the *tsaddik*'s primary *midda*. Since Yosef's *midda*, as we know, was "the *tsaddik* is the foundation of the world," which is particularly concentrated on preserving the sanctity of the *brit mila*, the Egyptians had to be circumcised—at least outwardly—if they were to benefit from the merit of Yosef.[4]

I have seen another reason advanced for what Yosef did, which also is very significant. Normally, the uncircumcised hold the circumcised in contempt. Yosef was apprehensive lest, when the Israelites later settled among them, the Egyptians would hold them in contempt and might even try to prevent them from practicing circumcision—the only mitzva which at that time singled them out as the people of Hashem. To avoid this, Yosef decided the Egyptians should experience circumcision themselves.

Yosef's actions during the famine, which resulted in the impoverishment of the Egyptian landowners and the amassing of great wealth in the hands of Pharaoh,[5] also seem puzzling. This, too, was a farsighted provision for something which would occur only much later. He wanted this wealth to be readily available for the time of the redemption when, as God promised, they would go out "with great riches."[6]

Another apparently incomprehensible act of Yosef was to move the population *en masse* from city to city. Our Rabbis tell us that he did this so that all the Egyptians would be "strangers." This, he hoped, would remove the stigma of being "foreigners" from his brethren when later they would be "strangers in a strange land."[7]

We see that in all his seemingly puzzling actions Yosef had only the best motives—to mitigate as much as possible the future suffering of his brethren in their long-predicted exile.

YOSEF'S DIFFICULT PROJECT

[This idea will also shed light on one of the most puzzling aspects of the narrative. Why did Yosef not notify his father of his whereabouts as soon as he could? And why did he, later on, afflict such mental anguish on his brothers by accusing them of being spies, with all that this entailed? It would be foolish indeed to think that he treated his brothers in this way as an act of vengeance, God forbid. The Torah banishes all such thoughts from our minds by emphasizing several times that Yosef was moved to tears at certain points in the story.[8]

The only clue which the Torah gives us to Yosef's motives is: "And Yosef remembered the dreams which he had dreamt about them and he accused them of being spies, etc."[9] Ramban explains that Yosef's motive in all this was to get his eleven brothers to bow down before him, thus fulfilling his dreams.

Rabbi Yitzḥak Arama, however, in his 'Akedat Yitzḥak[10] insists that a wise man does not allow his dreams to dominate his life. In his opinion, Yosef was not able to notify his father earlier; he was afraid that his sudden reappearance would lead to a rift which might break up the family. His purpose was to maneuver the brothers into a situation where they would have the option of leaving Binyamin in slavery or sacrificing themselves to save him. Through this test Yosef would know whether they had fully repented of their sin toward him. In this case, he could safely reappear without causing a rift in the family. But however good this explanation is, it does not explain the Torah's mention of the dreams as the apparent motive for his actions.

Rabbi Y. Arama's explanation is satisfactory on the ordinary level. But on a deeper level a different picture emerges. The dreams of a true tsaddik, say our Rabbis,[11] are likely to be true dreams. Ya'akov Avinu "took note" of Yosef's dreams,[12] meaning that he anticipated their fulfillment.[13] Now the first dream showed Yosef in a dominant position in connection with sheaves in a field. This is a clear reference to Yosef's future role as dispenser of grain. The second dream, however, showed the eleven brothers as stars. The first occasion when the descendants of Avraham are called "stars" is in the prophecy of the Covenant between the Pieces,[14] the same prophecy that foretells the Egyptian exile.[15] Yosef understood that he would dominate his brothers in this connection, too. As in the case of Pharaoh's dream, Yosef took this as an indication that some action was expected of him. (According to Maharal,[16] the sun and moon in the dream symbolize the forces of nature, and these too were to come under the dominance of Yosef and his descendant, Yehoshua.[17]) What could be the purpose of such an act of domination?

It is mentioned in our holy books that Yosef's motive in subjecting his brothers to false accusations and temporary oppression was to foreshadow the Egyptian exile. Here was a high Egyptian official ill-treating the representatives of the future tribes of Israel. But this was only outwardly. In truth, behind the Egyptian disguise was Yosef Ha-tsaddik, who loved them with all his heart and was moved to tears by their distress. (This symbolizes the nature of every exile; behind the outward form of the oppressor stands the loving presence of Hashem.[18]) The suffering of a *tsaddik* can atone for a whole generation.[19] Perhaps the suffering of these great *tsaddikim* could lighten the burden of the Egyptian exile from the shoulders of the coming generations.[20]

In this way Yosef undertook the most difficult—and perhaps the most dangerous[21]—of his projects to mitigate the forthcoming exile.]

notes

1 See *Strive for Truth!* IV, *Sanctuaries in Time*, pp. 16–17.

2 See Rashi on *Bereshit* 41:55.

3 *Bereshit Rabba* 91:5.

4 *Gur Aryeh* ad loc.

5 *Bereshit* 47:13–26.

6 Ibid. 15:14.

7 Ibid. 41:21, Rashi. In the next verse, we read that Yosef freed the Egyptian priests from taxes and gave them a special allocation of food. It seems strange that he should give special privileges to the idolatrous priests of Egypt. And what are we to learn from this? It has been suggested that this, too, was an example of his preparing for the forthcoming exile. He established a precedent that religious leaders should be exempt from taxation. He hoped that thereby the tribe of Levi, who were to be the religious leaders of Israel, would be exempt from any decrees that might later be imposed on the people of Israel. And as we know, this actually happened.—Rabbi Ya'akov Kamenetzky, *Emet Le'Ya'akov, parashat Vayigash.* (A.C.)

8 *Bereshit* 42:24, 43:30, 45:2.

9 Ibid. 42:9.

10 *Sha'ar* 29 and 30.

11 Zohar 199b.

12 *Bereshit* 37:11.

13 Rashi *ad loc.*

14 *Bereshit* 15:5.

15 Ibid. 15:13.

16 *Gevurot Hashem*, second introduction.

17 *Bereshit Rabba* 84:11.

18 See above on *parashat Vayishlah*.

19 *Bereshit Rabba* 33:3, see *Michtav Me-Eliyahu* IV, p. 201.

20 Compare the essay, "Causes of the Egyptian Exile" (end), above.

21 Because it is always dangerous to ill-treat people, even out of the highest motives. (A.C.)

Vayigash

Preparations for the
Egyptian Exile, II

Above we discussed Yosef's preparations for the Egyptian exile, which began well before the actual descent of his family into Egypt.

Our Father Ya'akov, too, made his preparations, all of which were of a spiritual nature.

"And the children of Israel carried Ya'akov their father."[1] This refers to the descent of the family to Egypt. Here the brothers are called "the children of Yisrael" while their father is called Ya'akov. What does this teach us?

Ya'akov as an individual is here called Ya'akov because he is going to end his life in Egyptian exile. The fact that the brothers are now for the first time called the children of Yisrael indicates that Ya'akov must have encouraged them to think of themselves as the future nation of Yisrael.

Indeed, Rabbi Ovadia Seforno writes: "They are called 'the children of Israel' because from now on they have to become the nation of that name. They have to strive with spiritual beings and men who will rise up against them now that they are going to a foreign country."[2] The meaning is that they will now have to elevate themselves to the level of "the children of Yisrael," the higher level; they cannot remain on the level of "the children of Ya'akov." They need this higher spiritual level in order to withstand the pressures of exile. This was Ya'akov's first preparation.

On the words "their father Ya'akov," Seforno comments: "[*Ya'akov* comes from the root *'akev*—"heel".] Now that he is going to his final joy [to meet his son Yosef] after all the troubles which had befallen him, he will be shown what will happen in the 'heel' of time—that is, at the end of days." The meaning is that through his joy in the recovery of Yosef, he was elevated to a height which enabled him to envisage the "end of days," that is the coming of the final redemption. This was the second preparation: to be in a state of joy and heightened emotion, through which he would be able to discern and envisage the coming of *Mashiah*.

When at last Yosef met his father, the verse tells us that Yosef wept a great deal when he kissed his father. But Ya'akov apparently did not kiss his son, nor did he weep.[3] Our Rabbis say that at that moment he was reading the *Shema*'. Why should he have been reading the *Shema*' just at that moment? Maharal explains: "When Ya'akov saw that his son was a king, the love and awe of Hashem filled his heart... This is the way of our Hassidim; on every occasion of happiness they enter into a state of *devekut* with Hashem in gratitude for all the good He has bestowed upon them. This is what is meant by 'reading the *Shema*'' [which contains the words 'and you should love Hashem...with all your heart and all your soul']... When he recovered Yosef after all the anguish which he had suffered on his account and when he now saw him to be a king, he loved Hashem who had given him all this and accepted His kingship with [reinforced] love."[4]

The *Sefat Emet*[5] explains this somewhat differently. "The reason [why Ya'akov did not kiss Yosef] was that he did not want his personal love for Yosef to make him forget his love for the Creator. Therefore he deliberately entered into a state of *devekut* with Hashem before he met Yosef; all physical love was forgotten [and he was therefore unable to show his love for Yosef]."

Earlier, Ya'akov did not mind showing his love for Yosef. He made him a special tunic and lavished his love upon him in other ways. This personal love became a vehicle for his feeling of gratitude and his desire to bless Hashem. A person should indeed enjoy himself in this world so that he can approach God in a state of gratitude and bless Him with a full heart. This is why *Hazal* tell us that a person who denies himself pleasure in this world is called a sinner.[6] What changed? The answer is that Ya'akov Avinu did all this when he was in Eretz Yisrael, the place of holiness. But in Egypt, the place of defilement, he preferred not to enter into any this-worldly enjoyment, even in the form of personal affection. He transferred all this to Hashem and converted it to the love of Hashem. He was afraid that otherwise it might be contaminated by the defilement of Egypt. Here we have another example of Ya'akov's extraordinary spiritual preparation for the benefit of his children, to strengthen their resistance to the evil influences of Egypt.

THE NEED FOR STRENGTH IN EXILE

The Egyptian exile was different in many respects from the exiles which Israel would subsequently experience.

The Egyptians were extremely proud of their science and wisdom, of their ability to create structures which would remain wonders of the world for thousands of years. They looked with contempt upon every other nation. This was the chief difficulty presented by Israel's exile in their land. Egypt was known to us as the *Gehinnom* of the spirit—the depth of moral degradation.[7] We see that in spite of all the preparations discussed in this and the previous essay, Israel eventually, under the influence of the Egyptians, descended to the "forty-ninth gate of defilement."[8] Why did Egypt have such an effect on them? Because being held in contempt by others can significantly cripple one's spiritual advancement. The redemption from Egypt essentially was a redemption from this state of mind. Freedom for Israel meant they would be free from the psychological pressures brought to bear by Egypt's culture. Redemption meant that they would be free to appreciate their own spiritual value as Israelites—the people of God.

In our time, too, we suffer from the destructive influence of the surrounding culture. Strange and distorted values dominate our streets and cities. And with what contempt do the proponents of these perverted values look upon us, the bearers of the truth of Torah! And what effort they expend trying to persuade us to adopt their twisted viewpoints! Any reader who is prepared to examine the depths of his heart will see to what extent they have succeeded. *This is the Egyptian exile of today.* To resist these inroads, we must summon up all the reserves of spiritual strength which are available to us through devoted attachment to our holy Torah.

notes

1 *Bereshit* 46:5.
2 See *Bereshit* 32:29.
3 *Bereshit* 46:29.
4 *Gur Aryeh* ad loc.
5 *Vayigash* 5637.
6 *Ta'anit* 11a, see *Michtav Me-Eliyahu* III, p. 153.
7 See *Strive for Truth!* IV, *Sanctuaries in Time*, p. 12.
8 Ibid.

Vayeḥi

[This essay is taken from *Michtav Me-Eliyahu* III, p. 187.]

| 181

Kelim for the Service of Hashem

We have already discussed the concept of *kelim* for the service of Hashem.[1] In His great goodness, Hashem has bestowed upon us innumerable *kelim*—vehicles and instruments which we can use to develop our spiritual service. These include parents, teachers, rabbis, books, ideas, places, and situations—everything and everyone we meet can be the means for our spiritual elevation.

Hashem has also bestowed upon us further *ḥessed* by allowing new *kelim* to emerge when needed. A great *tsaddik* may feel that the available *kelim* are not sufficient. Hashem may then help him produce a new type of *keli* which then can become everyone's property.

We find this idea in the *Midrash*:[2]

> Avraham asked for [the signs of] old age. He spoke before God: Lord of the Universe! A man and his son enter a place together and no one knows to whom honor is due. If You were to adorn him with signs of old age, this problem would be solved. God replied to him: By your life! You have asked for a good thing and it shall commence with you. From the beginning of the book

[Bereshit] until now ["And Avraham was old"³], old age is not mentioned. When Avraham arose, he was given old age.

Yitzhak asked for suffering. He spoke before God: Lord of the Universe! If a person has never suffered during his life, how will he face the attribute of justice? ...You have asked a good thing; it shall commence with you. When Yitzhak our Father arose, sufferings were given to him, as it says: "When Yitzhak became old, his eyes became dim and he could not see."⁴

Ya'akov asked for illness. He said: ...If a man does not fall ill a short time before his death, how will he be able to arrange matters between his children? If he is ill for two or three days, this problem is solved... You have asked a good thing; it shall commence with you. The first reference to sickness in the Torah is in the verse, "Yosef was told that his father was sick."⁵

Avraham's main characteristic, as we know, was loving-kindness—*hessed*. From *hessed* comes the desire to sincerely honor another person in order to give him pleasure. This is why it was Avraham who felt it was a problem that he could not immediately distinguish the person he needed to honor. He felt the need for a new *keli* and Hashem granted his wish. He truly and sincerely felt that the signs of old age would help him in his service of Hashem.

Our Father Yitzhak's main mode of service was in the aspect of strict justice—*middat ha-din*. From this view-point, he felt the need for a *keli* that would arouse a person to repentance. He needed a hint that all was not well with him; from his physical illness he would learn a lesson re-garding his spiritual deficiency. Therefore he asked Hashem for suffering, and blindness is certainly a form of suffering.

Ya'akov our Father was a "simple man."[6] His chief *midda* was truth, which—as we shall see—enables a person to make peace among conflicting factors and harmonize opposites. It was he who saw that there would be no peace among his heirs if he had no time before his death to give his personal instructions to his family and to sort out all possible points of conflict among them in the spirit of truth. People possess different characteristics and peace can never rule among them without the *midda* of truth. When striving for truth, each person yearns to fulfill his particular task in the world, which is the portion allotted to him personally by Hashem. Truth will show him how false it is to be jealous of someone else's portion. Under the influence of truth, he will see that only through the united effort of different people can the final result be attained. Each complements the other and peace and harmony will crown their efforts. Ya'akov felt that he needed a warning signal that death was near so that he would have time to insure that peace reigned among his heirs.

We see that each of our *Avot* invented the *keli*—for the benefit of all the people in the world who serve Hashem —which was most appropriate for his own particular characteristic.

notes

1 See above in the essay, "Avraham and the King of Sodom."
2 *Bereshit Rabba* 65:9.
3 *Bereshit* 24:1.
4 Ibid. 27:1.
5 Ibid. 48:1.
6 Ibid. 25:27.

Shemot

[This essay is taken from *Michtav Me-Eliyahu* III, p. 105.]

The Value of
Small Actions

In the *Midrash Rabba* on *Shemot*[1] we find an apparently puzzling statement.

> God does not give greatness to a person before testing him with a small matter. Only after this, does He raise him to greatness.
>
> Two of the greatest men in the world were tested by God with a small matter. When they were found trustworthy in this, He raised them to greatness.
>
> He tested David with sheep and he led them into the desert [the uninhabited part of Eretz Yisrael] in order to prevent them from trespassing on other people's property...
>
> And so with Mosheh: "He led the sheep into the desert"[2] to avoid trespass. And God took him to shepherd His people Israel, as the verse says: "You led Your people like sheep by the hand of Mosheh and Aharon."[3]

We have to understand why testing with a small action should be preferred to testing with a greater or more difficult action.

THE PURIM MONEY

The Gemara tells us another case of a "small action" eliciting an enthusiastic response from one of the *Tanna'im*.

> At the time of the Roman decrees against learning Torah, Rabbi Ḥanina ben Teradion risked his life by gathering large audiences to teach Torah in public. He paid a visit to Rabbi Yose ben Kisma, a great sage of his generation, who was gravely ill.
>
> As soon as he entered, Rabbi Yose said to him, "What's this I hear that you teach Torah to large audiences in public, with a *sefer Torah* in your arms? Do you not know that this nation [the Roman Empire] has been empowered by God to destroy the Temple and put to death the best of our people, and it is still as powerful as ever?"
>
> He replied, "May Heaven show mercy."
>
> Rabbi Yose answered: "My words are words of reason, and you say 'May Heaven show mercy'? I shall be surprised if they don't burn you at the stake together with the *sefer Torah*!"
>
> Rabbi Ḥanina replied, "Rabbi, what are my prospects for the World to Come?"
>
> Whereupon Rabbi Yose asked: "Can you tell me anything that you have done?"
>
> Rabbi Ḥanina told him that once he had money which he had set aside for his Purim meal and, beside it, money which had been collected for charity, and the two lots of money became mixed. Instead of repaying himself the amount he needed for his Purim meal, he distributed all of it to charity.
>
> Upon hearing this, Rabbi Yose exclaimed, "If this is what you did, I only hope that my share in the World to Come will be similar to yours."[4]

This again is very difficult. Why should this small act be greater than his readiness to sacrifice his life for teaching Torah? And why was Rabbi Yose ben Kisma so enthusiastic about the sacrifice of a few shekels?

The difficulty is even greater when we remember that Rabbi Yose ben Kisma was the *Tanna* who could not be tempted by a very large sum of money to leave his hometown. He said: "Even if you were to give me all the money and precious stones in the world, I would not leave a place of Torah."[5] Why should a man for whom all the money in the world meant nothing be so impressed by the sacrifice of a few shekels?

THE VALUE OF HALF A *PERUTA*

The solution is this. Large actions do not always reflect the true spiritual status of the person who does them. They may be done as a result of momentary enthusiasm, which may be external in nature. Again, great things may be undertaken with an eye to the public, giving no indication of the person's inner worth.

A person's true character—his true *madrega*—is revealed, rather, in the little things to which he may attach no special importance at the time. Our Rabbis say that Iyov's greatness was shown in the fact that he overlooked half a *peruta*. Say that he owed a workman half a *peruta* for some small job that he had done. There was no half-*peruta* coin, so Iyov suggested that they go to the nearest grocery store and buy a small loaf of bread or a couple of eggs to the value of a *peruta* and then divide them between them. When it came to that point, however, Iyov would not take his share. Instead, he insisted on the workman taking the whole loaf or all the eggs. He felt it would not be right to be particular about half a *peruta*.[6] This is not trivial, but shows Iyov's true character. Greed for money operates even in relation to insignificant amounts, and many shop-keepers tend to "even up" the odd coin in their own favor. A person's true character is revealed by his attitude to the smallest things.[7]

Since one's position in 'Olam ha-ba is determined by the degree of "inwardness"—*lishma*—that one has attained,[8] we understand why Rabbi Yose ben Kisma thought so highly of that apparently insignificant act of Rabbi Ḥa-nina. Giving one's life for Torah did not rate so highly in his eyes. After all, the person is well aware that he is doing a great thing which will make him a spiritual hero of Is-rael. The little act, which no one knew about and which flowed imperceptibly from his inmost heart, showed his true *madrega* in relation to 'Olam ha-ba.

notes

1 *Shemot Rabba* 2:3.
2 *Shemot* 3:1.
3 *Tehillim* 76:21.
4 *Avoda Zara* 18a.
5 *Avot* 6:10.
6 *Bava Batra* 15b and Rashi s.v. *minhag*.
7 Rabbi Dessler attributes this thought to his father, R. Reu-ven Dov, and terms it "a wonderful psychological insight."
8 Rambam, *Commentary on the Mishna*, end of *Massechet Makkot*.

Va'era

Hardening
Pharaoh's Heart

Our great commentators have given various interpretations of how God hardened Pharaoh's heart. We shall explain a few of them below.

RASHI—"Since he had already acted wickedly...and it is well known to Me [God] that the nations do not repent sincerely, it is better for Me that his heart should harden so that I can multiply my signs, etc."[1]

RAMBAM explains that because of his previous sins, justice required that the ways of *teshuva* should be unavailable to him. He writes: "It is possible that a person might commit...so many great sins so that the True Judge may decide that the just punishment for the sins he committed of his own free will is that repentance is withheld from him...so that he shall die and perish by his sins. In this sense we can understand what God said through the prophet Yesha'ya [6:10], 'Make fat the heart of these people. Make their ears deaf, turn away their eyes, lest they see with their eyes and hear with their ears and understand with their heart and repent and be healed.'...In this sense we are also to understand the words of the Torah,

'And I will harden the heart of Pharaoh.'"[2]

RAMBAN offers two explanations. In his first, he offers an explanation similar to Rambam's, but in his second he explains that God hardened his heart to enable him to withstand the plagues, so that he would not repent merely out of fear.[3]

IBN EZRA's explanation is somewhat obscure. The meaning seems to be that the hardening of his heart was a natural consequence of his own character. It is attributed to God only because all natural occurrences stem in the final analysis from God. Therefore, whether the verse says "Pharaoh hardened his heart" or "God hardened Pharaoh's heart" makes no difference. He is punished for this because a person has the power to change his nature.[4]

RABBI YITZHAK 'ARAMA maintains that the hardening of Pharaoh's heart does not mean that God prevented him from doing *teshuva*. It means, rather, that God gave him full rein to act out his evil intentions to the bitter end, and thus bring about his own destruction,[5] as the Rabbis say: "A person is led in the path that he chooses for himself."[6] This is attributed to God because God gave him every opportunity to pursue his evil designs to the full. He did this by bringing the plagues one after the other and by giving Pharaoh relief between each plague. This is consistent with *Hazal*'s statement: "If a person wishes to defile himself, the way is laid open before him."[7] Similarly, God "hardened the spirit of Sihon"[8] by showing him an apparent weakness in Israel, in that they showed no resistance to Edom.[9]

SEFORNO writes, "He prevented him from offering an insincere *teshuva*, coming merely from the severity of the plagues."[10] This is equivalent to Ramban's second explanation.

ANALYZING THE EXPLANATIONS

We know very well that the defilement brought about by the sin is itself the punishment for the sin—"The reward of a mitzva is the mitzva itself, and similarly the punishment of the sin is the sin itself."[11] Through a sin, the sinner loses his spiritual essence and all his pain and suffering are included in this. It emerges, therefore, that the explanations of Rashi, Rambam, and Ramban, in his first explanation, are all equivalent. Also, when Ibn Ezra and R. Yitzhak 'Arama insist that the punishment is a "natural" consequence of the sin, they are speaking from the external viewpoint which sees the punishment as something different from the sin. From the inner view there is no difference whether we call this natural or not. The "natural" consequence is part of God's decree concerning the consequences of sin.

A SIN REPEATED

The *Midrash Rabba* expounds this subject as follows:

> Rabbi Yohanan says: This verse seems to give heretics an opportunity to assert that Pharaoh was denied the ability to do *teshuva*... Rabbi Shimon ben Lakish replied: The wicked can say nothing. "God scoffs at the scoffers."[12] If God warns a person once, twice, or three times and he does not respond, He locks the doors of his heart in order to punish him for his previous sins. Similarly, Pharaoh was warned five times by God, but took no notice. God said to him: You have hardened your neck and deadened your heart; I will add to you defilement over and above the defilement you have caused yourself.[13]

A person sins because a spirit of madness comes upon

him.[14] Afterwards, he comes to his senses and regrets his act. The Rabbis say: "The wicked are full of regrets."[15] But "When a person has sinned and repeated his sin, the sin appears to him as if it were permitted."[16] The madness has established itself in his mind and has now become a matter of principle. This reminds me of a story I heard about someone who was seriously ill with diabetes. (This was before the discovery of insulin.) Unfortunately, he was very fond of eating sweet things. He saw some chocolate, could not resist the temptation, and began to eat it. At first he was annoyed with himself, knowing that he was endangering his life. After he had taken two or three pieces, he decided he might as well enjoy it, saying to himself: "Eat, drink, and be merry for tomorrow you may die."[17] And this is precisely what happened; within a year and a half, he was dead. His regret came only when the spirit of madness lifted for a moment. When he repeated the offense, it became a matter of principle, and then there was no more possibility of repentance.

This is the meaning of the above *midrash*. "The sin becomes as if permitted" and "I will add defilement to your own defilement" are identical.[18] The adding of defilement is not a new decree; it is a natural consequence.

TWO FORMS OF *TESHUVA*

Ramban's second explanation, which is identical to that of Seforno, may be explained by the following *gemara*.

> Rabbi Eliezer says: If Israel does *teshuva*, they will be redeemed; if not, they will not be redeemed. Rabbi Yehoshua replied to him: If they do not do *teshuva*, they will not be redeemed? [Surely God has promised Israel that *Mashiah* will come sooner or later?] But God will

raise up against them a king whose decrees are worse than Haman's and Israel will do *teshuva*...[19]

Maharal asks: It seems that both Rabbi Eliezer and Rabbi Yehoshua agree that Israel will do *teshuva*, so what is their dispute? He answers that there are two types of *teshuva*, one forced and one voluntary.[20]

The explanation is this. Suffering can have two effects. It may bring a person to *teshuva* because his experience arouses him to recognize the spark of truth in his own heart. Suffering may, however, simply break a person's will. His desires become weakened by his many tribulations. The difference is that in the second case, if the sufferings are removed, his desires—and his sins—will return. But even this is a kind of *teshuva*. At the moment, at least, he is not sinning. But it is not true *teshuva* because the evil is still established in his heart.

The true purpose of all punishments is that the person should learn from them to come to complete repentance and sincerely correct his ways. There is, however, a possibility that the person will merely be cowed by the suffering; he stops sinning, not because of repentance, but because he can no longer stand the suffering. If this happens, the true purpose of suffering has been frustrated. In His mercy, God acts to strengthen the heart of the sinner so that he is not subdued by the sufferings before learning from them to arrive at sincere repentance.

In the case of Israel at the end of the exile, when redemption can no longer be delayed and the "generation is totally guilty,"[21] even this second type of repentance will be accepted. The *yetzer ha-ra'* will be wiped out by the suffering and people will stop sinning. After this, God will reveal His glory by means of His righteous *Mashiah*, who will teach Israel the true ways of life.

THE GREATER THE PERSON, THE GREATER THE *YETZER*

Our Rabbis have said: "The greater the person, the greater his *yetzer ha-ra'*."[22] There is a simple reason for this. If the greater person, who has overcome all his trials, did not have his *yetzer ha-ra'* increased, he no longer would have any opportunity to exercise his free will. God, therefore, decreed that a person should never lose his *behira*. Whenever a person has achieved a spiritual triumph and has come out into the light, his horizon is darkened by renewed obscurity and a new challenge presents itself. This is the difference between a *tsaddik* and a *rasha'*. The *tsaddik* chooses good, even when the scale of good and evil is evenly balanced before him. The *rasha'*, on the other hand, will not choose good and shows no desire for it, even though he could easily have chosen it, since the good and evil are in equilibrium in his heart.

When Pharaoh saw all the wonders wrought by Mosheh and Aharon, all the miracles of the ten plagues, Pharaoh came to realize the power of Hashem. He became, in a sense, "greater." To balance this, God had to strengthen his *yetzer ha-ra'*—harden his heart—in order to restore the equilibrium of *behira*.

In conclusion: The hardening of Pharaoh's heart was not an extraordinary event. It is repeated in the heart of every person during his struggles with his *yetzer ha-ra'*. We should note that "I will harden Pharaoh's heart" is translated by Targum Yonatan as "I will harden the *yetzer* of Pharaoh's heart.[23] This whole episode teaches us a great deal about the workings of the *yetzer ha-ra'* in every human heart.

notes

1 On *Shemot* 7:3.

2 *Hilchot Teshuva* 6:3.

3 See note 1, above.

4 On *Devarim* 5:26.

5 *'Akedat Yitzhak, Sha'ar* 36.

6 *Makkot* 10b.

7 *Yoma* 38b.

8 *Devarim* 2:30.

9 *Bemidbar* 20:21.

10 See note 1, above.

11 *Avot* 4:2. See *Strive for Truth!* III, pp. 210–211.

12 *Mishlei* 3:34.

13 *Shemot Rabba* 13:3.

14 *Sotah* 3a.

15 See *Nedarim* 9b.

16 *Moed Katan* 27a.

17 See *Yesha'ya* 22:13.

18 *Maharal, Netivei Ha-teshuva*, Chapter 1.

19 *Sanhedrin* 97b.

20 *Netzah Yisrael*, Chapter 31.

21 See note 19, above.

22 *Kiddushin* 52b.

23 *Shemot* 7:3 and pass.

Bo

Instrumental Causes
and Underlying Causes

Say a person travels a long way from his hometown to Jerusalem. I happen to meet him and ask, "Oh, hi! What brought you here?" If he replies, "An airplane," I understand he is evading the true answer. But if he says, "To learn Torah," this is a good answer. I was not asking for the instrumental cause—Boeing jet or otherwise—but for the underlying cause, that is, the end or purpose he had in mind in coming here.

This seems very simple. But how often do we overlook this distinction when we are discussing our everyday affairs? We find that ordinarily we devote our main interest to the instrumental causes of things and think very little about the underlying causes. When someone is sick, God forbid, our questions are usually directed to the instrumental causes: How did he catch this disease? What were the circumstances? Had he been run down, etc.? Even if the question asked is, Why did he get this disease?, we still think in terms of the instrumental causes. Only very rarely do we pose the question, Why did Hashem allow me to catch this disease?

The materialistically inclined person sees in everything only the hand of chance. Ultimate purposes are beyond him. The spiritual person, on the other hand, is primarily interested in the purpose and much less in the instrumental causes. To such a person, it is as clear as the sun at noon that everything that happens in this world has a spiritual purpose. Its purpose may be to awaken us or to teach us or to challenge us. We can be quite sure that it has something to do with the purpose for which we were brought into this world, which is to sanctify God's name and reveal His greatness. Let us see how our Sages answer the question, Where did this thing come from?

The last plague before the striking down of the first-born was the plague of darkness. In the *Midrash*[1] our Sages ask, Where did the darkness come from? On this, there is a dispute between Rabbi Yehuda and Rabbi Nehemia. Rabbi Yehuda says it came from the darkness above—the darkness with which God shrouds His glory, as the verse says: "He makes darkness His secret place..."[2] Rabbi Nehemia says it came from the darkness below—the darkness of *Gehinnom*, as the verse says: "A land covered with darkness, the shadow of death, and disorder."[3]

Maharal[4] explains that *darkness* means nonexistence. In a human being there are two forms of nonexistence. Since he is a created being, there obviously was a time when he did not exist. This is an essential deficiency in the very definition of a human being. In addition, there is in every human being the deficiency which derives from all the things he has done wrong during his lifetime and all the time he has wasted. These, too, are forms of nonexistence. This means that from God's point of view, a person's life is punctuated by some regions of darkness—nonexistence.

The first form of nonexistence—the fact that there was a time when he did not exist—our Rabbis call "the darkness of above," the higher darkness. When we consider this fact, we come to realize that the whole world is, in itself, darkness. All our existence is surrounded by darkness. We exist only because God's full glory is obscured. The second form of darkness—the darkness of *Gehinnom*—teaches us that a person's actions cease to have true existence if they are tainted by evil.[5]

The plague of darkness, like all the plagues, came to teach us a lesson. The dispute between Rabbi Yehuda and Rabbi Nehemia is about which aspect of darkness are we most likely to learn from. Is it: reflecting deeply on the essential nothingness of man, whose origin is nothingness? Or is it: considering the vanity of man's actions and his failures to act appropriately? (This seems to be the intention of Maharal in his discussion of this *midrash*.)

TRUE CAUSES

We see that when *Hazal* pose the question, Where did this come from?, they were clearly talking about final causes. The lesson which we have to learn from a thing or event is its final cause—the purpose for which it was brought into the world.

The true causes of events are their spiritual causes. If we were to ask for example, What caused the death of the firstborn of Egypt?, it would be useless to look for microbes or other natural causes. These were not causes, but rather effects. The power which killed the firstborn and triggered the redemption from Egypt was the courage of the Israelites in slaughtering the lamb of the Pesah sacrifice before the very eyes of the Egyptians. Earlier on, Pharaoh had queried why they needed to travel a three-days journey away from Egypt in order to sacrifice to Hashem. He suggested that they could perform the sacrifice in the land of Egypt itself. Mosheh's reply was, "It would not be right to do such a thing. It is the abomination of Egypt [i.e., their god] that we sacrifice to our God. Surely if we were to slaughter the abomination of Egypt in front of their eyes, they would stone us."[6]

However, when God gave Israel the command to slaughter the *korban Pesaḥ*, He commanded them to slaughter it in front of the Egyptian's eyes. And not only that, but to keep the lamb in their houses for four days before the sacrifice so that their intention would be visible to all.[7] When he heard this, Mosheh was amazed. He said to God, "Lord of the Universe! How can I ask them to do such a thing? Don't You know that the Egyptians worship the lamb? If we slaughter it in front of their eyes, they will stone us!" Upon which God answered, "By your life! Israel will not leave this place before slaughtering the gods of Egypt in front of their eyes and showing to all that their gods are worthless."[8] The same night that they ate the *korban Pesaḥ*, death came upon the Egyptian firstborn. What was the cause of their death? God states it clearly: "You slaughter the *korban Pesaḥ*, and I slaughter the firstborn."[9]

notes

---

1 *Shemot Rabba* 14:2.
2 *Tehillim* 18:12.
3 *Iyov* 10:22.
4 *Gevurot Hashem*, Chapter 34. See also *Strive for Truth!* III, pp. 215–216.
5 For an explanation of this concept, see the first essay in this volume, "Adam's Test and Its Lessons for Us," subhead "Rambam's Solution."
6 *Shemot* 8:21–22.
7 Ibid. 12:3–6.
8 *Shemot Rabba* 16:3.
9 Ibid. 15:12.

Beshalaḥ

One Rises from
the Lowest Point

God said to Mosheh in *parashat Beshalah*: "See, I am standing before you there by the rock in Horev."[1] On which
our Rabbis comment: "The Holy One Blessed be He said
to Mosheh: Wherever you find signs of a human foot
—there I am before you."[2]

In order to gain some understanding of this very obscure *midrash*, we have to know something about the symbolism of our Rabbis. The foot is the lowest part of the
human body. Therefore, in the language of the Rabbis,
the human foot means the lowest level of a human being's
spiritual existence.

Speaking to the Serpent in *Gan 'Eden*, God said, "You
will attack him [the human being] at the heel."[3] The
meaning is that the Serpent—who is the *yetzer ha-ra'*—at-
tacks a person at the point of his greatest weakness. This
is the "heel" of the person: the sins which a person
crushes with his heel. There are things in a person's life
which he does not even call sins; he thinks them too small
to concern him. But in fact, "small" sins repeated innumerable times may cause more spiritual damage to a per-

son than greater sins, because he is aware of and concerned about the latter and will soon do *teshuva* for them, which is not the case with the "little" sins. It is, therefore, the unnoticed sins which constitute the person's lowest level.

But it is just at the lowest level that God stands. Right there is the place of the *Shechina*. As God said to Mosheh on a previous occasion: "Take your shoes off your feet; the place where you are standing is holy ground."[4] Wherever a person stands—there is his holy place: the place where he can begin his regeneration. His spiritual place —his *behira* point[5]—however low it may be on the scale of spiritual values is precisely the place from which he can begin his ascent. A person who discovers his lowest point can draw from this discovery the spiritual impetus which he needs for *aliya*. "Take your shoes off your feet" means, "Remove the covering which is hiding your defects from yourself." Only when this is done will "the place where you are standing" be "holy ground." There is no better place than that to begin one's ascent.

"WASH YOUR FEET"

In *parashat Vayera*, Avraham asked the visitors, whom he assumed to be desert wanderers, to wash their feet.[6] The Zohar explains that Avraham purified his guests in a *mikveh* as preparation for their entry under the wings of the *Shechina*.[7] "Washing of the feet" symbolizes purifying one's lowest level. Only after that did he invite them to "rest under the tree." This, according to the Zohar, alludes to the Tree of Life—the life-giving powers of the Torah.

The *Yalkut Shim'oni* states that as a reward for his saying "Let a little water be taken," his children merited that

Mosheh would strike the rock and release a great flow of water.[8] On this theme, the *Yalkut* comments in *parashat Beshalaḥ*:

> "You shall strike the rock" [*v'hikkita ba'tsur*: literally, "in the rock"]. From this verse Rabbi Yose ben Zimra used to say: Mosheh's staff was made of sapphire stone [which is very hard]. That is why it states, "You shall strike 'in' the rock"; the verse does not say "on the rock," but "in the rock." On Mosheh's staff was engraved the holy name of God, and with it he struck into the very depths of the rock.[9]

Here we have another example of *Ḥazal* using language symbolically. The holy name of God engraved upon the staff alludes to the desirability of doing everything for the sake of God. A sincere intention of this kind has the power to break through the mental barrier which one constructs around the truth in one's heart so that one's heart becomes a "heart of stone," impervious to holy thoughts. But if one's resolve is strong enough and sincere enough, one can break through this barrier and reestablish contact with the truth. This is what we mean by "returning knowledge into one's heart." We have discussed this idea in the essay entitled "Aiming for Greatness."[10]

MIRACLES DO NOT SOLVE ALL PROBLEMS

People like to say that if only God would perform miracles for us as in the times of the Torah, we would be much better people. But this is not true. A person may see open miracles and acquire great stores of knowledge about the wisdom and power of Hashem, but this may make no practical difference whatsoever to his life. He may remain sunk in his sins and his defilement without making any effort to apply this knowledge in his day to day living.

On the contrary, for a person in this state, great revelations may be a severe trial. When Israel was terrified by the divine revelation at Mount Sinai, Mosheh comforted them with the words, "Do not be afraid, for God has come to test [le'nassot] you."[11] There are many different interpretations of this verse, many of which take the word le'nassot away from its simple meaning. But Ramban writes: "In my opinion the simple meaning—'to test you'—is the right one. He is saying that after God has removed all doubts from your hearts, He will see whether you really love Him and desire Him and His commandments."[12]

We see here a most amazing fact. At *Mattan Torah*, God tore open all seven heavens and revealed His glory in a way that had never occurred before and will never occur again. The revelation was so great that all possible doubts about the power and glory of Hashem were completely removed. Nevertheless, this very fact posed a new test. Was the person who witnessed all this prepared to subdue his ego and follow God with love and devotion? Or did he prefer to reject all that he had seen and understood and choose to follow the inclinations of his own heart? At the moment of maximum knowledge, there was the point of maximum test. Amazing, but true!

EVERY PLACE IS A PLACE TO START

The truth is that wherever the person is standing, there is always the opportunity for ascent. That place, wherever it is, is his holy temple.

There are people who are occupied with important matters; projects which *Klal Yisrael* greatly needs. Very often they receive an extraordinary—even miraculous—

amount of heavenly aid. Fully aware of their own unworthiness, they are amazed at this. How is it possible, they think, that unworthy people such as we are can merit great mitzvot such as these and such an extraordinary amount of heavenly aid?[13] The answer is that God, in His great mercy, bestows heavenly aid on the person who steps forward to undertake a project needed by *Klal Yisrael*, in spite of his personal unworthiness. He may even have defiled his inner temple; he may—like King Menasheh—have erected an idol in the Holy of Holies. But still God is prepared to make miraculous events happen for him. We must remember that the ten miracles which occurred daily in the Temple in Jerusalem continued even after Menasheh introduced his idol. They continued until the destruction of the Temple.

So long as there still was a possibility that the Temple would remain, all the miracles still operated. Similarly, God is prepared to reveal Himself to any person so long as there is still hope that he will learn from this. He may have defiled his inner temple, but in spite of this, his *beḥira*-point may not have wavered far from the point of truth in his heart. *It is precisely his lowliness which may contain the seed of his spiritual regeneration.*

notes

---

1 *Shemot* 17:6.
2 *Mechilta* ad loc.
3 *Bereshit* 3:15.
4 *Shemot* 3:5.
5 See *Strive for Truth!* II, p. 52.
6 *Bereshit* 18:4.
7 *Parashat Vayera.*
8 *Yalkut, parashat Vayera.*
9 See note 2, above.
10 See *Strive for Truth!* IV, *Sanctuaries in Time*, pp. 39–41.
11 *Shemot* 20:17.
12 Ad loc.
13 Here Rabbi Dessler *zt"l* is clearly referring to his own experiences during the early period of his work in establishing the Gateshead Kollel in 5701 (1941). He disclosed that it was extraordinary how the amount of money he needed to keep the Kollel going arrived week by week, sometimes as a result of the approaches he had made to people many months earlier. He felt this was a reassurance from above that Hashem approved of his work. However, he was extremely surprised, in his humility, that he was considered to be worthy of such heavenly signs.

Yitro

[This essay is taken from *Michtav Me-Eliyahu* IV, pp. 53–55.]

Learning in Order
to Teach

In *Shemot Rabba parashat Yitro*,[1] on the verse, "And Mosheh went up to God,"[2] the Midrash comments:

> At that moment, the ministering angels wished to attack Mosheh [for invading their realm to obtain the Torah]. God made Mosheh's appearance similar to that of Avraham and said to them: "Are you not ashamed? Is this not the person whom you visited and in whose house you ate?" God then said to Mosheh: "You see, the Torah was only given to you by the merit of Avraham...the man who was great among the giants."

We know that Mosheh received his prophecy "through a clear lens."[3] Mosheh's great humility is described in the Torah.[4] As a result, the "glass" through which he saw his prophecy was clear; his ego caused no obscurities or distortions in his vision. (This was not the case with other prophets. However great they were, their "lens" was not completely clear.)

In spite of this, the angels wanted to attack him. They argued that even after his humility there still remained a residue of self which prevented him from attaining the level of perfect *lishma*. (In a similar sense, only forty-nine of the fifty gates of understanding were revealed to Mosheh.[5]) The angels thought that the Torah should not be given to anyone in whom the self had not been completely eradicated.

ACTIVE *HESSED*

What did God do? "He made Mosheh's appearance resemble that of Avraham." God demonstrated that Mosheh's *madrega* included the aspect of active *hessed* which characterized Avraham Avinu. In *hessed*, Avraham was "great among the giants." Even among people who were giants in *hessed*, Avraham would have towered over them as a giant towers over a normal person. Nevertheless, Mosheh's *madrega*, which was centered in Torah, included the same degree of selfless *hessed* that characterized Avraham. Mosheh was *rabbenu*—the teacher of all Israel in all generations. The microscopic amount of self which the angels may have discovered in Mosheh was utterly outweighed by the tremendous amount of active *hessed* which he invested in *Klal Yisrael* during their forty years of wandering in the desert.

There can be no greater *hessed* than teaching Torah. A person who looks after the physical needs of his fellow stands very high in the scale of Torah achievement. He has given life to a person in this world and "saving a life is equivalent to saving a whole world."[6] But a person who teaches other people Torah has given them life in this world and in the next, and there can be no greater *hessed* than this.

THE ANGELS AT AVRAHAM'S HOME

On the words "Torah of *hessed*" in *Aishet Hayil*[7], the Gemara notes that this implies that there can be a "Torah of _ḥessed_" and also a "Torah which is not of _ḥessed_." What is "Torah of _ḥessed_"? It takes two forms. One is Torah which is learned _lishma_—from completely selfless motives. Another is Torah which is learned in order to teach it.[8]

On the question of completely selfless motivation, the angels had occasion to criticize. Is anybody really completely selfless? But "Torah for the sake of teaching it," active Torah, is beyond the angels' experience. This is what they saw in the house of Avraham. God asked them, "Did you not eat and drink in his house?" meaning that the angels had much to learn from the active, practical _ḥessed_ of Avraham Avinu. When God showed them Mosheh in the guise of Avraham, they realized that the practical _ḥessed_ involved in teaching Torah was something they could never emulate. Here their challenge to Mosheh Rabbenu had to stop.

notes

1 _Shemot_ 19:3.
2 _Yevamot_ 49b.
3 _Bemidbar_ 12:3.
4 _Rosh Hashana_ 21b.
5 _Sanhedrin_ 37a.
6 _Mishlei_ 31:26.
7 _Sukka_ 49b.
8 Ibid.

Mishpatim

[This essay is taken from *Michtav Me-Eliyahu* IV, pp. 13–14.]

Aspects of Unity

In *parashat Mishpatim*, Hashem commands us: "If you lend money to My people, the poor man who is with you, you shall not behave to him like a creditor..."[1] On this, the *Midrash Rabba* comments:

> Happy is the man who stands his test. For there is no person whom Hashem does not test. The rich man is tested whether his hand is generously open to the poor. The poor man is tested whether he can stand suffering without becoming resentful... If the rich man stands his test and is generous with his charity, he enjoys his money in this world, the capital remains for him in the World to Come, and Hashem saves him from the judgment of *Gehinnom*... And if the poor man stands his test and does not rebel against his lot, he receives a double portion in the future world...

We have discussed this *midrash* elsewhere.[2] We explained there why the poor man who passes his test receives a double portion in the World to Come. (He receives one portion for observing his mitzva—accepting his fate without resentment—and another as a reward for the suffering he underwent in this world.)

Now we ask: Why does God have to "save the rich man from judgment of *Gehinnom*"? If he passed his test and was generous with his charity, why is he threatened with *Gehinnom* and need to be saved by the mercy of Hashem? The answer is that the rich man who "enjoys his money in this world" is in constant danger of becoming absorbed in his possessions and his pleasures. If he is not careful, they may become the dominant interests in his life. In this way, he would be erecting an idol in himself and this would be *Gehinnom* itself. This would mean that he was investing his whole life in nothingness and, as we have explained elsewhere,[3] a basic aspect of *Gehinnom* is indeed "nothingness." By placing his main interest in possessions which, in themselves, have no spiritual value — which, spiritually speaking, are nothing — he loses his own spiritual value and nothingness fills his soul. This is *Gehinnom*.

However, if that person tries to the best of his ability, sincerely and devotedly, to use his possessions as God wants him to use them, then God will bestow upon him the heavenly aid needed to avoid the pitfalls of his situation—to overcome the temptations and to act on the principle that the sole value of material possessions resides in the mitzvot that we do with them.

WITH ALL YOUR HEART

We know that a basic principle of the Torah is that "God is one."[4] But this must not remain merely an intellectual concept. We are immediately told to make this unity a reality in our lives: "To love God with all our heart, with all our soul and with all our possessions."[5]

"With all our heart" means not to let our love of ourselves turn into a barrier against the love of God. God created us with an ego in order to give us a driving force to bring ourselves closer to the will of Hashem. The elevated person who strives to achieve love of God will restrict his egoism as far as possible so that it is used only for its true purpose—to drive him to excel in the service of Hashem. With this, he has introduced unity into his mental and emotional life, since he is single-minded in his service.

WITH ALL YOUR SOUL

What is "loving God with all one's soul"? The Rabbis answer, "Love Him even if He takes away your soul—even if you are required to give up your life for *kiddush Hashem*.

Some people do mitzvot in order to live. Others live in order to do mitzvot. We should not look down on the one who does mitzvot in order to live. He is obviously a man of faith and understands that his life, his success, and the success of his family all depend upon his keeping the mitzvot of Hashem. However, it looks somewhat as if he had struck a bargain with Hashem. He will observe the mitzvot if, in return, Hashem will bestow upon him whatever he needs. This person may not realize that he is treating his private life as if it were something independent of God. This is certainly a defect in his concept of unity. Unity means that nothing in the world counts besides the will of Hashem.

What is the remedy for this? Once a person realizes that his attitude is far from what is expected of a true servant of Hashem, he will endeavor to make a radical change in his way of thinking. He will recall that the mitzva of *kiddush Hashem* means that his very life does not belong to him. His life was given to him for one sole purpose: for the service of Hashem. From the very fact that he must be ready to give up his life at any moment for the sake of *kiddush Hashem*, he should be able to deduce that life itself is nothing but a vehicle for mitzvot, not that mitzvot are a vehicle for life. In this way he will achieve unity in his whole relationship with Hashem.

WITH ALL YOUR POSSESSIONS

Loving God with all one's possessions means, as we have explained above, that all one's possessions should be considered to be God-given means to do mitzvot. A person who values possessions for their own sake is creating an even more powerful barrier between himself and Hashem. In his attempt to fortify himself with things which are outside himself, he is widening the region of his imagined independence, and so, widening the boundaries of his idolatry. The more he reduces the hold which possessions have over his mind, the closer he is to living a life devoted to practicing unity.

notes

---

1 *Shemot* 22:24.
2 See *Strive for Truth!* II, p. 162.
3 See *Strive for Truth!* III, p. 215.
4 *Devarim* 6:4.
5 Ibid. 6:5.

Teruma—Tetzaveh

[This essay is taken from *Michtav Me-Eliyahu* IV, p. 294.]

Mishkan and *Mikdash*

The Desert Tabernacle, the details of whose construction take up the whole of *parashat Terumah* and much of the succeeding *parshiyot*, is sometimes called "sanctuary" [*mikdash*] ("And they shall make Me a *mikdash*"[1]). More frequently, however, it is called *mishkan*, which means "dwelling place."[2]

The meaning of *mishkan*—the dwelling place (so to speak) of Hashem—is clearly expressed in the verse: "And so shall he (the *kohen gadol*) do to the Tent of Meeting which *dwells* with them in the midst of their defilement."[3] God rests His presence amongst us even in the midst of our defilement because He knows that we have the ability to raise and extricate ourselves from defilement. How? Through the Torah. The Tent of Meeting is so called because it is the meeting place of God and Israel—the place where Torah is transmitted. In *parashat Tetzaveh*, the Tent of Meeting is described as the place "Where I shall meet with you [plural, i.e. Israel], where I will speak to you [singular, i.e. Mosheh]."[4] "To speak to you" means to transmit Torah, and Torah learning creates a closeness between us and Hashem, a sense of joy and satisfaction. "The commands of God are straightforward and rejoice the heart."[5] All this is included in the term *mishkan*.

Mikdash, on the other hand, means a place of holiness. Holiness means transcendence. We feel the absolute gulf which separates the Creator from His creatures. Our response must be service—offerings and prayer—by which we recognize our lowliness before the grandeur of the Almighty. "My house shall be called a house of prayer for all nations."[6]

But nevertheless, we find that *mishkan* is sometimes called *mikdash* and *mikdash* is sometimes called *mishkan*.[7] How they are called reflects what they are in reality, for their meaning and existence are really one. If *mishkan* represents the joy in the presence of Hashem, and *mikdash* represents the awe one feels in the transcendence of Hashem, then together they form one whole. We have to "rejoice in trembling."[8] And the Rabbis say: "I experience fear in the midst of my joy and joy in the midst of my fear."[9]

notes

1 *Shemot* 25:8.
2 Ibid. 25:9.
3 *Vayikra* 16:16.
4 *Shemot* 29:42.
5 *Tehillim* 19:9.
6 *Yesha'ya* 56:7.
7 *Eruvin* 2a.
8 *Tehillim* 2:11.
9 *Tanna de-Be Eliyahu Rabba* #3.

Ki Tissa

[This essay is taken from *Michtav Me-Eliyahu* V, pp. 291–292.]

The Limited Power of the *Satan*

The *Satan* is an angel.[1] This means that he is a power created by God to serve God's purposes in the world. His task is to cause difficulties, temptations, and tests for people in order to challenge them and bring out the best in them.

The power of the *Satan* is very great, but it is limited too. Each step of a test he prepares for a person has to be approved by God. In general terms, the *Satan* in not permitted to attack a person with overwhelming force. He is permitted to launch just a weak attack the first time around. Only if the person who is being tested shows signs of succumbing is the *Satan* permitted to increase the intensity of his test.

We see this clearly in the development of the sin of the Golden Calf. It is difficult to understand how the people of Israel, who had achieved such tremendous heights at the giving of the Torah, could sink so low in such a short period of time. But great sins tend to commence with small failures. How did the sin of the Golden Calf begin?

"The people saw that Mosheh was late [*boshesh*] in descending from the mountain..."[2] Rashi explains that when Mosheh ascended the mountain, he told the people that

he would return after forty days, before the sixth hour
[that is, midday]. The people counted forty days after his
ascent, waited until midday, and when he did not arrive
by then, they felt a little uneasy. "At that point the *Satan*
came and confused the world. He showed them the appearance of thick darkness and confusion [at the mountain top]. They thought: Mosheh must have died; this
would account for all the confusion in the world. Then he
said to them, 'Mosheh is indeed dead; six hours of the day
have passed and he has not come.' Then he showed them
the appearance of Mosheh in a coffin being carried
through the heavens."[3]

We see there is a gradual process here. Each stage of the
test is more intensive than the previous one. What was the
commencement of the process? The feeling of unease at
the fact that Mosheh had apparently not returned at the
appointed time. This unease showed a lack of faith. If
they had looked at the situation through the eyes of truth,
they would have immediately understood that they had
made a mistake in their calculations. It should have been
obvious to them that it was impossible under any circumstances for Mosheh not to keep an appointment which he
had announced to them as the word of God. Instead of being surprised at Mosheh's delay, they should have been
surprised at themselves. If the truth had been operating in
them, they would have said to themselves: Look how
prone a person is to make mistakes. We were absolutely
sure that we heard him say that he would return today.
But since he has not come, we must have made a mistake.
(And in fact, they had made a mistake. Mosheh's words
meant that he would return forty full days after his ascent. But they wrongly took it to be forty days, including
the day of his ascent.)

However, since they did not make this correct deduction, and allowed a spirit of disquiet to enter their hearts, the *Satan* was permitted to increase the test and showed them—in their imagination—thick darkness and confusion at the top of the mountain. So they were led to make the next incorrect deduction and to think that only Mosheh's death could account for all this confusion. Only then was the *Satan* permitted to inform them emphatically, "Mosheh is dead because the time he stated has passed." And once this idea was clearly lodged in their minds, he was permitted to show them—in their imagination—Mosheh's coffin actually being carried through the air.

My teacher, Rabbi Zvi Hirsch Broide of blessed memory, told me in the name of Rabbi Yisrael Salanter that this episode is a classic example of how we ourselves strengthen the hands of the *Satan* and enable him to increase the severity of our tests step by step.

notes

1 *Iyov* 1:6.
2 *Shemot* 32:1.
3 Rashi ad loc.

Vayakhel—Pekudei

[This essay is taken from *Michtav Me-Eliyahu* V, pp. 415–417.]

The Secret of the Incense

"And they brought...the fragrant herbs...for the anointing oil and for the incense of aromatic spices."[1] The incense which was burned daily in the Holy Place and once a year, on Yom Kippur in the Holy of Holies, indeed possessed a unique fragrance. It hinted at the unimaginable sweetness of *devekut*—the experience of clinging in close attachment to the Holy One Blessed be He. (The root *katar*, besides its Hebrew meaning of 'burning,' also means 'binding' and 'attachment' in Aramaic.) We find fragrance used in this sense in the *gemara* which discusses the giving of the Torah: "With every word which came forth from the mouth of God, the whole world was filled with fragrance."[2] [One of the stated purposes of every offering in the Temple is to cause a "fragrant odor"—*reyah nihoah*—before Hashem.[3]] This being so, it would seem to follow that *ketoret* embodies the *reyah nihoah* of all the offerings.[4] As our Rabbis say: "All other offerings come because of sins or obligations, but *ketoret* comes only for joy."[5] The idea expressed by burning this incense is: It is our will to do Your will—to give You, so to speak, pleasure and satisfaction from our actions.

Ketoret is the offering of fragrance. Its perfect smell

symbolizes our *devekut* to Hashem without interference from any disturbing factor. It hints at a state of attachment to Hashem in which there is no hint of deception or intrusion of unworthy motives, in even the finest and most subtle form.

KETORET—UNITY OF THE HEART

The Zohar in *parashat Vayakhel* describes this in moving, eloquent terms.

> Whoever smelled the smoke of the *ketoret* ascending straight upwards as a result of the herb *ma'aleh 'ashan* felt his heart being clarified in light and in joy in the service of God. It removed from him all the defilement of the *yetzer ha-ra'* and left him with a single heart to greet his Father in heaven. *Ketoret* has the power of breaking the *yetzer ha-ra'*... There is nothing more beloved before God than *ketoret*.[6]

This is one of the wonders of the Holy Temple and the heavenly aid which was manifested in it. It enabled every heart to experience what the pure and loving service of the Almighty could mean.

The *ma'aleh 'ashan* mentioned in the Zohar describes an herb, a small amount of which was included in the *ketoret*, which caused its smoke to rise straight up like a staff.[7] This symbolizes how *devekut* requires a "straightening of the heart," i.e., complete honesty and sincerity. The heart "goes straight up" to Hashem without being diverted by any hint of selfish or unworthy motives.

We are told that one of the eleven main ingredients in the *ketoret*—*helbenah*—did not have a fragrant odor.[8] It nevertheless had a strong odor which lent pungency to the whole.[9] The message here is that in order to arrive at the state of *devekut*, one needs strong willpower in order to overcome any imperfections of character which may prevent or disturb this. The exercise of willpower to overcome imperfections involves hard spiritual work—it does not possess a "sweet odor"—nevertheless, united with all the other ingredients, our difficulties are dissolved and the wonderful odor of *ketoret* emerges stronger than ever.

THE POWER OF *KETORET*

We find that *ketoret* can counteract a plague. Aharon stopped a plague by burning *ketoret* "between the living and the dying."[10] *Ketoret* symbolizes the heart of Israel which, essentially, is unified in the love of Hashem.[11] We recall the wonderful words of Rambam: "Every Jew desires to be part of the people of Israel and to perform all the mitzvot and to refrain from all the *averot* and [if he sins] it is his *yetzer* which has attacked him."[12] When a person experiences this truth, in spite of all appearances, he creates a favorable atmosphere in which Hashem forgives the sins of his people, seeing that they have not sinned with all their heart, but have merely stumbled into sin. If this fact is "seen" here below, it will also be "seen" in heaven. This can bring about the cessation of a plague.

On the other hand, we see that *ketoret*, improperly used, can cause death. This was demonstrated in the case of Nadav and Avihu[13] and also in the case of Koraḥ and his assembly.[14] There is no contradiction. An individual who personally offers *ketoret* in front of Hashem, but who had not purified himself, is acting with great impudence. By bringing *ketoret* as a personal offering, he is declaring that he is the one who has completely unified his heart in perfect attachment to Hashem, whereas in fact, he has done no such thing. This act is a desecration of holiness and can result in his death.

We see that *ketoret* is an extremely powerful tool. May we merit to experience its life-giving powers in the rebuilt Temple speedily in our days.

Notes

1 *Shemot* 35:27–28.
2 *Shabbat* 88b.
3 *Vayikra* 1:9; see *Mishnah Zevahim* 4:6.
4 Rabbi S. R. Hirsch commentary on *Shemot* 30:1.
5 *Tanhuma Tetzaveh* #15.
6 II, 218b.
7 *Yoma* 53a.
8 *Keritot* 6b.
9 *Radvaz, Ta'amei Ha-mitzvot, mitzvat Ketoret.*
10 *Bemidbar* 17:11–12.
11 See *Strive for Truth!* IV, *Sanctuaries in Time* on "The Day of Atonement" pp. 129–133.
12 *Mishneh Torah*, Laws of Divorce 2:20.
13 *Vayikra* 10:2.
14 See Rashi, *Bemidbar* 17:13.

Glossary

The following glossary provides a partial explanation of some of the Hebrew words and phrases used in this book. The spellings and explanations reflect the way the specific word is used herein. Often, there are alternate spellings and meanings for the words.

AISHET ḤAYIL: "a woman of valor," *Mishlei* (*Proverbs*) 31:10-31; praise of the perfect wife.

AKEDA: Abraham's binding of Isaac on the altar.

ALIYA: ascent.

AVEROT: transgressions.

AVODAT HASHEM: serving God.

AVOT: lit., fathers; the Patriarchs.

BA'AL ḤESSED: one who performs acts of kindness.

BEḤIRA: free will; free choice.

BEIT HA-MIDRASH: the study hall of a yeshiva.

BERACHA: a blessing.

BERESHIT: the Book of Genesis.

BITTUL TORAH: the misuse of one's time in non-Torah pursuits.

BRIT MILA: the ritual of circumcision.

DEVEKUT: devotion and attachment to God.

DIN: Divine judgment.

EMET: truth.

EMUNA: faith in God.

GAN 'EDEN: the Garden of Eden.

GEHINNOM: hell.

GEMARA: commentary on the Mishna; together they comprise the Talmud.

GEVURA: strength of character.

HASSID: a pious, righteous man.

HAZAL: an acronym meaning "Our Sages, of blessed memory."

HESSED: lovingkindness.

HILLUL HASHEM: desecration of the Divine Name.

HUTZ LA'ARETZ: outside of the Land of Israel.

KABBALA: ancient Jewish mystical philosophy.

KAVVANA: concentration in prayer.

KIDDUSH HASHEM: sanctification of the Divine Name.

KLAL YISRAEL: the Nation of Israel.

KOHEN GADOL: the High Priest.

KORBAN(OT): sacrifice(s).

KORBAN PESAH: the Passover offering.

KOTEL HA-MA'ARAVI: The Western Wall.

LE'SHEM SHAMAYIM: for the sake of Heaven.

LISHMA: "for its own sake", from unselfish motives.

MADREGA: a spiritual or moral level.

MASHIAH: the Messiah.

MATTAN TORAH: the giving of the Torah.

MIDDA: a character trait; a positive attribute.

MIKVEH: a pool for ritual immersion.

MUSSAR: moral discipline; the ethical movement founded by R' Yisrael Salanter in the 19th century.

'OLAM HA-BA: the World to Come.

PARASHA: the weekly Torah portion.

RASHA': a wicked person.

RUA<u>H</u> HA-KODESH: the Divine Spirit.

SEFIRA (-ROT): the ten mystical spheres or levels described in Kabbala.

SHECHINA: the Divine Presence.

SHEMA': "Hear O Israel," the opening words of the fundamental Jewish prayer which proclaims the unity of God.

SHEMOT: the Book of Exodus.

TALLIT KATAN: ritual fringes tied onto each corner of a four-cornered garment.

TANNA (-'IM): scholars of the Mishna and earlier periods.

TESHUVA: penitence; a return to Jewish practice and observance.

TSADDIK: a righteous man.

TZEDAKA: charity.

YETZER HA-RA': the evil inclination.

YETZER HA-TOV: the good inclination.

YIR'AH: fear; awe.

Now available
in pocket size!

Masterplan

JUDAISM: ITS PROGRAM, MEANINGS, GOALS

Rabbi Aryeh Carmell

Drawing on Talmudic and midrashic sources, the insights of *mussar* and *chassidut* and the writings of S.R. Hirsch, *Masterplan* shows how every mitzva is a building block in the Master Architect's plan for a better world and each is as relevant and applicable today as it was on the day the Torah was given to the People of Israel thousands of years ago.

Rabbi Aryeh Carmell provides explanations for the individual mitzvot but shows how they form a dynamic training program designed to advance the human spirit from selfishness towards selflessness. It emerges that the goal of Judaism is no less than the establishment of a just and caring society which can be a model for all mankind. 424 pp.

Now available
in compact size!

Challenge

TORAH-VIEWS ON SCIENCE AND ITS PROBLEMS

Edited by Aryeh Carmell and Cyril Domb

*Published in conjunction with the
Association of Orthodox Jewish Scientists*

Challenging many preconceived notions about Orthodox
Judaism and modern science, the 34 articles in this book
show that essentially there is no conflict between the two.
Dealing with the interaction between Torah and science,
Genesis and evolution, "the secular bias," and ethical dilemmas
arising out of recent scientific advances, the book portrays
the Torah Jew as facing the secular world with assurance,
guided by his age-old tradition. 538 pp.